A History of the Quaker Movement in Africa

A History of the Quaker Movement in Africa

ANE MARIE BAK RASMUSSEN

BRITISH ACADEMIC PRESS

An imprint of I.B.Tauris & Co Ltd
London · New York

Published in 1995 by
I.B.Tauris & Co Ltd
45 Bloomsbury Square
London WC1A 2HY
175 Fifth Avenue
New York NY10010

In the United States of America
and Canada distributed by
St Martin's Press
175 Fifth Avenue
New York NY10010

A CIP record for this book is available from the British Library

A full CIP record is available from the Library of Congress

ISBN 1 85043 904 4

Typeset in Monotype Ehrhardt
by Lucy Morton, London SE12

Printed and bound in Great Britain by WBC Ltd,
Bridgend, Mid Glamorgan

Contents

Preface
by Harold V. Smuck vii

Foreword
by Joseph Wasike Mululu ix

Introduction
by Kathleen Staudt xiv

Maps xviii

Kenya xviii
Western Kenya xix
The Western Province Administrative Divisions xx

1 Background to the Quaker Mission to Kenya 1

The Development of Evangelical Quakerism 1
Revival among American Friends in the Late Nineteenth Century 13
Eagerness for Mission 19

2 The Early Years: Friends Africa Mission 26

The Peoples of Western Kenya and Their Religion 26
The Colonial Setting 32
The Arrival of the First Missionaries 39
African–Missionary Interaction in the Development of the Church 44
Revival in the Late 1920s 58
The Aftermath of the Revival 66
Crisis in the mid-1940s: Dini ya Msambwa 70

3 The Church under African Leadership 94

The Establishment of East Africa Yearly Meeting of Friends 94
The Influence of Later Missionaries 101
Administration and Property in African Hands 107
A Split in 1973: Elgon Religious Society of Friends 114
The Division into Four Yearly Meetings 127
Questions Outstanding in 1987 135

Conclusion
by Kathleen Staudt 155

Theoretical Perspectives 155
Historical Summary 157
Significance and Implications 161

Index 163

Preface

HAROLD V. SMUCK

The Religious Society of Friends (sometimes called Friends Church or Quakers) are a very small group originating in seventeenth-century England and spreading in the first generation to North America. Yet by far the largest population is found in Kenya, East Africa. The author estimates that there are two hundred thousand Friends in Kenya, fairly consistent with David Barrett's (University of Nairobi) estimate almost thirty years ago. This would mean that more than half the Quakers in the world are in this one African country. Obviously there are per capita many times more than in any other place. While Friends are known out of all proportion to their numbers, and probably far beyond what they deserve, they do have a major place in the modern history of Kenya, and it is therefore appropriate to offer this in-depth study.

Ane Marie Bak Rasmussen has done an excellent job of tracing how this large Quaker population came about as she studies their development in Kenya (and tangentially in Tanzania and Uganda). She has also provided valuable insights into conditions and developments which led to the Holy Spirit bodies. Virtually all the mainline mission-developed churches in Kenya (Catholic and Protestant) experienced defections. The study of why this happened is instructive – and, to me, fascinating.

When this manuscript reached me I began by reading the numerous footnotes. I met authors and interviewees, most of whom were known to me and a few of whom were not. Rasmussen's extensive use of correspondence and colonial government documents is illuminating. She demonstrates an excellent grasp of the development of American evangelical Quakerism from which the foreign missionary programmes sprang; catching the shift in the 1950s and 1960s from the mostly non-specialist evangelizing missionaries in Kenya to the extensive use of specialists, including educators from England. She treats with care and insight the cultural differences between 'the north' (Busuku) and 'the south' in the original Quaker territory in western Kenya. The differing timing and activities of missionaries in these two areas had results crucial to subsequent developments, as the book clearly shows. Kathleen Staudt has provided a very helpful introduction and conclusion.

My modest personal assistance to Ane Marie is a source of real satisfaction. My path crossed hers in Kenya, and I was able to arrange housing for her American research with our next-door neighbour, a ten-minute walk from the Quaker records in Earlham College library, and not far from Friends Central Offices.

It is a pleasure to commend this study, while feeling a twinge of regret that something like it was not available to me when I went to work with Kenyan Friends in the 1960s.

Foreword

JOSEPH WASIKE MULULU

This book forms part of a larger manuscript, 'Contextualization of the Church in Kenya, Illustrated through the Society of Friends and the Holy Spirit Churches in Western Kenya', which Ane Marie Bak Rasmussen had planned to complete by the end of 1993. At her death on 19 October 1992 only the first part, on the Society of Friends, was fully completed. Ane Marie had already done fieldwork for the second part, on the Holy Spirit churches, and parts of her Master of Arts thesis, 'The History and Present Characteristics of Four African Independent Churches in Western Kenya: Holy Spirit Church of East Africa, African Church of Holy Spirit, Gospel Holy Spirit of East Africa and Lyahuka Church of East Africa' (1976), were planned to be integrated in the second part of the manuscript. Owing to technical difficulties, this thesis was withdrawn from Nairobi University without examination. Plans are therefore under way to have the second part on the Holy Spirit churches, 'The History and Present Characteristics of Four African Independent Churches in Western Kenya', published separately.

Ane Marie Bak Rasmussen began her fieldwork in Western Kenya in 1974. She was fascinated by the Holy Spirit churches – African independent churches which broke away from the Friends Church. She was especially fascinated by the members' experiences of being filled with the Holy Spirit, a closeness to God, and thereby overcoming evil. Ane Marie first spent two years – from 1974 to 1976 – in Kenya; thereafter – until 1991 – she did research there for longer and shorter periods in order to follow developments within the Friends churches and Holy Spirit churches, and to see points of contrast and similarity between them.

In order to learn how Friends think and live – in America, where most missionaries came from, as well as in Great Britain, where it all started (in the seventeenth century) – and to learn about the historical development of Friends, Ane Marie went in 1985 to the Wider Ministries Commission under Friends United Meeting in Richmond, Indiana and Friends' Study Centre at Woodbrooke College, Selly Oak, Birmingham, England.

These are Ane Marie's own acknowledgements, written shortly before her death:

My interest in Western Kenya was first sparked off by discussions with my husband, Joseph Wasike Mululu. He and I have done all field research together since 1974, and without his intimate knowledge of the area and its people I would not have been able to make so many valuable contacts nor to reach the same level of understanding. Whenever we have visited the churches in Kenya, whether Quakers or Holy Spirit churches, we have felt that we were coming back to good friends. This has made it possible to share intimate feelings and knowledge about what was going on. And in spite of all the splits that have occurred and which in some cases have made it difficult for people from different groups to meet and talk together in a constructive way, we have been received everywhere as friends and have been given the information that was necessary to allow us to form a balanced view of the situation. I thank my husband for his tireless work and all our good friends in Kenya, Quakers as well as members of the Holy Spirit churches, for the trust that they have put in us. And I hope that what I have written in this book may reflect and respect their trust. I should like to mention specifically a few of the persons with whom I have talked several times over the years, such as G. Jeremiah Lusweti, Thomas Ganira Lung'aho, Elisha Wakube, Ezekiel Wanyonyi, George Kamwesa, Salomon Adagala, Temeteo Hazekiah Shitsimi, and the late Kefa Ayub Mavuru, Japheth Zale Ambula and Eliakim Kiverenge Antonya. The names of many others are to be found in the notes, but I have talked with so many people that it has been impossible to mention all of them.

Outside Kenya, I should like to thank the staff of Friends United Meeting in Richmond, Indiana, USA, for giving me access to their records where I learnt much about the missionaries who went to Kenya and, through their writings, about the history of Friends churches in Kenya. I also thank the librarians in Earlham College, also in Richmond, Indiana, for allowing me to use their library and its facilities. A number of Friends in Richmond helped me in many practical ways as well as in trying to give me an understanding of the life of Quakers both historically and presently. I give special thanks to Louise and Jay Beede who received me as a guest in their house during the entire period of about six weeks that I spent in

Richmond. And also to Evelyn and Harold V. Smuck who had arranged everything for me before my arrival.

Likewise, I learnt very much about the origin and development of Quakerism in England during my stay at Woodbrooke College, Selly Oak, Birmingham, in late 1985, and I thank the staff of Woodbrooke College for all the help that they gave me.

Finally, I want to thank my supervisor at the University of Aarhus through these many years of studies, professor, dr. theol. Johannes Aagaard, for his readiness to give advice and help at all times. I also appreciate very much the help by professors Anna Marie Aagaard, Lars Thunberg and Holger Bernt Hansen in going through my manuscript and giving much valuable advice.

In addition to these acknowledgements, expressed by Ane Marie herself, I want to mention some further names of people and organizations who deserve our appreciation. This book could not have been completed without the goodwill and assistance of the Kenyan government and the Friends Church in Kenya. My thanks are due to officials in the Office of the President in Nairobi who issued the research permit and made it possible to collect relevant information, and to the authorities of the Provincial Administration for Western Province, Kakamega, and the Bungoma District, students and staff at the Friends Bible Institute, Tiriki, St Paul's United Theological College, Limuru, Friends Centre, Kalokol-Turkana, Lodwar, Kenya National Archives, the National Council of Churches of Kenya, Nairobi, All Africa Conference of Churches, Nairobi, John Padwick, Organization of African Instituted Churches, Nairobi, the Head of the Roman Catholic Church His Eminence Maurice M. Cardinal Otunga, Nairobi, The Sisters of Tindinyo Carmel, Kaimosi, Sister Rita Itebete, Headmistress, Mukumu Girls High School, Khayega, and the late Father Agapitus Muse. I also want to express my gratitude to Professor Dr J.G. Donders, Dr Samwel G. Kibicho, Dr Ezekiel Kasiera, Department of Philosophy and Religious Studies, and Dr Atieno-Odhiambo, Department of History, University of Nairobi, Dr (Sister) Anne Nasimuyu, Philosophy and Religious Studies Department, Kenyatta University, Nairobi, Julius M. Wasike, Dr Chris W. Mukwa, Faculty of Education, Moi University, Eldoret, Professor Julius Wangila Mukhwana, Faculty of Business, Victoria University of Technology, Melbourne, Australia, Lenah and Hon. Joseph Muliro, Dr James A. Bukhala, John Kitui, E.P. Nakitare, Director of Culture, Nairobi, Haiderali Bhanji Noormohamed, J.J. Shiundu, J.K. Mulira,

Ezekiel Kw. M. Wekesa, Enock Imbuye, E.M. Waliáula, Marko Mukhweso, Lene and Dr Martin McWere, the late Tomasi K. Mukonambi, Jeremiah Wafula, Timothy Bilindi, Semeon Shitemi, T.W. Wamunyokoli, the Reverend Musa Musoga, S.E. Bunyali, R.A. Ambeba, Inga and Sven Rasmussen (Danish Quakers), Marte Kari, Aage and Kristian Berntzen (Norwegian Pentecostal Church). Ane Mette Jensen, Jens and Anne Vibeke Mou, Rigmor and Preben Frederiksen, Vita and Hans Bak Rasmussen, Ex-Senior Chief Johathan and Ruth Barasa, Benjamin S. Wegesa, Hezekiah Ngoya, Nathan Munoko and L. Mansure, Zephaniah W. Wekesa and Amos M. Yiminyi, London, Graham Garner, Friends Book Centre, Martin Wilkinson, Friends House, and Roger B. Sturge, Friends World Committee for Consultation, London, M.W. Furaha, Beth Tomkinson, Oxford, Ambassador of the Republic of Kenya to Sweden and other Nordic countries, Professor A.I. Salim and his wife Monira Salim, for perspective.

I wish to express sincere appreciation to the Reverend Dr Lissi Rasmussen, Copenhagen, Lecturer Cand. theol. Hans Raun Iversen, Institute of Systematic Theology, University of Copenhagen, Bente Stær, Secretary at the Institute of Systematic Theology, University of Aarhus, Professor Kathleen A. Staudt, Department of Political Science, University of Texas at El Paso, USA, Professor Dr.Phil. Holger Bernt Hansen, centerleder, Center for Afrikastudier, University of Copenhagen, Professor Anna Marie Aagaard, Institute of Systematic Theology, University of Aarhus, Harold V. Smuck, Friends United Meeting in Richmond, Indiana, USA, and Dr Lester Crook, British Academic Press, London, for editorial advice. They all committed themselves in order to facilitate a speedy publication of Ane Marie's work, and for this I want to thank them.

Appreciation also goes to various institutions that funded Ane Marie's research for different periods, and the publication of this book: The Lutheran World Federation, Geneva, Switzerland; the Scandinavian Institute of African Studies, Uppsala, Sweden; Institute of Systematic Theology, University of Aarhus; the Danish Research Council for the Humanities, and Jens Nørregaards og Hal Kochs Mindefond, Copenhagen.

Finally, a word of sincere thanks goes to our two sons, Hans Peter Bak Wasike Mululu and Zakarias Bak Wasike Mululu, for their forbearance during the period of research in Kenya, the USA and the UK. They have known many days when we were absent from home and play, and many evenings when we worked late. I hope one day they will find inspiration in what their mother was applying herself to.

We continue to look back and cherish the years of companionship and friendship, love and affection, within our family.

Aarhus, May 1994

Introduction

KATHLEEN STAUDT

Ane Marie Bak Rasmussen, my colleague and my dear friend, has produced a scholarly work of extraordinary depth and breadth. She tells the long and rich story of the Society of Friends in Kenya, beginning with historical perspectives on the Quaker Mission in Kenya, moving to the interaction between western Kenyan peoples and missionaries of the Friends Africa Mission in a colonial context, and concluding with the ongoing organizational development and separation of the African Friends in independent Kenya.

Before I go any further, I must say something about Ane Marie as a person, for it is her remarkable character that makes this study the full and even-handed account it is. Many shared my sense of shock and tremendous grief when they learned of Ane Marie's tragic and untimely illness and death in 1992.

Although we were born five days and six time zones apart, our paths crossed in Kenya in 1974. We met in Nairobi, began going to Government of Kenya Archives together, and soon became close friends. Once our reading tasks were completed, we journeyed to Western Province, parting temporarily as we pursued separate research interests – hers on the Friends; mine on farmers and agricultural policy. Periodically, Ane Marie and her husband, Joseph Mululu, would invite me to attend church meetings and visit compounds in the Province. Once my interviews with farmers were completed, I stayed with Ane Marie near Kakamega to analyse the data and prepare my report on preliminary findings to the University of Nairobi. By this time, we had become like sisters. This sister–friend of mine was the kindest and most generous person I have ever known. She was genuinely honest and scrupulously fair, and these personal qualities are exemplified in her research methods and emerge in her analysis. She moved with grace, integrity and trust among the many different Friends in Kenya. This manuscript and its documentation are a shining example of these characteristics.

After leaving Kenya, we sustained our relationship through correspondence and visits to one another's families and homes (the latter in 1985 and 1991). She, of course, returned to Kenya many times. This book is the intellectual project of her life, and in absorbing its insights we both learn about the Friends and treasure her memory.

This story of the Friends in Kenya has multiple layers and strands of meaning and complexity, and Ane Marie's comprehensive, interdisciplinary approach reveals these many dimensions. The book addresses a profound question scholars and practitioners ask about religion: How can we explain conflict among people who share a spiritual community? The answers are not simple; they require immersion in the lives and contexts in which people live, combined with rigorous historical and social scholarship.

On one level, this is the history of particular ideas about people's relationship to their deity, and how those ideas are transformed in different contexts. Among the Quakers in pre-twentieth-century Britain and the United States, we learn about a religiosity so intensely experienced that its adherents disagreed and separated into different organizations. One stream of faith produced an evangelicalism that transcended national boundaries. Religious intensity which commits adherents' ideas to their everyday life practices produces splits among Friends in many parts of the world. Whatever the decade, Friends disagreed over the meaning, practice and priority of particular principles in their everyday life. Ane Marie methodically documents these differences, culling evidence from historical texts, letters, government archives and oral histories, interviews and observations with Friends in the late- and post-colonial historical periods. On another level, Ane Marie has written a sociological analysis of African people, their changing political economy, and the ensuing new forms of social stratification. Rifts within the Church reflect the growing differentiation of Luyia peoples by class, region, gender and language. Material inequality and poverty undermined members' spiritual equality.

The other side of Ane Marie's sociological analysis is her focus on structural characteristics such as church size, growth, and organizational hierarchy. She describes leadership styles and strategies hitherto only known regionally in Kenya or buried in records.

This story is also a political one. How do leaders relate to one another? To their members? What is the relationship between Church and state? What are the international relations of missions and churches around the world? For long periods of the twentieth century, the colony in which Friends lived denied them democratic rights. Friends turned to the institution – the Church – in which they did have the moral and organizational right to expect accountability. The Church had both spiritual and material development missions, the latter including industrial and agricultural training, education, and loans – invariably distributed unequally to men and women in different regions. In the context of limited opportunities and scarce resources, Friends agonized over the classic social question: Who benefits? And the answers to this question involved intense struggle – intense because the incentives that propelled the growth of membership in this organization were not merely material but also ideological: the kind of ideological incentive that called for personal transformation in one's everyday life. It is no wonder that in the face of conflict, 'exit' became an option exercised as much as 'loyalty' and 'choice'.[1]

In her thorough distillation of the language of official records, in the bureaucracy and between correspondents, Ane Marie compels readers to wonder at the discourse that one cultural group uses about the other, and the distance such discourse – embedded in an elaborate hierarchy – creates between human beings. These insights are produced not through polemic, but simply through Ane Marie's painstaking revelation of language across time, space and social division. Her scholarship is a social science – a science not of national statistics, rigid survey research instruments and quantitative analysis, but of intimate knowledge of the people, academic literature, and life in Kenya and the areas she writes about. Many villages and towns mentioned in this book are towns that Ane Marie visited, from those on well-traversed roads to those off the beaten track. She not only interviewed church leaders but spoke with hundreds – maybe thousands – of ordinary people in the course of conversation, shared meals, and work together. Before contemporary scholars began calling for analyses of ordinary people and their agency in history, Ane Marie was there, merging her intellectual project with personal qualities to produce an analysis that fully covers people's everyday lives.

Ane Marie's analysis is an inclusive one, revealing the experiences of leaders and members, rich and poor, Africans and non-Africans, men and women. Because women, despite their strong allegiance to and membership in Friends activities, have limited voice in theological alliances and disputes, it is ironic that a woman such as Ane Marie gives voice to this fascinating history for an international readership.

African Friends will go forward, making their own history in ways that replicate some of the alliances and conflicts of the past. Will another voice bear scholarly witness to that story with Ane Marie's depth, sensitivity and care? The analytic gift she has bequeathed us will last a long time, leaving indelible insights – insights that all humans and Friends can use to bring a just and noble meaning into their lives.

Kathleen Staudt, Professor of Political Science,
University of Texas at El Paso

Note

1. The conceptual language of these last two sentences comes from the work of political scientist James Q. Wilson and economist Albert O. Hirschman.

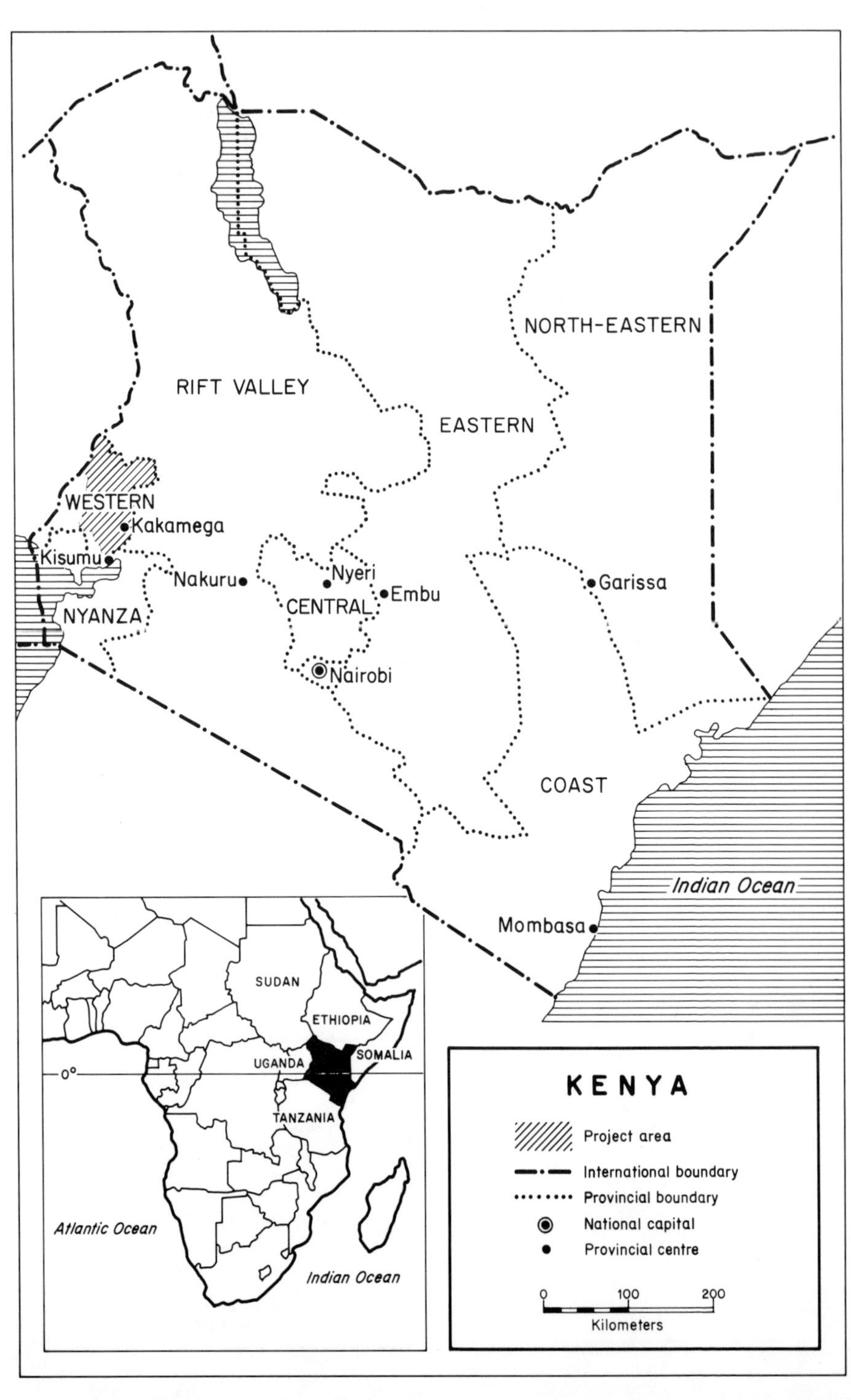
RIFT VALLEY
NORTH-EASTERN
EASTERN
WESTERN
Kakamega
Kisumu
Nakuru
Nyeri
Embu
Garissa
CENTRAL
NYANZA
Nairobi
COAST
Indian Ocean
Mombasa
SUDAN
ETHIOPIA
SOMALIA
UGANDA
0°
TANZANIA
Atlantic Ocean
Indian Ocean
KENYA
Project area
International boundary
Provincial boundary
National capital
Provincial centre
0
100
200
Kilometers

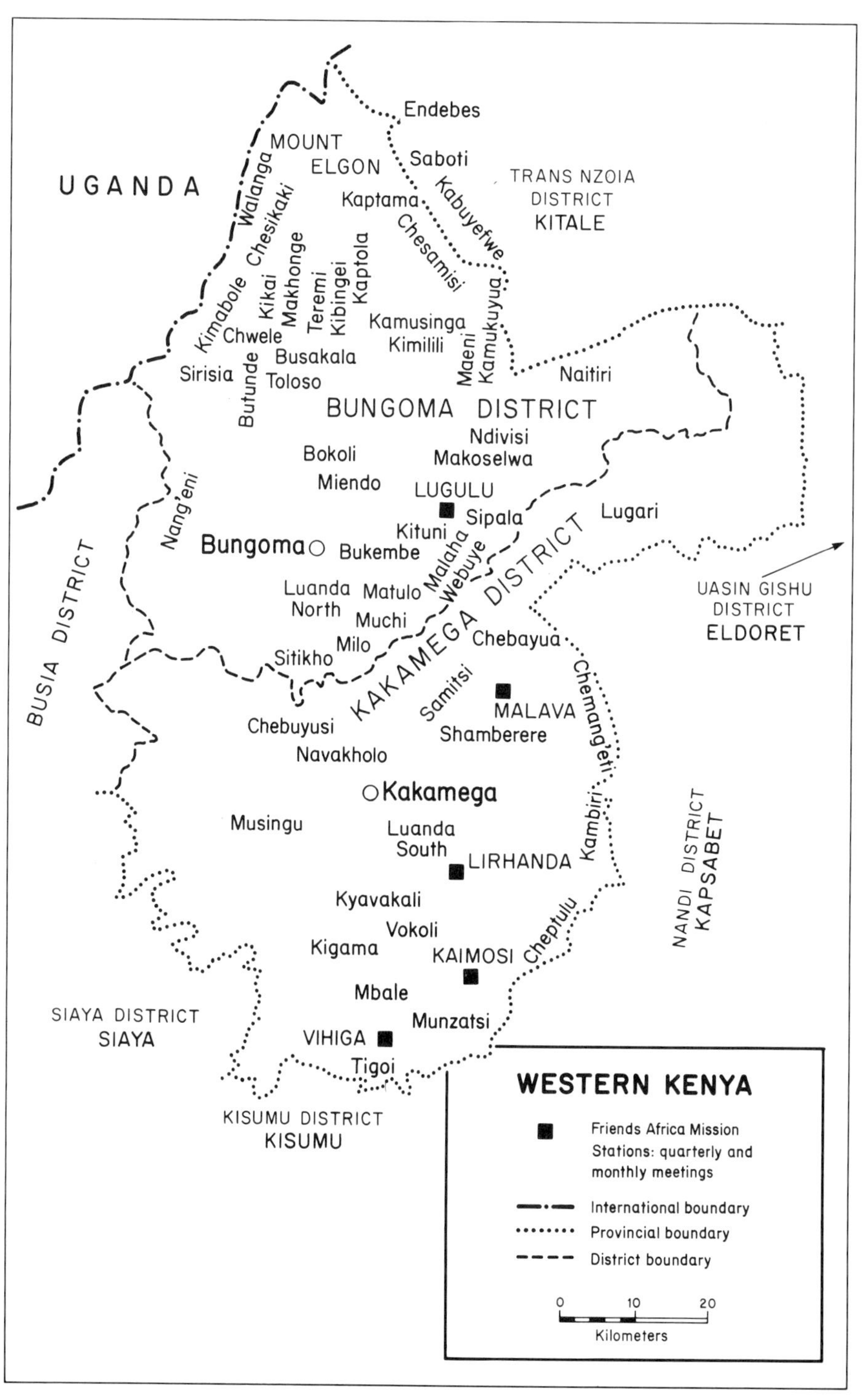

UGANDA
MOUNT ELGON
Endebes
Saboti
TRANS NZOIA DISTRICT
KITALE
Walanga
Chesikaki
Kaptama
Kabuyefwe
Chesamisi
Kimabole
Kikai
Makhonge
Teremi
Kibingei
Kaptola
Kamusinga
Kimilili
Kamukuyua
Maeni
Chwele
Busakala
Sirisia
Butunde
Toloso
Naitiri
BUNGOMA DISTRICT
Ndivisi
Makoselwa
Bokoli
Miendo
LUGULU
Sipala
Lugari
Nang'eni
Kituni
Bungoma
Bukembe
Malaha
Webuye
KAKAMEGA DISTRICT
UASIN GISHU DISTRICT
ELDORET
Luanda North
Matulo
Muchi
Milo
Sitikho
Chebayua
BUSIA DISTRICT
Samitsi
MALAVA
Chemang'eti
Chebuyusi
Shamberere
Navakholo
Kakamega
Musingu
Luanda South
LIRHANDA
Kambiri
NANDI DISTRICT
KAPSABET
Kyavakali
Vokoli
Kigama
KAIMOSI
Cheptulu
Mbale
Munzatsi
SIAYA DISTRICT
SIAYA
VIHIGA
Tigoi
KISUMU DISTRICT
KISUMU
WESTERN KENYA
Friends Africa Mission Stations: quarterly and monthly meetings
International boundary
Provincial boundary
District boundary
0
10
20
Kilometers

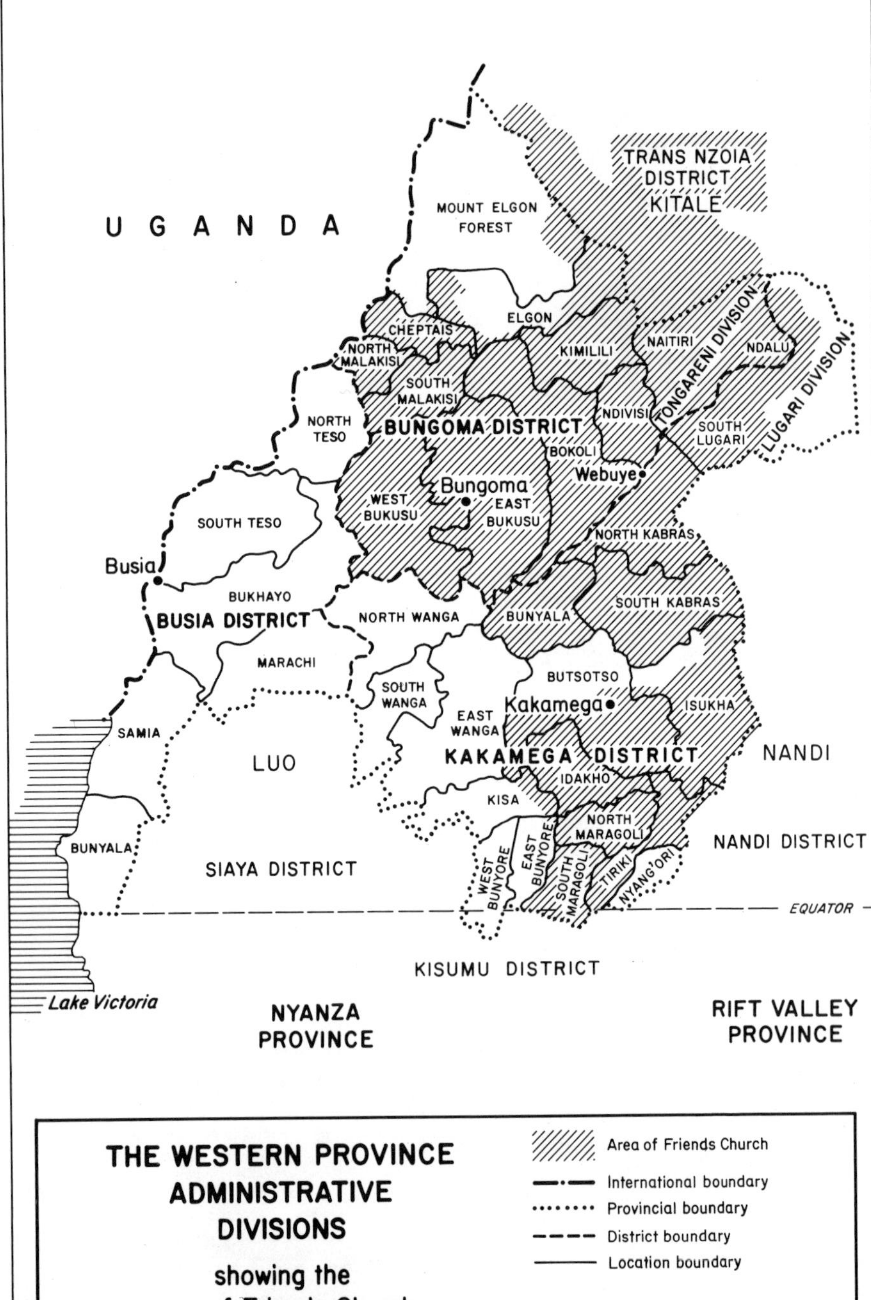

UGANDA
MOUNT ELGON FOREST
TRANS NZOIA DISTRICT
KITALE
ELGON
CHEPTAIS
NORTH MALAKISI
SOUTH MALAKISI
KIMILILI
NAITIRI
TONGARENI DIVISION
NDALU
LUGARI DIVISION
NDIVISI
SOUTH LUGARI
NORTH TESO
BUNGOMA DISTRICT
BOKOLI
Webuye
Bungoma
WEST BUKUSU
EAST BUKUSU
SOUTH TESO
NORTH KABRAS
Busia
BUKHAYO
BUSIA DISTRICT
NORTH WANGA
BUNYALA
SOUTH KABRAS
MARACHI
BUTSOTSO
SOUTH WANGA
Kakamega
ISUKHA
SAMIA
EAST WANGA
LUO
KAKAMEGA DISTRICT
NANDI
IDAKHO
KISA
NORTH MARAGOLI
NANDI DISTRICT
BUNYALA
WEST BUNYORE
EAST BUNYORE
SOUTH MARAGOLI
TIRIKI
NYANG'ORI
SIAYA DISTRICT
EQUATOR
KISUMU DISTRICT
Lake Victoria
NYANZA PROVINCE
RIFT VALLEY PROVINCE
THE WESTERN PROVINCE ADMINISTRATIVE DIVISIONS
showing the area of Friends Church (Quakers)
Area of Friends Church
International boundary
Provincial boundary
District boundary
Location boundary
0
10
20
Kilometers

A History of the Quaker Movement in Africa

I

Background to the Quaker Mission to Kenya

The Development of Evangelical Quakerism

The Society of Friends in Kenya belongs to that large part of the Quaker family which has programmed meetings for worship and appoints pastors to care for its congregations. On the surface at least, this is a radical departure from the principles of the early Quakers of the seventeenth century. 'Hireling priests' and fixed rituals were features of church life which were abhorrent to the early Quakers, because they prevented the free expression of religious experience by all members of the meeting, and they represented some of the aspects of established church life in England at the time, against which the Quaker fathers and mothers rebelled.

When those same factors that were important in provoking the protest out of which the Society of Friends emerged begin to appear again within the Society of Friends itself, we need to analyse the historical development which led Quaker meetings to adopt such seemingly unquakerly practices, yet without losing their essentially Quaker character.

The Rise of Quakerism

England in the mid-seventeenth century, with its great political and religious turmoil, was the background for the rise of Quakerism. From 1642 the Civil War raged between King Charles I and his supporters among the nobility and gentry, on the one hand; and Oliver Cromwell and his New Model Army, supported by the merchant class, on the other. The king was defeated and finally executed in 1649, after which Cromwell assumed power over the whole country, from 1653 as Lord Protector.

Cromwell's New Model Army contained within its ranks representatives from all those groups in society that were opposed to the oppressive power of the king and the established Church. At that time the whole of England was divided into parishes of the Church of England, to which everybody was expected to belong. But a rebellion was going on. The Puritans wanted a 'pure' church, free from priests who worked only for money, and freedom from the control of the bishops. Many tried to reform the Church by working within the existing parish structure. But there were many who were in favour of abolishing the parish system altogether and forming new communities of true believers, free from any control by religious or political authorities. Those groups were often seeking a more inward type of religion based on individual experiences rather than on the authority of the Bible as interpreted by the priests. They were especially strong in the poor northwestern part of the country, where the control of the civil and ecclesiastical authorities was less rigid than further south, and their radical religious ideas often went hand in hand with equally radical political ideas of opposition to the landowning nobility and to the king.

Quakerism arose in the midst of this political and religious upheaval. A number of its early leaders had been soldiers in the New Model Army, and were strongly influenced by the radical ideas which were prevalent there, and many early Quakers were recruited from groups of 'Seekers', 'Ranters', and other separatists opposed to the religious and social oppression of the ruling classes and the established Church.[1]

The man who is considered, in Quaker history, to be the founder of the Society of Friends is George Fox. A number of other people had experiences similar to his, and probably played as important a part in creating the Society. However, Fox's spiritual discoveries, as related in his Journal, serve as a good illustration of the type of spirituality that characterized the early Quakers. Also, his Journal has come to assume an authoritative position in later Quaker thought, and for these reasons his experiences are related here in some detail.

George Fox was born in 1624 in a small town in Leicestershire where his father was a weaver and a churchwarden. From his early youth he found no satisfaction in the parish church life in which he grew up, and in 1643 he decided to leave home and travel around, seeking a true relationship with God.[2] At first he found some truth in various Puritan priests. But he soon began to see their reliance on the

Scriptures, which they regarded as infallible, and the fixed rituals in their church services, as too outward a form of religion; he then turned to the separatist groups, hoping to find what he was searching for in them. But even there he found nobody who 'could speak to his condition'. Finally, in 1647, after four years of seeking, came his central experience, which he describes in his Journal in these words:

> And when all my hopes in them and in all men were gone, so that I had nothing outwardly to help me, nor could tell what to do, then, Oh then, I heard a voice which said, 'There is one, even Christ Jesus, that can speak to thy condition', and when I heard it my heart did leap for joy. Then the Lord did let me see why there was none upon the earth that could speak to my condition, namely, that I might give him all the glory; ... For though I read the Scriptures that spoke of Christ and of God, yet I knew him not but by revelation, as he who hath the key did open, and as the Father of life drew me to his Son by his spirit.[3]

This experience showed him that neither the words of any person nor reading the Scriptures could reveal God to him. God could be known only when Christ revealed himself directly to a human being, without any intermediaries. And when this happened, that person was taken up into a different sphere of existence, leaving the sinfulness of the world behind. Fox says:

> I knew nothing but pureness, and innocency, and righteousness, being renewed up into the image of God by Christ Jesus, so that I say I was come up to the state of Adam which he was in before he fell.[4]

Fox had experienced what, in Quaker terminology, came to be described as 'the inner Light' which was seen as Christ revealing himself directly to a human being, or 'the Seed' planted by God inside a person which could grow only when it was activated by the Holy Spirit.[5] He believed that for those who repented there was no longer any need to wait for the Second Coming of Christ. Christ was already here, and he could be known through the inner Light. After sixteen hundred years of apostasy, when only remnants of the true, believing Church had remained within the structures called churches, the same Spirit that had spoken to the apostles had now come back to direct the lives of individuals. The Day of the Lord was nigh, and the whole world had to be turned to the Light in preparation for it.[6]

Fox immediately began to preach about his new discovery, often in the open, at markets or in other places where many people gathered.

He also used to go into parish churches, which he called 'steeple-houses' in order to indicate that he saw nothing of the true, holy Church in them, and here he would speak after the sermon against what he saw as the lifeless words of the 'hireling priest' who worked for pay but had no real spiritual understanding of the matters about which he preached. Fox saw the Scriptures which the Puritan priests emphasized as the only true guide to life as dead letters if they were not interpreted by the Spirit of Christ within.[7] In the same way, he was against the 'ordinances' of baptism and communion. He saw these as further examples of the practice of dead, outward rites without spiritual content. What mattered was the true baptism in the heart of the believer, and true inner communion with God.[8]

A number of people found in Fox's message the answer to their search for truth. Many of them belonged to already established but often isolated groups of 'Seekers' or other religious radicals, especially in northern and western England, and they formed the nucleus of the new movement.[9] Many of them had already, for some time, held their own meetings for worship, apart from the meetings they held in parish churches, where they would sit and wait for a message from God to be given to any one of them, and then to be passed on from that person to the rest. When these people heard Fox preaching they recognized an experience of inward truth very similar to their own, and many joined forces with him and formed groups of 'Children of the Light', as they called themselves. A number of them went out, like him, as itinerant 'Publishers of Truth' to other parts of England, and even abroad, to spread the good news of the Light of Christ, which could lighten the darkness of the human heart and bring people into real communion with God, without the use of any priests as intermediaries. Their meetings for 'waiting on the Lord' – which seem to have been characterized by much enthusiasm during the early years but gradually developed into silent gatherings broken only by an occasional message about a revelation from God – became the backbone of the new movement, and in 1667–68 George Fox went around from one group to another, reorganizing and gathering them into monthly meetings.[10] This became the beginning of the Quaker hierarchy of preparative, monthly, quarterly and yearly meetings,[11] and the basis for the organization of the Society of Friends as a denomination.[12]

But not only did their meetings differ radically from the familiar parish church services. The Children of the Light quickly developed a new and characteristic lifestyle which set them apart from their surroundings. At the root of this new lifestyle was their belief that God did not mean the experience of the inner Light of Christ to be restricted to a few people: all human beings, both high and low, could be enlightened by it and receive its revolutionary power to transform their lives according to the will of God. And because they did not see the parish priests as in any way superior to others in this respect, nor able to guide others in matters of Truth, the Children of the Light refused to pay tithes which were used for the priests' upkeep. This refusal constituted a legal offence and became one of the reasons for the persecutions they were to suffer.

Their belief in the equality of all human beings in the eyes of God also led them to treat everybody as a social equal. Consequently they refused 'hat-honour' – doffing one's hat in the presence of social superiors – and instead of addressing higher-ranking persons with the customary 'you' they insisted on using the pronouns 'thee' and 'thou' to everybody, although these were normally used only in talking with social equals or children. This 'plain speech' went hand in hand with plain living in every sense. 'Plain dress' became another Quaker characteristic: dressing in the type of clothes used by ordinary working people, without unnecessary decorations or bright colours. And just as no one was supposed to show her- or himself superior to others in her or his way of dressing, so no one should take advantage of others in her or his business dealings. Absolute honesty in measuring and weighing, and refusal to bargain, became strict Quaker principles.[13]

In Quaker tradition a distinction is made between such customs as plain speech and plain dress, on the one hand, and the 'testimonies' which might often lead to suffering, and which therefore served as 'winnowing tests' of the real quality of the membership, on the other.[14] These testimonies were the refusal of tithing and the refusal of hat-honour, and also the refusal of oaths and war. The Quakers believed that Christ himself had forbidden his followers to swear. Those who had been liberated by the Light of Christ could no longer go back to the bondage of the oath, but must speak the truth plainly as revealed to them by Christ.[15] The testimony against war was developed as a consequence of the belief in the dignity of every human being in the eyes of God as one who had the potential to receive His Light. Nobody, therefore, had the right to kill anybody else. As mentioned above, a number of the early Quakers had been soldiers in Cromwell's New Model Army. But as early as 1651 George Fox refused to do military service,[16] and testimony against war soon became a commonly accepted Quaker principle for which the Quakers were willing even to suffer persecution.

And they were persecuted almost from the beginning, on various grounds. Many were outraged at the preaching and behaviour of these people: at what was seen as disturbance of public worship and insubordination to people in authority. Their belief that Christ revealed himself directly to people through the inner Light which elevated them to a state of sinlessness led to charges of blasphemy, and on all these charges they could be arrested and often kept in jail for long periods of time. George Fox was arrested in Derby in 1650, accused of blasphemy, and it was here, according to his Journal, that the group first got the name 'Quakers' when the judge used it as a nickname after Fox had told him to tremble at the name of the Lord.[17] The name 'Friends' seems to have come into use around 1652.[18]

Throughout most of the second half of the seventeenth century the Quakers were persecuted. Thousands were jailed, and a few even died from the hardships they suffered in prison. During the first few decades this did not, however, detract from their missionary zeal. On the contrary, they would openly defy orders against their meetings, and continue their public preaching in spite of threats from the authorities. But gradually, as the Quakers realized that their message was not going to be universally accepted and revolutionize the whole world, their eagerness to preach to everybody faded. They were still determined to stand up for their principles, they still held on to their testimonies, their silent meetings for worship, and their special way of life. But activities aimed at converting other people gradually ceased, and they concentrated on preserving the type of life they believed that God had revealed to them. At the time of Fox's death in 1691 this tendency was already apparent, and from around 1725 Quakers settled into the period of Quietism which was to last about a century.

The weakening of the revolutionary spirit among Friends and their disillusionment concerning their potential to change the world were expressions of a general tendency in English society at the time. Cromwell's republic had not lasted long. In 1660, two years after his death, came the Restoration, when anti-royalist forces had to give up their fight and the monarchy was reinstated. Cromwell had shown a certain understanding of Quakers and other dissenting groups; nevertheless they had been persecuted during his Protectorship because they were often seen as a threat to the state and to national stability.

The same fear continued after the Restoration and led to fierce persecution for another twenty to thirty years. But as political opposition to the monarchy crumbled, there was a general wish to conform to the authorities' demands. Many dissenting groups ceased to exist, and those that survived, including the Quakers, turned their attention more and more towards spiritual matters and consolidation of their own ranks, and away from attempts to bring an unresponsive society into line with their ways. The authorities, on the other hand, stopped seeing these people as a threat; consequently, the persecutions decreased.

In 1689 an Act of Toleration was passed which gave freedom of conscience, and although there were still areas of disagreement between the state and the Quakers – over tithing and oaths, for example – on the whole the Society of Friends was now left to live peacefully according to its own principles.[19]

Quakers had stopped preaching the judgement of God over unbelievers, and trying to convert them to the true principles of the Light. But they continued to be open to God's guidance in matters of conscience, and this led them to develop a strong sense of justice and to work actively for social reform. Friends started aid for poor people and work for prison reform very early – first in order to help their own members during the years of persecution, but later the experience they gained from this work was used for the benefit of the wider society. They were also among the pioneers in work for the liberation of slaves and for establishing proper, peaceful relations with Indians in America.[20]

The Spread of Quakerism in America

The broadcasters of truth did not limit their activities to England. As early as 1655 some of them went to the continent of Europe and as far as Jerusalem and Constantinople, though they did not win many converts.[21] More successful were those who went to America. The first to go there were two women, Mary Fisher and Ann Austin, who arrived in Boston, Massachusetts, in 1656. On the whole, women played an important role as broadcasters of truth right from the beginning, constituting about half of their number.

When the two women arrived in Boston they were immediately imprisoned. Massachusetts had been set up as a Puritan colony, and its rulers wanted to keep it free from any other religious influence.

The Quakers were seen as a threat to their theocratic government, so they wanted to get rid of them as soon as possible. After five weeks in jail, Mary Fisher and Ann Austin were sent away on the same boat that had brought them. This did not help the Boston authorities much, though: two days later another boat brought eight more Quakers from England who were treated in the same way, and others followed them.

In 1658, in order to rid themselves of the Quaker intruders, the Massachusetts authorities passed a law which made it a capital offence for a Quaker to return to the colony after being banished. But rather than preventing them from coming, this law made a number of Quakers decide to challenge it openly, and as a result four Friends were hanged in Boston between 1659 and 1661. At that time the new English king, Charles II, who wanted to suppress the Puritanism of Cromwell's period, interfered and ordered the executions of Quakers to stop. But for many years thereafter Friends were still being persecuted in various ways in Massachusetts.[22]

Persecutions took place in a number of other American colonies as well, although they were not as fierce as those in Massachusetts. By around 1675, however, Friends had been accepted in most places, and they now began to come in larger numbers and to establish their settlements in the colonies along the Atlantic coast. In some they even came to hold most of the positions of authority – for example in Pennsylvania, which was set up by William Penn as a 'Holy Experiment' aimed at establishing a true Christian colony according to Quaker ideals. The experiment lasted until 1756, when Pennsylvania's involvement in the Seven Years War with the French and the Indians brought Friends into conflict with their peace testimony, and most of them resigned their seats in the governing assembly.[23]

Towards the end of the eighteenth century many Friends felt that the institution of slavery in the eastern colonies was a burden on their conscience, and in 1787, when the Northwest Territory[24] was opened up for colonization, with the rule that slavery was not to be introduced there, many saw migration into the new areas as the solution to this problem, as well as a means of getting good farm land. Thus Quakers, together with many others, started the Great Migration westwards, settling in small farming communities, and wherever they went they established new meetings. Soon their numbers were sufficient to set up new yearly meetings, and in 1813 Ohio Yearly Meeting was created as an offshoot of Baltimore Yearly Meeting. In 1821 Indiana Yearly Meeting sprang up from Ohio, and other yearly meetings further west were established during the nineteenth century, all for purely geographical reasons.[25]

The Hicksite Separation, 1827–28

Meanwhile, new social and religious developments on the east coast gradually led the Society here into a crisis which could not be resolved through peaceful means, and finally resulted in a serious schism that had implications for the whole of the Society of Friends.

In the city of Philadelphia a number of Friends had attained powerful positions within the business community. Their influence in the Quaker meetings was also considerable, and they held the majority of positions as elders. During the last decades of the eighteenth and the first decades of the nineteenth century, they – as well as many other people in the city – gradually came to accept evangelical doctrines as the true interpretation of Christianity, and for these Friends the acceptance of such ideas was facilitated through the visits of English travelling ministers who combined evangelical views with adherence to Quaker customs.[26]

In the countryside these ideas had not penetrated to the same extent as in the city. The majority of Friends here held strongly to the old Quaker belief in the all-important role of the inner Light as the only true guide to God. At the same time, they had been influenced by a new democratic spirit which gave them a feeling of independence in the face of the elders' authority. Their most prominent spokesman was Elias Hicks, a farmer and preacher from the State of New York. He was an eloquent speaker who had travelled in the ministry for about fifty years before anyone began to challenge his views. For him, and for many of his followers, the evangelical emphasis on the importance of the death of Jesus Christ for salvation, and on the authority of the Scriptures, was too 'outward' a form of religion. He believed that the only true authority was the inner Light working in human hearts, and the real cross was this Light of Christ in the soul calling for the crucifixion of self-will.[27]

The peaceful coexistence of these two groups within the Society of Friends could not last. When, around 1820, Elias Hicks came to preach in Philadelphia and criticized the elders there for not ordering their lives according to established Quaker principles, the difference between them came out into the open, and they in turn attacked his theological views, which they saw as false and unorthodox. After a number of clashes between the two groups, where neither would give in to the other, the inevitable schism finally came at the yearly meeting in Philadelphia in 1827. Hicks' supporters could no longer submit to the authority of the elders, who were unwilling to allow their views within the Society, and when the yearly meeting showed signs of wanting to impose the 'orthodox' position, the 'Hicksites' decided to make a 'peaceful retreat' and set up their own, separate yearly meeting.

The separation in Philadelphia Yearly Meeting had consequences for all other yearly meetings. When the two groups, both claiming to be Philadelphia Yearly Meeting, now sent the customary yearly meeting 'epistles' to all other yearly meetings, those were, in turn, forced to decide which one to recognize. The same controversy between an orthodox and a Hicksite group existed in some of them, and it now came out into the open, resulting in separations in New York, Baltimore, Ohio and Indiana Yearly Meetings in 1828, while the rest of the yearly meetings, both in America and in England, confirmed their orthodox positions. These separations showed that evangelical views had taken firm root in the Society of Friends. The majority of the yearly meetings were now orthodox, Hicksite supporters having outnumbered the orthodox only in Philadelphia, New York and Baltimore Yearly Meetings, and Ohio having divided into two almost equal parts.

The Second Separation in America 1845–55

The Hicksite Separation was the first major split within the Society of Friends. For the first time, yearly meetings existed which claimed to be truly Quaker meetings, yet did not enjoy the recognition of London Yearly Meeting, which had hitherto taken the position of parent yearly meeting to all others. But the Hicksite Separation was to be only the first of a number of schisms during the nineteenth century. The second major one occurred between 1845 and 1855; later ones were determined by the same controversies.

The separation that began in 1845 took place within the orthodox wing of the Society of Friends. In England, evangelical beliefs came to occupy an increasingly important place among Quakers; and in America, the extent to which evangelicalism permeated the Society of Friends was evident when a prominent English Quaker, Joseph John Gurney, went to America in 1837 on a visit which was to last nearly three years. Although he was a 'plain' Quaker who adhered to the peculiar customs of his Society, he was strongly influenced by the evangelical views held by Low-Church Anglicans. This meant that he emphasized the importance of the Scriptures to a greater extent than was customary among Quakers, while at the same time he de-emphasized the inner Light as the only true guide to God. Like other evangelicals he believed that a person could be justified by the grace of God at a specific point in life through belief in the sacrificial death of Jesus Christ, and this moment of justification – or conversion – could be followed, through the influence of the Holy Spirit, by sanctification as a second gift of grace:

> The serious and enlightened Christian of every name, will readily confess that it is only through the influence of this Holy Spirit, that he is enabled rightly to apprehend God, to know himself, and to accept Jesus Christ as his all-sufficient Saviour – that it is only through such an influence that he is converted in the first place, and afterwards sanctified and prepared for his heavenly inheritance.[28]

Although Gurney viewed sanctification as a gradual process taking place in the person after conversion and did not, like many evangelicals, believe that it had to be experienced at one specific moment, his distinction between justification and sanctification was nevertheless at variance with the Quaker belief that the Light of God, identified by many with the Holy Spirit, would work in a human being throughout his or her life, suppressing that which was opposed to the ways of God and giving the person power to act according to God's will. Justification, or acceptability in the eyes of God, was, for the traditional Quaker concept, indistinguishable from sanctification, since it was the same Light of God that justified a human being precisely through the process of sanctifying him or her. And this Light, or Holy Spirit, was the same one that had inspired those who wrote the Scriptures. Even though the Scriptures were regarded as important, therefore, they could not be held up as the only authority for the Christian life, since no one should exalt the letter of the Scriptures above the Spirit that gave them.[29]

When Gurney came to America and began to preach his views, people flocked to his meetings and he received a huge response. There were some, though, who did not agree with him so wholeheartedly, and saw his theology as a departure from Quakerism. Most important among them was John Wilbur, who belonged to New England Yearly Meeting. Although he was himself influenced by evangelical views, he felt that Gurney was leading Friends away from their belief in the inner Light. In a series of letters to his friend George Crosfield, written as early as 1832, when he was visiting English Friends, he says:

> Now … I would ask if it is not alike dangerous to man and dishonourable towards God, to deny that Jesus Christ has done anything for our salvation without us, and to deny that he is doing anything for us, within us, for the same purpose…[30]

Wilbur wanted to strike a balance between on the one hand the views of Elias Hicks, who tended to overemphasize the inner Light at the expense of the Scriptures, and on the other the extreme evangelical position – as he saw it – represented by Joseph John Gurney: that only the Scriptures were important. The latter, according to Wilbur, led to a too one-sided view of Christ's sufferings as the only condition for salvation. For him:

> what Christ has done for us without us, has not … in the least exonerated us from obedience, or from fulfilling as much of the conditions as devolves upon us.[31]

And he warned:

> where good works or obedience are struck altogether from the account … and implicit confidence being placed on Christ's redemption without us, then comes in the doctrine of universal salvation without any condition.[32]

Although he agreed with the general evangelical view of the possibility of sanctification, saying that the plan of our salvation and redemption consists of three things: repentance, the atoning blood of Christ, and the Holy Spirit which sanctifies,[33] he nevertheless found that the teaching of Gurney and other evangelicals about justification by a simple act of faith, separating it from sanctification, reduced the importance of the obedience worked in human hearts by the Holy Spirit.

Wilbur spoke strongly against Gurney in defence of what he saw as traditional Quaker beliefs. The majority in New England Yearly Meeting, however, were pro-Gurney, and they tried to persuade Wilbur's monthly meeting to disown him. When the monthly meeting was not willing to do this, the yearly meeting went to the extent of having it dissolved and affiliated to another monthly meeting which then withdrew his membership in 1843. This, however, did not solve the problem. A number of other members of New England Yearly Meeting supported John Wilbur. Thus there were splits in several of its monthly and quarterly meetings, leading to the setting up in 1845 of a separate yearly meeting composed of 'Wilburite' Friends, who numbered about five hundred, while the 'Gurneyites' remained with about six-and-a-half thousand members.[34]

Again the problem arose for the rest of the Society: to decide which of the meetings should be recognized when they both sent epistles to the other orthodox yearly meetings. Most of them, including London Yearly Meeting, were strongly evangelical, like the large body in New England. Therefore they chose to recognize the New England meeting, although this led to a number of small schisms in some of the yearly meetings. This decision was particularly painful for Philadelphia and Ohio Yearly Meetings. Both had experienced serious splits in the earlier Hicksite Separation, and wanted to avoid a second division among their members; they therefore postponed the decision. But in the Ohio Yearly Meeting of 1854 the issue could no longer be left undecided when both Thomas B. Gould, a strong supporter of John Wilbur in New England, and Eliza P. Gurney, widow of Joseph John Gurney, were present, each providing a focusing point for the two groups, and it now came to a schism between the larger Wilburite and the smaller Gurneyite body, each of them setting up its own Ohio Yearly Meeting. This event again made it more urgent for Philadelphia Yearly Meeting to decide which course to take, and although it was divided between a strongly anti-Gurney group and an influential minority of his supporters, finally, in 1857, it came to the decision that in order to preserve unity within its own ranks it would suspend all epistolary correspondence with other yearly meetings, thereby to a large extent isolating itself from the rest of the Society of Friends.[35]

Revival among American Friends in the Late Nineteenth Century

After the second separation, American Friends were now divided into three groups: Hicksites, Wilburites (also called Conservatives) and Gurneyites, or Orthodox. The latter group was to become strongly engaged when a revival swept through the country from around 1860 onwards.

The Protestant churches in America had experienced a number of revivals before this, but the Society of Friends, which since the early eighteenth century had been an exclusive group, dedicated to the perfection of its own inner life, had not been influenced by these earlier revivals because Quakers attended only their own meetings.[36] As we have seen, however, Friends were gradually becoming more open towards members of other denominations, and on the 'frontier' in the Midwestern and Western states, where members of many different churches settled as neighbours, the isolation of Friends was no longer possible. This had led to the incorporation of evangelical views into the beliefs of the Society, and when other denominations experienced a renewal of revival efforts, Orthodox Friends had become so much a part of them that from around 1860 they, too, became involved.

One of the leaders of this revival was Charles Grandison Finney, a Presbyterian-Congregational lay preacher. Finney believed that a revival 'is not a miracle, or dependent on a miracle.... It is a purely philosophical result of the right use of the constituted means.'[37] He was convinced that if only the proper methods were used, a revival would follow. And all through his fifty years as a revivalist, starting in the mid-1820s, he made extended use of such methods as 'protracted meetings', often lasting for several days, emotional preaching, calls for individual decision to accept Jesus as a personal saviour, and the use of a 'mourners' bench' where those who were repenting their sins could come to be prayed for by the leaders.[38] These methods were originally used by Methodists, but they were now taken over by Finney and other revivalists, and thereby given wider acceptance.[39]

A number of Friends attended meetings where such methods were used, and some of them experienced conversion of the type preached by the revival leaders, where justification, or regeneration, was experienced at a specific moment, often accompanied by emotional outbursts. Those Quakers who had been converted in this way carried their enthusiasm over into their own Society, where they began to preach in the same manner as other revival preachers, and often with the same results.

Certain religious practices had been developed within the Society of Friends which prepared the ground for this revival. From the late 1830s – to a large extent because of the influence of Joseph John Gurney – Friends had begun to study the Bible seriously. Before that, as we saw above, their fear of formality in worship and their wish to remain open to the promptings of the Spirit had made them limit their use of the Bible. That attitude was now changing. Although the meetings for worship remained silent, other types of meetings were developed which could accommodate the new interests. A number of people, the majority often young Friends, would come together in the evenings to read the Bible and tracts together, and it was in these more informal groups that the revival among Quakers started. The restraint of the silent meetings for worship, where to stand up and speak was considered a very serious matter, was not felt here; therefore, those who had been converted in revival meetings of other denominations would freely give testimonies, and there would be vocal prayer.

One of the first revival meetings among Friends took place in Richmond, Indiana, during Indiana Yearly Meeting of 1860, when a group asked permission to hold an evening meeting for worship for the younger Friends. Despite a good deal of opposition, permission was granted and the meeting was held, with more than a thousand people in attendance. For many, this became the first time that they had spoken in a religious meeting, and there were hundreds of testimonies and prayers.[40] This meeting led to the permanent institution of evening meetings in Richmond, and the practice spread to many other areas. One other centre of the new revival right from the beginning was Ohio Yearly Meeting. In these and other places the new type of meeting gradually gained more acceptance, resulting in many meeting houses opening their doors to them as an addition to their silent meetings for worship.[41]

In 1867 there was a strong revival in Walnut Ridge, Indiana, and in Bangor, Iowa. In Iowa:

> many hearts were reached and all broken up, which was followed by sighs and sobs and prayers, confessions and great joy for sins pardoned and burdens rolled off, and precious fellowship of the redeemed.[42]

These emotional outbursts paralleled those in Indiana, where the revival spread to the regular meetings for worship and manifested itself in emotional praying, testimony, shouting and even singing, which hitherto had been almost unheard of in Friends meetings. At Walnut Ridge many older members, and even elders and overseers, were converted; and here, for the first time among Quakers, a 'mourners' bench' was used.[43]

Soon similar revivals took place in other Quaker communities, in most places sweeping the majority of the membership along with them. In a number of places, however, there was opposition, especially among the older members who until then had been the leaders of their meetings, and led them in what they saw as the true Quaker ways of silence and simplicity. The new emotional meetings were alien to these older Friends, and in a number of cases they were forced to see themselves left behind when the new practices, which to them were unquakerly, swept over their meetings. They wanted to stand up for essential Quaker truths, and in so doing they sometimes found it necessary to break the unity of their meetings and form new meetings where their viewpoints would be respected. This led to the setting up of 'Conservative' yearly meetings which were gradually recognized by the older Wilburite bodies.[44]

In the majority of Orthodox meetings, however, the wave of revivalism could not be stopped. This implied the acceptance by Friends of new measures that completely revolutionized their meetings for worship. Not only that: inseparably connected with the new patterns in worship, a different theological emphasis also came into the Society of Friends. The interdenominational revivalism was dominated by Holiness Methodism, with its fourfold gospel of conversion, sanctification, faith healing, and the expectation of Christ's Second Coming, and this influence was strongly felt among Friends, too. There were different degrees in the acceptance of the latter points, while the first two became generally accepted.[45] As we have seen, the idea of the possibility of sanctification was not new to Friends. What was new was the revivalists' insistence that sanctification could be experienced at a definite moment in a person's life, subsequent to and separate from the experience of conversion. And these beliefs were based on a fundamentalist reading of the Bible which left little or no room for the traditional Quaker doctrine of the inner Light.

The yearly meeting that adopted the fourfold gospel most fully was the evangelical Ohio Yearly Meeting, which went so far as to state that there was no 'principle or quality in the soul of man, innate or otherwise', that could in any way 'save a single soul'.[46] And their full acceptance of the general evangelical beliefs, including a strong emphasis on Scriptures, made many in Ohio Yearly Meeting even receive baptism and take part in communion, contrary to established Quaker practice.[47] Other yearly meetings strongly opposed the use of the 'ordinances', nor could the majority of them go to the extent of denying the validity of the inner Light, as Ohio had done. Nevertheless, the Gurneyite yearly meetings had been caught up in the evangelical revival, and adopted many of its theological beliefs. Both socially and theologically, evangelical Friends had adjusted to the society around them. They no longer saw themselves as a peculiar people, and many of their peculiar customs disappeared during the revival years.[48]

The revival did not mean only a change in the beliefs and religious practices of Friends. It also meant that large numbers of people who had not previously been Quakers were converted in Friends meetings, and thereafter decided to become Friends. For these people, coming from completely different denominational backgrounds, the silence of the traditional Friends meeting and its openness to the ministry of any of its members meant nothing. They came from backgrounds where it was natural to have a pastor leading the church service. They had in many cases been converted through the preaching of revival leaders, and they expected this leadership to continue. Quakers of longer standing also began to feel the need for one person to be in charge of the meeting, because of their wish to sustain the revival spirit and care for the many new members. As a result, from 1878 a number of meetings began to employ pastors.[49] This was a departure from the traditional Quaker collective responsibility – to a large extent taken care of by elders and overseers – for the meetings for worship and the spiritual welfare of members. John Punshon points out that there were economic reasons for this new practice, in addition to those mentioned above: farmers in the Midwest, where the pastoral system started and became most widely accepted, were moving from subsistence farming to commercial production of a single crop. They were therefore more vulnerable and, as a consequence, too pressed timewise and economically to be able to devote themselves to the task of following up the gains of the revival. Thus, instead of a number of them sharing the responsibility, it was natural to delegate the work to one particular person, and to pay him a maintenance salary.[50]

In the discussion among Friends as to whether it was right for them to accept the pastoral system, it was pointed out that there is a difference between preaching for pay and being paid for preaching. Furthermore, it was emphasized that this did not mean the introduction of 'hireling priests' into Friends meetings; it did, however, mean that once it was decided that someone's services were required, it was fair to pay him for his work, since many ministers were poor and were leaving their families unprovided for.[51] For these reasons, the pastoral system was widely accepted throughout the Gurneyite yearly meetings during the 1880s and 1890s. With the advent of pastors there was also a change in the set-up of meetings. Elders and overseers who had earlier been the guardians of the spiritual and moral welfare of the meetings, respectively, lost much of their influence, since both aspects of their leadership were largely taken over by the pastors. Furthermore, as Friends followed the example of other denominations and employed mostly men as pastors, women lost many of the opportunities for service they had had before – not only as elders and overseers, but also as ministers. On the whole, there was a decline in spontaneous vocal ministry by ordinary members because the pastors, since they were being paid for their work, felt that it was their responsibility to preach in the meetings.

Hence, as a result of the influence of the revival and the introduction of the pastoral system, Friends meetings became not unlike the church services of other Low-Church Protestant denominations. Although they did not introduce a fixed liturgy, meetings nevertheless followed a relatively fixed pattern laid down by custom and consisting of preaching, vocal prayer and singing of hymns, sometimes broken by periods of silence. These 'programmed' meetings, as they are called, had become normal and accepted among all evangelical Friends by the end of the nineteenth century, as opposed to the 'unprogrammed' meetings of Hicksite and Conservative Friends.[52]

Those yearly meetings that had been involved in the evangelical revival and adopted the pastoral system began to feel the need for more co-operation and unity at this time of great change, and in 1887 a conference was convened in Richmond, Indiana, for all yearly meetings in correspondence with London Yearly Meeting, where they drew up their common theological stand in the Richmond Declaration of Faith. The yearly meetings that took part in this Richmond Conference decided to meet at five-yearly intervals thereafter, and at their meeting in 1902 they formed the Five Years Meeting for the purpose of co-operation in various fields. Of all the Orthodox yearly meetings, only Ohio Yearly Meeting did not join, for fear that the basis for membership was not evangelical enough. Later, other yearly meetings or groups left the Five Years Meeting for the same reason. But it is still the largest body of Quakers in America, known since 1966 as Friends United Meeting, and now holding its meetings every three years.[53]

Eagerness for Mission

Foreign Mission Work – a Concern for Evangelical Friends

The evangelical influence which led to the great revival among Friends also aroused in them an interest in foreign mission work. Individual American Friends had done some work among Indians, but without calling themselves missionaries, and it was characteristic that there was no organized mission work. This was prevented by the Quaker fear of 'creaturely activity': any effort originating in people's own minds and not in a divine call. And an individual's 'concern' to follow a specific course of action might very well, however, be recognized by his or her meeting as a genuine call from God, and therefore receive its practical support. In a number of cases, therefore, individual concerns to go to foreign countries as missionaries received the support of the meetings to which the individuals belonged, before those same meetings were willing to set up any missionary organizations.

In this way, from around 1830 onwards, a few individual Friends, from both England and America, travelled to different parts of the world, mostly visiting the mission stations of other denominations, and the reports they brought home led to an increased interest in foreign mission work among Friends, and gradually also to a feeling that a collective effort was needed. This development went hand in hand with the revival which, as we have seen, led a majority of Friends in America to accept the pastoral system and reduced the fear of 'hireling' priests, thereby also making more acceptable missionaries who were to be financially supported in their work of spreading the Gospel. At the same time, the effects of the revival changed Friends' attitude towards active service in the world outside their own Society and made them less afraid of 'creaturely activity' so that their unwillingness to establish mission organizations gradually broke down.[54]

In 1870, at about the same time as the setting up of a Friends Foreign Mission Association in England, Indiana Yearly Meeting formed its own Foreign Missionary Society, which soon started work in Mexico, and before long other yearly meetings followed its example and established mission boards which took up work in various countries. In 1892 seven yearly meetings had their own mission boards operating seven different mission stations around the world; therefore, one of the main questions under discussion at the second quinquennial conference of the Orthodox yearly meetings in that year was that of unity in mission, since a co-ordination of all these efforts seemed desirable.

After recommendations had come from all the yearly meetings involved, in 1894 a conference was convened at which the American Friends Board of Foreign Missions was formed. And when the Five Years Meeting was set up in 1902, the American Friends Board of Foreign Missions became its official board of missions, gradually taking over most of the missionary activities of the individual yearly meetings.[55]

The Setting up of Friends Africa Industrial Mission

One of the mission boards that was later to be incorporated into the American Friends Board of Foreign Missions was the Friends Africa Industrial Mission Board. It was formed on the initiative of a group of students at the Friends Bible Institute in Cleveland, Ohio, who had been inspired by Willis R. Hotchkiss, who had spent four years, from 1895 to 1899, in Ukambani in the eastern part of Kenya with the Africa Inland Mission. His experiences in this mission – which had proved a failure, apparently in large part due to lack of organization and the mission's inability to offer relief during a severe famine in Ukambani – had taught him that a mission in Africa, if it was to be effective, must aim at creating 'a self-supporting, self-propagating native church'.[56] The African Church should, in the long run, be able to support itself and not be dependent on aid from the mission organization. Hotchkiss also believed that the ideal way to achieve this aim was for the missionaries to set up an industrial mission where their role would be not only to preach but also to teach the Africans practical skills which could help them to earn an income for the benefit of the Church. An additional argument offered by Hotchkiss in favour of this policy was that although he was convinced that 'what the world needs first and above all is, not changed social conditions, but Christ', he nevertheless believed that, 'there never can be a *real* change of heart that is not followed by a radical cleansing of the social conditions which immediately encompass it'.[57] And this 'cleansing' of the social conditions, which he describes in terms such as 'barbarism pure and simple, with its social anarchy, lawlessness, and consequent instability of character',[58] could be done precisely through the work of an industrial mission.

When Hotchkiss, himself a Quaker, came home to America in 1899, he first approached the American Friends Board of Foreign Missions in order to seek their support. But at that time they were about to take up new work in Cuba, and were unable to consider work in yet another country. He therefore brought his ideas to Friends Bible Institute in Cleveland, where he had been a student before he went to Kenya, and here he received an enthusiastic response. One of the students there was Arthur B. Chilson, who for some time already had felt a call to go to Africa as a missionary. When Hotchkiss described his plans he immediately joined forces with him, and they travelled around together to all American yearly meetings, gathering support for a mission in Africa. The result was that in 1901 nine yearly meetings formed the Friends Africa Industrial Mission Board, and in April 1902 Hotchkiss and Chilson, together with a trustee of Friends Bible Institute, Edgar T. Hole, left for Kenya.[59]

The new mission organization had accepted Hotchkiss's idea of an industrial mission, and stated in its records:

> The primary aim of the F.A.I.M. is the evangelization of the heathen.... The industrial feature is introduced into the work for the purpose of exerting a continuous Christian influence over the natives employed with the hope of obtaining the following results, viz: teaching them habits of industry and ultimately establishing a self-supporting native Christian Church.[60]

Notes

1. For an important description of this period and the role of religious groups in it, see Christopher Hill, *The World Turned Upside Down: Radical Ideas during the English Revolution*, Temple Smith, London, 1972. See also Susanne Gregersen: *Kvækersamfundet. Historisk, social, religiøs og politisk baggrund*, Kvekerforlaget, Ås, 1979. Quakerism's emergence from this background, and the subsequent history of the Society of Friends, are described in Barry Reay, *The Quakers and the English Revolution*, Temple Smith, London, 1985; Hugh Barbour, *The Quakers in Puritan England*, repr. by Friends United Press, Richmond, IN, 1985 (1st edn Yale University Press, New Haven, CT, 1964); Elfrida Vipont, *The Story of Quakerism through Three Centuries*, Friends United Press, Richmond, IN, 3rd edn 1977 (1st edn The Bamisolale Press, London, 1954); Elbert Russell, *The History of Quakerism*, Macmillan, New York, repr. 1943 (1st edn 1942); John Punshon, *Portrait in Grey: A Short History of the Quakers*, Quaker Home Service, London, 1984; Hugh Barbour and Arthur O. Roberts in their introduction to *Early Quaker Writings 1650–1700*, William B. Eerdmans Publishing Company, Grand Rapids, MI, 1973 (pp 13–46), and in William C. Braithwaite's very thorough volumes, *The Begin-*

nings of Quakerism, 2nd edn prepared by Henry J. Cadbury, Cambridge University Press, 1955 (1st edn 1912) and *The Second Period of Quakerism*, 2nd edn prepared by Henry J. Cadbury, Cambridge University Press, 1961 (1st edn 1919); and Rufus M. Jones, *The Later Periods of Quakerism*, vols I and II, Macmillan, London, 1921.

'Ranters' had a pantheistic view of the universe and believed in God's direct revelation to each individual human being. 'Seekers' were also seeking a first-hand knowledge of God's will. Other groups were 'Levellers', who wanted to level out social and economic differences, and 'diggers', who began to dig and cultivate unused areas of land.

2. George Fox, *The Journal of George Fox*, revised edn John L. Nickalls, Cambridge University Press, 1952, p 3.

3. Ibid., p 11.

4. Ibid., p 27.

5. Ibid., pp 12 ff.

6. Ibid., pp 103 ff.

7. Ibid., p 109.

8. Ibid., e.g. pp 45 f., 134.

9. It was important for the early Quakers to maintain a distance between themselves and, for example, Ranters; see Robert Barclay, 'The Anarchy of the Ranters', in *Truth Triumphant* (Collected Works), Benjamin C. Stanton, Philadelphia, PA, 1831, vol I, pp 457 ff. (first published 1674). This is an indication that there were similarities which might make it difficult for outsiders to distinguish between them. George Fox, when he preached to Ranters, found that they had 'tasted of the power of God' but had become 'dry', and were now misguided in their practices; he describes how he convinced many of them (Fox, *Journal*, e.g. p 79). The Westmorland Seekers were part of 'a great people to be gathered', according to the revelation he received on Pendle Hill in 1652, and they became an important part of the new movement.

10. Fox, *Journal*, pp 511 ff.

11. The preparative meeting for worship is the smallest local unit. The monthly meeting for business is often made up of a number of preparative meetings. This is the most important administrative unit, since membership always means association with a particular monthly meeting, and a monthly meeting is free to decide its own matters independent of other monthly meetings. Quarterly meetings for fellowship and business take place three or four times a year, and the highest level of co-operation is the yearly meeting to which all member monthly meetings send representatives.

12. It was important for Friends to emphasize what they saw as a fundamental difference between themselves and other churches. Those were part of the age of apostasy, with outward forms and rituals that could not awaken a real faith in their members, whereas Friends were a community of true believers; they therefore chose to call themselves a 'Society' rather than a church.

13. Braithwaite, *The Beginnings of Quakerism*, p 139; Fox, *Journal*, pp 169 f.

14. Jones, *The Later Periods of Quakerism*, vol I, pp 146 ff.

15. Braithwaite, *The Second Period of Quakerism*, p 15.
16. Fox, *Journal*, p 65.
17. Ibid., p 58.
18. Braithwaite, *The Beginnings of Quakerism*, p 73.
19. Punshon, *Portrait in Grey*, p 100.
20. See, for example, John Woolman's writings in Phillips P Moulton (ed.), *The Journal and Major Essays of John Woolman*, Oxford University Press, New York, 1971.
21. Braithwaite, *The Beginnings of Quakerism*, pp 406 ff.
22. Braithwaite, *The Second Period of Quakerism*, pp 401 ff.; Rufus M. Jones, assisted by Isaac Sharpless and Amelia M. Gummere, *The Quakers in the American Colonies*, Macmillan, London, repr. 1923, pp 26 ff.
23. Isaac Sharpless in Jones *et al.*, *The Quakers in the American Colonies*, pp 417 ff.; Braithwaite, *The Second Period of Quakerism*, pp 399 ff.
24. Later this territory became the states of Ohio, Indiana, Illinois, Wisconsin and Michigan.
25. Russell, *The History of Quakerism*, pp 269 ff.; Errol T. Elliott, *Quakers on the American Frontier: A History of the Westward Migrations, Settlements, and Developments of Friends on the American Continent*, Friends United Press, Richmond, IN, 1969, pp 60 ff.; Jones, *The Later Periods of Quakerism*, vol I, pp 377 ff.
26. This description of the Hicksite separation is based mainly on Jones, *The Later Periods of Quakerism*, vol I, pp 274 ff., 435 ff.; Robert W. Doherty, *The Hicksite Separation: A Sociological Analysis of Religious Schism in Early Nineteenth Century America*, Rutgers University Press, New Brunswick and New Jersey, 1967; and H. Larry Ingle, *Quakers in Conflict: The Hicksite Reformation*, University of Tennessee Press, Knoxville, 1986; but also on Russell, *The History of Quakerism*, pp 280 ff.; William Hodgson, *The Society of Friends in the Nineteenth Century: A Historical View of the Successive Convulsions and Schisms therein during that Period*, Smith, English & Co., Philadelphia, PA, 1875, vol I, pp 58 ff.
27. Jones, *The Later Periods of Quakerism*, vol I, pp 455.
28. Joseph John Gurney, *A Peculiar People: The Rediscovery of Primitive Christianity*, Friends United Press, Richmond, IN, 1979, p 75 (first published 1824 under the title *Observations on the Religious Pecularities of the Society of Friends*).
29. Thomas D. Hamm, 'The Transformation of American Quakerism, 1800-1910', unpublished PhD thesis, Indiana University, 1985, pp 22, 29, 51 ff.
30. John Wilbur, 'Letters on Some of the Primitive Doctrines of Christianity', in Meeting for Sufferings of New England Yearly Meeting of Friends, *Republication of the Letters of John Wilbur to George Crosfield; together with Some Selections from His Correspondence and Other Writings*, J.A. & R.A. Reid, Providence, RI, 1879, p 50.
31. Ibid., p 30.
32. Ibid., p 41.

33. Ibid., pp 31 f.

34. Jones, *The Later Periods of Quakerism*, vol I, pp 522 ff.

35. Ibid., p 526 ff.; vol II, pp 49 ff.; Hodgson, *The Society of Friends in the Nineteenth Century*, pp 292 ff.

36. Jones, *The Later Periods of Quakerism*, vol II, p 892.

37. Charles Grandison Finney, *Lectures on Revivals of Religion*, ed William G. McLoughlin, Harvard University Press, Cambridge, MA, 1960, p 13.

38. Ibid., p vii; William G. McLoughlin, *Revivals, Awakenings, and Reform: An Essay on Religion and Social Change in America, 1607–1977*, University of Chicago Press, Chicago and London, 1978, pp 122 ff.

39. Richard Carwardine, *Trans-Atlantic Revivalism: Popular Evangelicalism in Britain and America, 1790–1865*, Greenwood Press, Westport, CT, 1978, pp 10 ff.

40. Jones, *The Later Periods of Quakerism*, vol II, pp 885 ff.

41. Russell, *The History of Quakerism*, p 423.

42. Louis T. Jones, *Quakers of Iowa*, Iowa City, 1914, p 164, quoted from Russell, *The History of Quakerism*, p 426.

43. Jones, *The Later Periods of Quakerism*, vol. II, p 900; Russell, *The History of Quakerism*, pp 426 f.

44. Russell, *The History of Quakerism*, pp 429 ff.

45. J. Brent Bill, *David B. Updegraff: Quaker Holiness Preacher*, Friends United Press, Richmond, IN, 1983, pp 34 ff.; Hamm, 'The Transformation of American Quakerism', p 198.

46. *Ohio Yearly Meeting Minutes, 1879*, pp 28 f., quoted from Hamm, 'The Transformation of American Quakerism', p 246.

47. Brent Bill, *David B. Updegraff*, pp 23 ff.; Russell, *The History of Quakerism*, p 488.

48. Hamm, 'The Transformation of American Quakerism', pp 158 ff.

49. Russell, *The History of Quakerism*, p 483; Jones, *The Later Periods of Quakerism*, vol II, p 915; Hamm, 'The Transformation of American Quakerism', pp 248 ff.

50. Punshon, *Portrait in Grey*, pp 201 f.

51. Edwin B. Bronner (ed.), *An English View of American Quakerism: The Journal of Walter Robson (1842–1929). Written During the Fall of 1877, While Traveling among American Friends*, American Philosophical Society, Philadelphia, PA, 1970, p 87.

52. Russell, *The History of Quakerism*, pp 485 f.

53. Jones, *The Later Periods of Quakerism*, vol II, pp 930 ff.; Francis B. Hall (ed.), *Friends in the Americas*, Friends World Committee, Section of the Americas, Philadelphia, PA, 1976, pp 14 f., 22 f.

54. Christina H. Jones, *American Friends in World Missions*, American Friends Board of Missions, Richmond, IN, 1946, pp 25 ff.; Jones, *The Later Periods of Quakerism*, vol II, pp 870 ff.; Henry T. Hodgkin, *Friends Beyond Seas*, Headley Bros, London, 1916, pp 23 ff.

55. C.H. Jones, *American Friends*, pp 38 ff.; Russell, *The History of Quakerism*, pp 438 ff. In 1927 the American Friends Board of Foreign Missions was

merged with the American Friends Board of Home Missions, set up on the initiative of the Five Years Meeting of 1917, to form the American Friends Board of Missions (C.H. Jones, *American Friends*, pp 57 f.), now renamed the World Ministries Commission, under Friends United Meeting (Punshon, *Portrait in Grey*, p 219; Hall, *Friends in the Americas*, p 28 f.).

56. Willis R. Hotchkiss, *Sketches from the Dark Continent*, Headley Bros, London, 1903, p 111 (first published in America in 1901).

57. Ibid.

58. Ibid., pp 112 f.

59. C.H. Jones, *American Friends*, pp 186 ff.; Errol T. Elliott, 'J. Walter Malone', in *Quaker Profiles from the American West*, Friends United Press, Richmond, IN, 1972, pp 158 f. In 1911 the Friends Africa Industrial Mission Board was incorporated into the American Friends Board of Foreign Missions (C.H. Jones, *American Friends*, p 188).

60. C.H. Jones, *American Friends*, p 188.

2

The Early Years: Friends Africa Mission

The Peoples of Western Kenya and Their Religion

The area chosen by the Friends Africa Industrial Mission for its activities was the country of the Luyia, a group of Bantu-speaking peoples who occupy what is now the Western Province of Kenya. The Luyia are made up of about twenty different groups who, although related, are distinguished from each other by certain differences in language and customs. This study is concerned with the eastern Luyia peoples, because they were the ones who came under the influence of the Quaker missionaries. As a consequence, the Holy Spirit churches came into existence among some of them. They include the Logoli, Tiriki, Isukha, Idakho, Kabras, Tachoni, and Bukusu peoples.[1]

In the centuries before the British established their rule over the area there had been many migratory movements, resulting in the occupation of the country by the Luyia peoples. Most of them have traditions saying that their forefathers originated in Misri, normally identified as southern Egypt or northern Sudan, whence they migrated until, after many generations and after being settled for a number of years in various places, they arrived in their present country. These migratory movements were often undertaken by smaller groups – occasioned, for instance, by quarrels between members of a lineage which made one part of the lineage move to a different area, or by pressure from enemies which drove a group of people to seek refuge elsewhere. And even up until the time when the British took control of the country, it was common for families or lineages to move away from their land into unoccupied or sparsely populated areas whenever population pressure or other factors made this desirable.[2]

Wherever they arrived, the Luyia peoples would clear a plot of ground and settle down to perform their traditional economic activities of cultivating the land and taking care of their cattle and smaller animals. All Luyia were agriculturalists who combined growing crops with cattle-raising, the pastoral element being strongest in the northern part of the country, which was less densely populated than the southern parts. The basic economic unit was the elementary family, which was self-sufficient, except for a few items produced by specialists such as iron tools and pottery. Through their male members individual families were grouped in lineages and, on a larger scale, in clans which were patrilineal and exogamous, and often occupied a continuous stretch of land.[3]

Under normal circumstances, the clans were the most important political and ritual units among the majority of the Luyia peoples. Only the Wanga, immediately to the west of the groups discussed here, had a ruler, 'nabongo', whose power extended across all the clans to the whole of the Wanga people,[4] while among the Tiriki the clans were somewhat less important than among other Luyia because of a strong age-grade organization.[5] Among the other peoples, for defence of their territory, a number of clans might choose to co-operate in making arrangements for war, just as inter-clan co-operation was necessary if members of one clan had a judicial case against those of another. But in no case except that of the Wanga was there any centralized 'tribal' leadership before the colonial era.[6]

The most important leadership roles in most traditional Luyia societies, therefore, were to be found at clan level. Each clan had a council of elders whose members judged cases arising between different people in the clan, performed ritual functions, gathered people to war if need be, and on the whole took care of the proper running of community affairs. Often one man would rise above the rest of the elders and assume special authority, dependent on various factors such as wisdom, old age, wealth, reputation as a warrior, and possibly possession of special religious qualities such as those of a diviner or a dream prophet. But this person would never make decisions on important matters without consultations with the rest of the elders, who together shared the responsibility for the well-being of the clan, and there appears to have been no institutionalized distinction between different types of leaders such as war-leaders, judges, and priests. Even in those areas – most notably among the Tiriki, where community organization was not primarily based on membership of a specific clan – leadership structures were similar, a council of elders being the most important decision-making body.[7]

The authority wielded by the elders was derived from their important ritual status in that they were the ones who, because of their old age, were considered to be closest to the ancestors of the clan, and therefore to hold stronger religious power than the younger people. At each important new stage in life an individual would go through a rite of passage initiating him or her into the new status and conferring the religious sanction and power belonging to that status. Each new stage was considered higher than the previous one and carried with it increased social and religious responsibilities, and when a man had gone through all the different stages of initiation and had become an elder, his religious powers had reached their height, and he was entitled, together with other elders, to perform the most important ritual functions of his clan or community. Since all aspects of life were believed to be of religious significance, this meant that – as we have seen – together with their ritual roles, the elders were the ones to decide on all types of matters in the community.[8]

The ancestors of a clan or a lineage, therefore, were very important for the lives of its living members. Not only was their help invoked at all crucial stages of life when a person was initiated into a new status in society, but they were also believed to be able to give their blessings or show their disapproval of their descendants' activities. Possession by the spirit of an ancestor, observable through various phenomena such as trance behaviour, violent trembling, persistent diseases, or dreams, might be a sign that the person in question was destined to take up the practice of one of the specialized ritual functions such as that of a diviner, a dream prophet, a circumciser, an iron-maker, or a rain-maker.[9] On the other hand, an ancestor also had the power to show his or her disapproval of the behaviour of a living relative by making that person sick, and it was believed that such a disease could be cured only if the appropriate measures were taken to appease the angry ancestor.[10]

Upon death, the 'heart' and 'shadow' of a person were believed to leave the body and thereafter to form the 'spirit' of the deceased.[11] The spirit did not immediately leave the dead body but lingered on to see that it was buried properly, and for some years after death remained in a sort of intermediate situation when it was not yet fully accepted in the spirit world. Günter Wagner and Gideon S. Were, in their descriptions of Luyia religious beliefs, both agree that the transition from this life to the afterlife was seen as a change for the worse – that the world of the spirits was harsh and full of solitude until four to five years after death, when the last funeral rites were performed and they were fully integrated into the community of the dead. It was during this period that the spirit was believed to harbour most feelings of jealousy and anger against its living relatives. After its full acceptance into the spirit world,[12] however, it was thought to have 'cooled off' and was now believed to be willing to help the living.[13]

In order to secure the goodwill of the ancestors or to restore a good relationship where it was believed to have been disturbed, the living would offer sacrifices to the dead. Most of these rituals were performed at family shrines,[14] and presided over by the lineage or clan elders. They took the form of offering meat from the sacrificial animal and drink to the ancestor or ancestors in question, apparently with the aim of establishing a community with the spirits of the dead.[15]

Ezekiel Kasiera, in his study of the development of Pentecostal Christianity in western Kenya, argues that it is incorrect when a number of scholars say that the Luyia worshipped their ancestors. According to him, once people were dead they had lost their power and become dependent on the living, and the ceremonies performed served the purpose of reassuring the dead that the living still remembered them, not of praying for their help, since they were no longer able to assist their living relatives.[16] Gideon Were asserts that religion among the Luyia revolved around the Supreme Being, and it was this god – generally known as Wele among the northern Luyia and as Nyasaye among the southern peoples – who was the real object of worship, although worship was usually channelled through the spirits of dead relatives as effective intermediaries.[17] He still believes, however, that ancestors were important and powerful agents in human life who could be invoked in times of distress:

> because they were deemed to be more powerful than human beings and were capable of influencing their lives. Moreover, they were still regarded as active relatives so that, in death, their help was as much valued as in real life.[18]

From my observations it seems obvious that ancestors were, indeed, regarded as powerful influences on the lives of the living, clearly illustrated by the large number of cases in which diseases were – and are – seen to be caused by the anger of dead relatives.[19] But although

I am not, therefore, able to support Kasiera's view that ancestors were not regarded as powerful, nor his claim that people did not pray to them for help, I do nevertheless believe that he is right in his fundamental assertion that the Luyia did not worship their ancestors. This view is supported by Were's theory that what on the surface might appear to be ancestor worship was in reality worship of the Supreme Being, channelled through the ancestors. And Walter Sangree writes of the Tiriki that the supplications made to the ancestors correspond in form to the traditional way of showing friendliness and hospitality – namely, to serve food and beer – so, he says, it was only appropriate that this should be done for the ancestral spirits in trying to restore their favour and invoke their help.[20]

The Luyia peoples, then, seem to have regarded their ancestors not as godlike beings who should be worshipped but, rather, as close relatives who, although dead, were still interested in the world of the living and able to influence it, and now with greater power than when they were alive. The living would, through their sacrifices and other ceremonial rites, make sure that their relationship to their dead relatives remained good and, through these same relatives as intermediaries, ask the Supreme Being for help at crucial stages of life.

The Supreme Being was seen as the ultimate religious reality among the majority, if not all, of the Luyia peoples.[21] He was believed to be all-powerful, benevolent, creator and protector of all people and creatures, and the source of all life, health, prosperity, wealth, and so on. In so far as any sex was ascribed to him he was seen as a masculine god who was omnipresent, but residing in the sky, invisible, and capable of making his presence and his wishes known.[22] According to Wagner, the concept of a Supreme Being was most elaborate among the northern Luyia peoples, especially among the Bukusu, who saw Wele as 'an ever-present and ever-effective force working exclusively for the well-being of his creation'.[23] Every adult Bukusu person, whether male or female, greeted each new day by spitting east and west and saying a prayer addressed to Wele, and a number of other prayers were also directed to him. Wagner finds the concept of a Supreme Being among all the Luyia peoples, however, and he refers specifically to the Logoli, whose ideas of the High God were, according to him, much less definite than among the Bukusu but who, nevertheless, performed sacrifices apparently addressed to him, most important among them being those performed twice a year on behalf of the whole Logoli people in order to secure an ample harvest.[24] As we have seen, both Kasiera and Were confirm the belief in a Supreme Being among all the Luyia, although they do not confirm Wagner's theory that the Bukusu had a more developed concept of him than the others did.

Wele was believed to have a number of helpers, spirits of people who had died long ago and were now favourably disposed towards living human beings. On the other hand, there was 'wele gumali' or 'wele evimbi', the black or evil god, who was Wele's opponent and also had his helpers. These, likewise, were the spirits of people who had died, but they were the spirits of people who had been witches or sorcerers while alive.[25]

On the whole, it was believed that the universe was filled with evil powers of various kinds. Physical health, material well-being, and success in various undertakings was seen as the normal state of affairs. But these good conditions could easily be threatened, as we have seen, by the interference of angry ancestors, and also by other living persons who might make use of various techniques of witchcraft or sorcery[26] in order to harm others. The Luyia believed in a number of different categories of such evil-minded people who might be thought to be the driving force behind all sorts of misfortune, bad health, or death.[27]

Consequently, the fight against the various evil powers was a very important aspect of life among the Luyia peoples. If angry ancestors were believed to be the cause of a particular misfortune, the remedy was to perform a sacrifice to them. On the other hand, if witchcraft or sorcery was suspected, the person in question had to consult specialists who were believed to be able to detect and destroy the evil magic, reverse its direction to harm the originator, or perform counter-magic.[28] Furthermore, it might be thought that a person had suffered misfortune because he or she had fallen into a state of ritual impurity. This could happen through an act of the person himself or herself – for instance, in the case of shedding blood – but it might also be caused by an event completely outside the control of any human being – for example, if an infant cut its upper teeth first. In these cases a purification ritual had to be performed in order to restore the full ritual status of those concerned, as such persons were otherwise believed to be a danger both to themselves and to others.[29]

It is evident, therefore, that the fight between good and evil forces was of great importance in the religion of the Luyia peoples. In order to combat evil influences, the living would bring prayers and sacrifices to the Supreme God, often through their ancestors as intermediaries, or to the ancestors themselves; and if the harm was believed to have been caused by evil-minded people, measures were taken to destroy their magic or to apply counter-magic – all according to the cause of the misfortune as detected, for instance, by a diviner. Those who performed the sacrifices and other rituals were the elders of the clan or community, since they, because of their age and because they had passed through all the stages of life, possessed a higher degree of ritual power than other people.

The Colonial Setting

With the advent of colonial administration, many changes took place in the lives of the Luyia peoples. Their society had not been a stationary one. As we have seen, wars with neighbouring peoples and internal problems between related groups had forced them time and again to migrate to new areas where they could live in peace, and find suitable agricultural land. Pre-colonial society had been one in which the authority of the elders was the guarantor of stability, but opposing tendencies towards segmentation were always present, and groups of people would move away from their former homes in order to escape this authority and set up new communities under new leaders somewhere else.[30]

Into this society, towards the end of the nineteenth century, came the British. At first, the area that is now western Kenya was not important for them in itself but served only as a caravan route and supply area on the way to Buganda. But with the setting up of the Protectorate of Uganda in 1894, it became essential to secure the long supply route and bring it under more effective control, so in 1895 the British declared a protectorate over the land between the coast of the Indian Ocean and Uganda, and named it the East Africa Protectorate. Western Kenya belonged to the Uganda Protectorate until 1902, when it was transferred to the East Africa Protectorate.[31]

Imposition of colonial rule in this area came to follow a different pattern from that which the British had followed in West Africa and also in Uganda, where there were strong traditional rulers with whom they could make agreements, and so carry on 'indirect rule' through them. In western Kenya, as we have seen, only the Wanga people had a ruler who commanded the respect of, and could claim effectively to control, the entire people. It so happened that the caravan route followed by the British on their way to Buganda passed through the Wanga area, and their first attempts at control over western Kenya took the form of agreements with the Wanga leader, Mumia. He soon proved incapable of controlling the rest of the Luyia peoples, however, so in order to secure their interests the British waged wars of 'pacification' against a number of them in which the Luyia had to accept defeat, despite strong opposition in several places.[32]

Those areas that were thus 'pacified' had to accept the imposition of chiefs and, under them, headmen through whom the British could administer them and secure permanent control over them. Also, in 1900 a hut tax was introduced, partly as a sign of subjugation and partly as a source of revenue for the administration. During the first few years of British rule, tax collection, together with the maintenance of law and order, became the main tasks of the newly imposed chiefs and, therefore, the ways in which the new administration first made itself felt by the ordinary people. But other duties were soon added to the work of the chiefs when the British government's wish to have the Protectorate pay its own expenses made them open it up for European farmers who came in large numbers and settled in the 'White Highlands' – in some cases on land that was apparently unoccupied at the time of their arrival, in others on land from which the original African occupants had first to be driven. These settlers needed Africans as labourers, and although the government declared a 'dual policy' of economic development of both European and African areas, in practice the needs of the settlers were given the highest priority, and Africans were strongly encouraged – and in some cases directly forced – to seek employment at the white-owned farms. It was to the chiefs that the task of ensuring a sufficient number of labourers fell, and in time this became an important part of their work as the area of the Luyia peoples developed into one of the most important labour-supplying districts in the country. At the same time, the dual policy meant that the administration wanted the African areas to produce more crops for export, and chiefs were given the duty of encouraging African farmers to grow new crops for commercial purposes.[33]

All these new measures gradually had a strong effect on the everyday lives of the Luyia peoples. Instead of producing only enough food for their subsistence needs, they were now urged to grow new types of crops and to sell them for money, and a completely new system of work was introduced, with the opportunity – which for many became an economic necessity – to work for European settlers. Some moved with their families to the White Highlands and became 'squatters', living on land provided by a European farmer and performing a certain amount of work for him every year. But the majority went there as individual labourers, leaving their families behind in the 'reserve', as the areas demarcated for Africans came to be called. And for this last category of labourers there was a great change in their social lives, since for a large part of the year they would be away from their families and from the authority of their elders, often working together with people from other ethnic groups.

The Luyia generally responded positively to the new economic demands, one reason being their wish to satisfy new needs – for instance, for clothes, bicycles or better houses – created to a large extent through the activities of missionaries. Cash could also be used for paying bride-wealth, and apart from these considerations it became a necessity, because people were now forced to pay taxes, although they got very few services in return. Probably because many Luyia saw some advantages to be gained from working for settlers, they did not protest against migrant labour as such. But there was much dissatisfaction with measures aimed at forcing people to become labourers and at controlling them, especially with the 'kipande', a registration certificate which the British introduced shortly before 1920 and which all labourers had to carry and to have endorsed by their employers in order for the administration to check the movement of people in and out of the reserves.[34]

The chiefs and headmen who became the vehicles for introducing all these changes in Luyia society were, as we have seen, imposed by the British. Their positions were new ones, divorced from the traditional councils of elders which in pre-colonial days had come together on an ad hoc basis, whenever the need arose, to determine people's course of action. They were now allowed to play only a secondary, unofficial role, dealing with matters outside the interest of the administration. During the early years of the Protectorate the British did, however, make an attempt to practise indirect rule and to channel their innovations through local great men. In order to do this they chose many of the first chiefs and headmen from among the relatives and supporters of Nabongo Mumia, and in 1909 he himself was appointed 'Paramount Chief' over all the Luyia. This system, however, soon proved very unpopular among the rest of the Luyia peoples, who saw the Wanga rulers as foreigners and, consequently, as illegal usurpers of power; so they were gradually replaced by local people, generally chosen from among the dominant clans in their areas. In the process other clans were left out of the power hierarchy and, therefore, without influence. They often reacted to the new order of things by demanding a headman of their own, and by refusal to follow the chiefs' orders. Even when, from 1911 onwards, an attempt was made to remedy the situation by having local councils of elders to assist the chiefs, this meant the institutionalization of something which had previously been informal and was not, therefore, identical with the traditional councils of elders. As a consequence of these innovations, certain men gained influential positions while many of those who had earlier shared in decision-making processes were now left out of them. And as the chiefs consolidated their positions over the years through taking advantage of the new economic opportunities and through the education of their sons and relatives, the beginnings of social and economic stratification of the Luyia society had appeared.[35] The new authority structure was further extended and differentiated with the setting up of a Local Native Council in 1925,[36] and of a number of tribunals which from 1937 were made into independent bodies, divorced from the chiefs' authority.[37]

Not only did the British introduce a much more fixed authority system over the Luyia peoples, they also fixed the boundaries of their area. The free flux of groups of people, which in pre-colonial time had provided a means of escaping the elders' authority and overcrowded conditions in one area and the opportunity to find new land in another, was stopped. With the setting up of the White Highlands, the boundaries of the African reserves were laid down, and within the reserves each local 'tribe' was given its own 'location' or administrative unit.[38] The area of the Luyia peoples became what was called North Kavirondo District until 1948 and subsequently North Nyanza District, within Nyanza Province.[39] This amounted to a freezing of the boundaries of each people's area more or less at the place where they had been when the British arrived, and it soon led to serious overcrowding and land shortages, especially in the southern Luyia locations where, by 1923, the number of people per square mile had reached nearly seven hundred in North Maragoli, and more than a thousand in neighbouring Bunyore.[40] Some people, especially from Maragoli, found an escape from these conditions when they were allowed to migrate and settle in the less populated eastern locations of Tiriki and Nyang'ori, while others, including a good number of Bukusu people from the northern locations, moved as squatters to the White Highlands. Nevertheless, the density of population in many North Kavirondo locations was high, and this was one factor that played an important role in shaping the response of the various Luyia peoples to the new demands and opportunities put before them by the colonial administration and by Christian missionaries.[41]

Fixing the boundaries of each people and creating new authority systems, directly under their control, was a means by which the British could dominate the peoples of the East Africa Protectorate, including the Luyia. This fragmentation of the African areas also served the purpose of keeping each people in some degree of isolation, thereby making the formation of large scale opposition movements against the colonial administration more difficult.[42] Other developments within the same colonial situation, however, worked towards more unity between the different peoples. The wider outlook gained by those who went to the White Highlands to work for the settlers, often together with people from other parts of the country, gave them a greater understanding of their common grievances and interests, and at the same time freed them from some of the restraints experienced under the authority of the elders and under the new local administrative system.[43] Service in the Carrier Corps of the British troops during the First World War was another experience which widened the outlook of those participating in it, and was to have important consequences for the formation of an African opposition against the colonial administration.[44] Carriers from many different ethnic groups had worked together; many had died; and when the survivors returned home after the war they found themselves faced with unemployment because of the postwar slump, which also hit the white farmers and therefore limited employment opportunities for Africans. At the same time, the prices of their own agricultural produce fell, taxes were raised, currency changes were followed by inflation, and in 1920 the East Africa Protectorate changed its status and became Kenya Colony, an event which provoked African fears that this new status would make it even easier for the British to alienate African land and give it to white settlers.[45]

These common grievances, together with the new knowledge of peoples from outside their own local areas, made a number of those most affected try to create opposition movements against what they felt to be abuses of power by the administration, and in some cases there were attempts to involve a number of ethnic groups in the same movement, although large-scale mobilization of African opposition on a country-wide basis did not take place until after the Second World War. But a number of more local opposition movements came into existence during the 1920s and 1930s, and by now the Christian missions and the education that they brought with them had become important factors in the formation of new loyalties among people belonging to different subgroups of the Luyia, as well as between them and other peoples of Kenya, although the large number of different missionary societies operating among them also led to the formation of new barriers. This is illustrated by the fact that in many cases membership of the opposition movements against the colonial administration at this time, consisting as it did of people who had been educated at mission schools, did not fall within only one of the Luyia peoples but, rather, followed the lines of church membership. For instance, two of the most important associations, North Kavirondo Taxpayers' Welfare Association and North Kavirondo Central Association, were formed among members of the Anglican Church Missionary Society and of Friends Africa Mission respectively, with only few members drawn from other churches.[46]

Probably only a relatively small percentage of the Luyia, however, became members of these and other sociopolitical organizations before the late 1930s. But at that time, membership of African political organizations increased and became more broadly based. They also tended to become more radical in the face of new measures which the colonial government wanted to introduce in order to prevent soil erosion in the reserves. With the closing of location and reserve boundaries, the traditional Luyia land use – cultivation of a piece of land until it could yield no more, then cultivation of another piece – was no longer possible. Each people now had to stay within the area of their own location. As we have seen, this led to serious overcrowding in some places. Land became scarce, there was no new land to move to when the old piece was exhausted, and at the same time, the growing of cash crops had intensified the use of the land. As a result, during the 1930s there were signs of serious soil exhaustion and erosion; consequently, the administration wanted to force the people to carry through soil conservation measures and cattle culling, to an increasing degree through the help of their own European agricultural officers, bypassing the African chiefs and other administrative personnel. This direct interference with their methods of cultivation, coupled with fears that it was prompted by the Europeans' wish to alienate even more of their land, made a large number of the Luyia join those associations that protested against the commands of the colonial power – often with the tacit approval of the chiefs. With the outbreak of the Second World War, however, these activities came to a stop.[47]

During the war the administration concentrated on getting North Kavirondo to contribute as much as possible towards the upkeep of the Allied troops in East Africa. Apart from the fact that large numbers of men were conscripted for service in the British army, agricultural production was stepped up in order to feed the troops and increase revenue. As a result, soil deterioration was an even greater problem after the war than before it, and many of the administration's efforts in the postwar years went into measures aimed at improving the quality of the land. But by now the experiences of the war and the resulting greater awareness of the vulnerability of the Europeans, coupled with a better understanding of the other peoples of the colony, had changed the focus of African politics away from local problems and attempts to remedy them. To a much larger extent African politics now aimed at gaining influence on national politics rather than improving the local situation.[48]

Although the agricultural policies of the administration did not result in local political opposition, as they had before the war, they had other wide-ranging effects within North Kavirondo District. Thus they contributed to an increasing differentiation between, on the one hand, the group of people who had benefited from the colonial situation; and, on the other, a large number who had not. The former, as we have seen, were those who had received their education from the Christian missions, and now occupied influential positions within the colonial authority system, or had become teachers, clerks or traders. They used their positions and their knowledge of colonial society to take advantage of the opportunities that society had to offer, and thereby to consolidate the economic position of themselves and their families. The majority of the latter were uneducated, and had therefore not been able to improve their economic and social standing.[49] These disparities were now further accentuated as a result of the soil conservation measures carried out by the colonial administration after the Second World War. In order to demonstrate the methods to be used, and make sure that they would be effective, the administration decided to concentrate their efforts on the better farmers, who were given advantages over others in return for putting the new measures into effect. They were offered rewards in the form of cash, and given farm tools and implements free of charge, or at low prices.[50] The people who benefited from these policies were those who had already established good farms – that is, those who had consolidated their positions through membership of the new elite; whereas those who were already disadvantaged did not qualify for any such help. On the contrary, a cess was deducted from the price paid to African farmers for their produce, thereby securing an advantage for the European farmers, who received the full price. The cess was paid into an Agricultural Betterment Fund, and this money was used to assist the progressive farmers, resulting in a widening gap between the two groups.[51]

As Kathleen Staudt has pointed out, the development of Luyia society, even after Kenya achieved national independence in 1963, has in many ways followed the same pattern as before it. Those already established in prominent positions have generally been able to hold on to, and often extend, their social and economic privileges, while those who had no such privileges at the time of independence have found it very difficult to turn the resources available in the community to their own advantage. And she shows that the group of people who are given the fewest opportunities for economic advancement are the already poor rural women.[52]

The Arrival of the First Missionaries

When Willis Hotchkiss, Arthur Chilson and Edgar Hole of the Friends Africa Industrial Mission arrived in British East Africa on 24 June 1902, they followed the newly completed railway line from Mombasa to Kisumu, where they were assisted by the District Commissioner, C.W. Hobley, in their attempts to find a suitable site for a mission station. On one of their journeys in the North Kavirondo area they arrived on 10 August at Kaimosi, just east of the Luyia area. At first they camped there, because both Hole and Hotchkiss had fallen ill, but they soon discovered that the place was ideally suited for the kind of industrial mission they wanted to establish. They found the falls of the Goli Goli river, which could be used for water power. There was a big forest that could supply wood for a sawmill. The land was fertile, and this would make it possible to grow crops in the mission. And the altitude, 5500 feet above sea level, made the climate well suited for the American missionaries. With the help of Mr Hobley they obtained about 1000 acres of land, and here they began to build their mission station. At the time of their arrival there were hardly any Africans living around Kaimosi, which was in a kind of no-man's-land between the Tiriki and the Nandi. However, the presence of the mission station and further attempts by the British to 'pacify' the Nandi soon brought the inter-ethnic fighting to an end, and as a result many Tiriki moved into the area and settled around Kaimosi.[53]

At the beginning the missionaries had to use a very large part of their time in establishing the industrial mission they wanted. As soon as possible a dam was built across the Goli Goli river, and a watermill was erected for sawing timber and grinding grain. Forest was cleared, crops were planted, and many houses were built. In later years the large sums of money invested at Kaimosi became an important factor in determining mission policies, leading to the concentration of the majority of Quaker institutions there.[54] Some of their supporters at home soon began to criticize the missionaries for spending so much time on practical work instead of preaching the Gospel. But for the missionaries themselves, with their background in pioneer rural communities of the American Midwest, it was natural to set about creating a physical environment suitable to their needs, and they saw no conflict between this type of work and their wish to preach Christianity to the Africans. On the contrary, when Arthur Chilson went home on furlough in 1905 and was criticized along these lines, he ignored his critics and took a new water turbine back to Kenya with him.[55] And a few years later, when he was constructing roads north of Kaimosi, he saw his presence at the road site and the opportunities it afforded for preaching the Gospel to the workmen as a legitimate part of his work as an evangelizing missionary, and as a means of stopping the advance of the Roman Catholics who had shown an interest in starting work in the same area.[56]

In spending so much time on construction and other practical work the Quaker missionaries had adopted Willis Hotchkiss's plans for an industrial mission which, as described above, was intended to serve the double purpose of 'cleansing' the Africans' social conditions and enabling them to earn an income from which they could support their church.[57] They believed, like many other missionaries, that in order for Africans to become true Christians it was necessary not only to preach the Gospel to them but also to teach them many aspects of the Western way of life.[58] And, as Ezekiel Kasiera has pointed out, this double emphasis on evangelism and social development was in keeping with the traditional humanitarian attitudes of Friends, whereas some other missionaries, notably those from the neighbouring Pentecostal mission, were simply forced by circumstances to take the social element into consideration 'at a time when they could be talking about heaven', not as an integrated part of their task as missionaries.[59]

Even for the Friends, the relationship between the four departments of their work – the evangelical and the industrial together with the medical and the educational, which were soon added – was not always without problems as the work developed over the years. But from the outset, all four departments appeared necessary, and missionaries engaged in them with great energy. Willis Hotchkiss left Kaimosi after only about six months because of disagreements with the other two missionaries.[60] But already in that same year, in 1903, a missionary doctor, Elisha Blackburn, arrived, with his wife and Edgar Hole's wife. In 1904 Emory and Deborah Rees came, and in 1907 Edna Chilson, wife of Arthur Chilson. All these missionaries took part in all aspects of the work, but as time passed, and some kind of specialization became necessary, Arthur Chilson concentrated more and more on evangelization, while Emory Rees used a good deal of his time translating the New Testament into Luragoli together with the first African convert, Akhonya, later on with Yohana Amugune, and finally for many years with Joel Litu.[61] The women missionaries were active in educational and evangelizing work among women. Meanwhile, the industrial work assumed a relatively independent position with the arrival in 1912 of Fred Hoyt, who took charge of the milling and building activities, and in 1913 of C. Frank Conover, who was an agriculturalist. Medical work was continued when Dr Archie Bond took over from Dr Blackburn in 1917, while the educational department, which at first developed alongside the evangelistic work, gradually became more and more important. In 1929 Everett Kellum arrived to supervise all Friends educational institutions. All these and other missionaries, together with their wives, took part in evangelization, and often saw their own departments as serving the overall purpose of converting the Africans to Christianity. But the two missionaries who became the most prominent preachers were Arthur Chilson and Jefferson Ford, who came to Kenya in 1914. It was Jefferson Ford who, together with Joel Litu, translated the Old Testament into Luragoli.[62]

All the early Quaker missionaries to Kenya were strongly influenced by the revival which, as we have seen, swept over the United States and also made a strong impact among Friends from around 1860.

They had taken part in revival meetings, and gone through conversion experiences. A number of them were not birthright Friends,[63] but decided to become Quakers after being converted in Friends meetings. After conversion many of them had, in addition, experienced sanctification, and all felt a clear call to go to Africa as missionaries.[64] Edna Chilson gives a vivid description of her husband's experiences. In 1889, when he was sixteen years old, there was a revival meeting in the local Friends church, and here he 'went to the altar and was converted'. He received no special emotions or feelings that night, but the following day 'a full realization of God's saving grace swept over him and he was filled with joy and peace, and knew that he was a redeemed soul'. His call to become a missionary came not long afterwards:

> One Sabbath morning not long after he was saved, he was sitting in the meeting and heard the Lord's voice, clear and distinct asking, 'Will you be willing to go to Africa as a Misssionary?' His answer was quick and clear, 'Yes, Lord.'

However, Arthur Chilson still found something within him 'that did not make victory easy'. But after much praying, he went one evening – approximately three years after these first experiences – to visit his pastor, and here 'the light began to break upon his soul; he saw that there was complete victory for him when he was sanctified and baptised with the Holy Ghost'. He dropped on his knees, 'and there he made his consecration, laid his all on the altar, and received the blessed Holy Ghost in all His fullness. From that day – from that hour – the Holy Ghost was a definite, real personality to him.'[65] Jefferson Ford describes his experiences in terms less coloured by Pentecostal-type vocabulary:

> I would not leave the impression that there have not been struggles and battles in my Christian life since then. There have been, but I have found the secret of victory is to 'Walk in the light as He is in the light' (I John 1: 7) ... In the sanctified life there are two things for me to do: First, keep my consecration completed, that is, keep all on the altar (Matt. 23: 19). Second, to be obedient. Should I disobey Him I must come to Him for forgiveness (I John 1: 9).[66]

Although sanctification did not mean that the person would no longer be tempted to sin, these Friends believed, nevertheless, that the indwelling of the Holy Spirit, received at the time of sanctification, brought people into a very close communion with God, and that as long as they remained open to God's promptings, He would protect them from sin. Chilson and Ford, as well as the rest of the early missionaries, therefore had a strong conviction that God had called them and was leading them, and that they were serving Him. This made them extremely dedicated to their work but could also lead to conflicts between them, since each individual followed the course that he or she believed to have been shown by God, and was often unwilling to accept criticism.

The Gospel they brought to the Luyia people was the revival Gospel which had meant so much to them personally. The central point was their belief in Jesus Christ's atoning death on the cross. They regarded those who were unconverted as sinful and in need of the saving grace which Jesus had won for them, which they could receive if they repented and confessed their sins. And from the point of view of the missionaries, this Gospel was exactly what the Africans needed. Arthur Chilson talks about 'dark, dark, despairing Africa',[67] and describes how, a few years earlier, those who were now Christians had been 'steeped in immorality, vice and superstition, naked and debauched'.[68] Although not all the missionaries regarded African society as quite so dark and evil,[69] the attitude permeating much of the early missionaries' correspondence implies, nevertheless, that unless people are converted to Christianity they will be lost and go to hell. One example is a letter from Helen Farr Ford, wife of Jefferson Ford, in which she describes her talk with a father and mother whose child has died. Her argument is that the child is in heaven because children are pure, whereas the parents will go down to live with Satan unless they ask Jesus to forgive their sins and cleanse their hearts, in which case they can go to heaven and see their child again.[70] And the terminology used by Jefferson Ford's second wife, Helen Kersey Ford, and by Edna Chilson, to describe the deaths of their husbands brings out their belief that after death those who are saved are taken to heaven immediately. Helen Kersey Ford writes about her husband that he 'entered heaven',[71] and Edna Chilson says that her husband 'went in to see the King'.[72]

Once Africans had heard and accepted the Gospel, they could receive salvation along exactly the same lines as Christians in America, as Arthur Chilson says in his diary:

> Here we are, with all of this sin and superstition about us ... The Gospel of the Crucified Son of God is just suited for these Africans and they are

> finding forgiveness for sins, sanctification for believers, and the indwelling of the Holy Ghost, just as people, who believe and trust, are finding in our own home-land.[73]

Africans could be converted and find forgiveness for their sins, and they also had the opportunity to experience sanctification with the indwelling of the Holy Ghost following upon their conversion, in the same way as the missionaries themselves had experienced it. Therefore, as soon as a few people had become Christians, Chilson began to preach about this second blessing, and to pray for an outpouring of the Holy Spirit. As early as 1909, when there were probably only eleven African converts,[74] Chilson reports that he and his wife held Sunday afternoon services for Christians only, and here, 'We have felt led to give special lessons on the baptism with the Holy Ghost.'[75]

Chilson's expectation, as well as that of at least some of the other missionaries, was that Christ's Second Coming was imminent, and his goal was to prepare the Africans to be ready when Christ came again. He says in a letter in 1917:

> There are things that make us wonder if Jesus is not coming soon; we look for His early return... and we desire that these, who sit in such darkness, may be found ready and waiting, with us and you, when He appears.[76]

And Chilson probably believed that the Second Coming of Christ was to institute the millennium. This, at least, was the opinion of some of the missionaries, as is evident in a letter from Archie and Mira Bond in which they describe how Edgar Hole had preached on the coming of Christ and emphasized that when Christ returned Satan would be bound for a thousand years.[77]

African–Missionary Interaction in the Development of the Church

When the Quaker missionaries arrived in western Kenya in 1902 the Luyia peoples had not yet been influenced by any missionary teachings. But on the completion of the railway line to Kisumu in 1901, it became easy for missionaries to travel to the area, and soon a number of societies showed their interest. Friends Africa Industrial Mission was the first missionary society to arrive among the Luyia, quickly followed by the South African Compounds and Interior Mission (later Church of God), the Church Missionary Society, and the Roman

Catholic Mill Hill Fathers, all of whom started work in around 1905. In 1909 a Pentecostal mission was added; from 1924 this came under the control of the Pentecostal Assemblies of Canada.[78] Some years later, Seventh-Day Adventists and the Salvation Army also started activities among the Luyia.[79]

As pioneers in a new – and, to them, unknown – country, the Friends missionaries had to make their own experiments to find out how best to carry through their evangelizing mission. With very little previous knowledge of the peoples they had come to, and with no other missionaries' experiences in the same area to build on, they had to try to find their own ways of reaching the people.

From the beginning, the industrial and building activities at Kaimosi became a contact point between the missionaries and the Luyia peoples, since a number of young people were attracted by the new happenings and came to work for the missionaries. Some of the first to come were Akhonya and Lung'aho, both from Isukha, Amugune from North Maragoli, and Maraga from Tiriki, who later married Lung'aho.[80] Missionaries and Africans communicated with each other through a teacher from Pemba by the name of Kwetu, who knew English. This he translated into Kiswahili, which Akhonya and Lung'aho understood, and they in turn translated the Kiswahili into Luisukha. The communication process was eased when the missionaries had learnt enough Kiswahili to talk with those among the Africans who understood that language. Arthur Chilson preached his first sermon in Kiswahili in February 1903,[81] and the language situation improved further when Emory Rees arrived in 1904. He realized the importance of missionaries using the local language, and very soon started to learn it, and to reduce it to written form. After this, texts for reading lessons in the Friends schools could be written in the vernacular. Thus, after four to five years of using Kiswahili, the missionaries began to teach in the local language. Since Rees and his wife soon came to live in Maragoli, the language they learnt and into which he helped to translate the Bible was Luragoli, and this therefore became the dominating language in Friends Africa Mission for many years.[82]

From the beginning, the missionaries held daily services with the people employed at the mission station, and public worship services on Sundays. These services attracted large numbers of people. More than three hundred came to a public service on one Sunday in May 1903, and attendance increased over the years.[83] This great interest, however, was not immediately reflected in a corresponding number of converts. The experiences of missionaries in other parts of East Africa proved valid here: that the first converts were to be found among people who had, in one way or another, been separated from their normal surroundings. Mass conversions, however, did not take place until the impact of colonialism on society had been felt to such an extent that traditional authorities had lost much of their power, and people had obtained connections beyond their own ethnic groups.[84] The first Africans to be converted by the Quaker missionaries were those mentioned above who worked together with them and were therefore more exposed to their teachings than anybody else.[85] Furthermore, since they were living at the mission station they did not feel the authority of the traditional elders and the ancestors to the same extent as did those who lived outside, and this undoubtedly made it easier for them to sever their connections with the past and embrace the new way of life and the new religion. But it was quite a few years before a significant number of people less closely connected with the missionaries became Christians. It was 1905 before the first five converts were received into church membership. In 1906 five more were added, in 1907 one more, and in 1911 the number of African Christians was reported to be still only sixteen.[86] From around 1914 when thirty-five new converts were received, there seems to have been a steady, though slow, increase in the number of members, in spite of a setback in normal mission activities because of the First World War and smallpox and influenza epidemics, together with famine, in 1917–18.[87]

Those Africans who had become Christians, however, showed great eagerness to spread the new Gospel to those who lived in the villages away from the mission station, thereby laying the foundations for the great increase in membership that was to come after the First World War. They began to go out on Sundays to various places in the surrounding area to preach to the people there, often two and two or a group together, and it soon became a fixed practice to start very early on Sunday mornings with a teaching session at the mission station for those who were to go out and preach, after which they would go to their preaching points and tell the Bible story they had just heard.[88]

The missionaries were also eager to spread their message over as large an area as possible, and they had already set up two new mission stations in 1906, when Emory and Deborah Rees went to live in

Vihiga in South Maragoli, and the Holes moved to Lirhanda among the Isukha people.[89] In 1913 another mission station was opened at Lugulu among the Bukusu, and in 1919 one at Malava in Kabras. Arthur Chilson had camped in Kabras since 1915, building roads while he waited for government approval for a mission station there, and he and his family were the missionaries who moved into this new station when it became permanent, while the Fords spent most of their time in Kenya at Lugulu.[90] When African Christians began to move out from these stations to preach in the same way as they did from Kaimosi, the effect was that quite a large number of people got the chance to hear the Christian Gospel.

But probably the most important factor in evangelization was the emergence of the Friends school system. The first school was set up by Edgar Hole at Kaimosi as early as February 1903, with fifteen boys and young men in attendance.[91] And with the establishment of the new mission stations, schools were started there as well. After some years, 'out-schools' were added away from the mission stations when those who had already acquired the most elementary learning went out to surrounding villages to teach and establish schools.[92] Usually it was the same person who acted as both evangelist and teacher, opening a school and a meeting point for religious services at the same place. For instance, Yohana Amugune started going to Mbale to establish evangelism and literacy training there around 1908, and Daudi Lung'aho acted as a teacher as well as a preacher in at least three different places, moving on to a new location once the work had become well established in one area.[93]

From the point of view of the early missionaries, the school work was a part – and an important one – of their evangelizing mission. When they were teaching Africans to read they had the same purpose in mind as they had in their industrial work, that of the general 'development' of the people. Alta Hoyt says:

> All are needed in the healthy growth of the people in Africa. Teaching them the love of God first, accepting Christ as their Savior, and the study of the Bible, and in order to grow as Christians they must learn to read, teach and develop along all lines.[94]

But first of all, reading was an essential skill for the all-important purpose of studying the Bible. For the early Quaker missionaries, as we have seen, were evangelicals and strong fundamentalists who saw a thorough knowledge of the Bible as a necessity for Christians.

Therefore, literacy training, along with the ability to read the Bible, was an important element in their work of spreading the Gospel.

The curriculum of the Friends schools as described by Arthur Chilson in a letter in 1921 gives a good illustration of the kind of education they offered:

> Our Mission Stations have thousands of scholars in scores of schools for most part taught by native teachers, who are evangelists first and teachers afterwards. The Bible is used as a Text book in the schools continuously. In every session there is a Gospel service in which Bible truth is presented and sinners urged to seek forgiveness of sins.
>
> Education is used merely as a means to the conversion of the individual and the building up of a strong, self supporting, self propagating, native, Christian church.[95]

This quotation also shows that by 1921 there was a great interest in the Friends school work, a strong contrast to the situation only five years earlier when Fred and Alta Hoyt reported: 'The work is growing a little in interest but very slowly ... The attendance is small at all of them but it is beginning and we trust for increased interest as the schools continue.'[96]

As we have seen, chiefs and headmen were some of the first people to realize the importance of the education offered by the missionaries, and they soon began to send their sons and relatives to school in order to prepare them for assisting them in their work, and eventually taking over from them as rulers. They were also the ones through whose help schools were established in new areas, and their requests for schools and teachers often even surpassed the missionaries' ability to train new teachers quickly enough.[97] But the real breakthrough in interest for education and for church membership came shortly after the First World War when the Africans began to understand the full implications of the colonial situation. As we have learnt, many who had served in the Carrier Corps during the war had experienced personally the hardships which the British colonial power was capable of inflicting upon them. When they returned home after the war they were faced with economic problems such as unemployment, reduced prices for their agricultural products, increased taxes, and inflation. As a consequence, the missionaries reported unrest among the Africans during these years, in particular in Maragoli. Here, the proximity of Kisumu offered good possibilities for the development of trade, and the high population density, with the corresponding land shortage, made people eager to take advantage of the new educational and employment opportunities. Therefore, the Maragoli people were very much exposed to the new influences under the colonial system, and consequently also reacted to the strains they experienced under it by spreading 'propaganda of an undesirable sort'.[98] On the other hand, from the mid-1920s the missionaries also report a growing interest in the work of the Church and a 'deepening in the things of God',[99] an indication that at this time people found the missionaries' message and activities relevant to their needs.

By now the traditional elders and ancestors had been proved powerless when it came to solving the numerous problems which people encountered as colonial subjects, and many turned to Christianity for help in improving their lives under the new conditions. This connection between the hardships people suffered and their wish to become Christians is brought out in Benjamin Wegesa's description of the life of Abraham Sangura. Sangura, a Busuku, had been taken in around 1920 by Chief Murunga, a Wanga who ruled North Bukusu for many years, to perform forced labour in his fields, and Benjamin Wegesa says of him:

> He wanted to help abolish this slavery which he himself was suffering. There was no freedom in Kenya then. People were ruled by force, and they obeyed from fear. Because of these conditions that haunted the lives of African men and women, Abraham made up his mind to become a Christian, if he could get the chance. He wanted to help his people understand the value of the human soul. He wanted the African courts to learn what justice means in human lives.[100]

Here Christianity is seen as the religion which was able to liberate those who were oppressed, and bring justice to its followers under the new social system. This view of Christianity – that it offered an opportunity for change in people's lives at personal as well as social levels, away from that which kept them in bondage and towards greater freedom – explains why even a large number of old people, who had nothing to gain from the missions' educational programmes in terms of employment, began to show an interest in learning about Christianity and becoming Christians in the 1920s. Emory Rees reports that in 1922 there was a movement towards Christianity of about a hundred old people in Maragoli,[101] and in 1927 Chilson tells of meetings for old people, also in Maragoli, with four to six thousand people attending.[102] While this movement seems to have started in Maragoli, a similar interest among the old people is reported at both Lirhanda and Kaimosi in 1927.[103]

For many young people, however, it was the missionaries' school work which brought them into contact with Christianity. This was where they saw new opportunities opening up, since a mission education would enable them to be employed as clerks or teachers, and on the whole taught them the skills necessary for playing an active role in modern society. For these reasons there was a great inrush of new pupils to the Friends schools in the early 1920s, and here they learnt the basic elements of reading, writing and Christianity side by side; as a result, a large number of them were eventually converted and became Christians. Therefore, because people came to see that Christianity as presented by the Quaker missionaries had much to offer in terms of a theology which was suited to their new experiences in colonial society as well as an educational programme that fitted the conditions of that society, Friends Africa Mission experienced a great increase in membership in the 1920s. In 1920 the number of full members and people on probation for membership combined was reported to be 1013,[104] while in 1926 it had increased to about 4100,[105] and in 1929 to about 7500.[106]

As the school system of Friends Africa Mission was extended to meet the great demand for education,[107] and as the same development took place within other missions, a large number of schools were spread over the Luyia area. During the early years of missionary enterprise, the Protestant missionary societies had divided the area between them, creating separate 'spheres of influence',[108] and although there were occasional attempts by one mission to start work in the area of another,[109] on the whole all the societies respected this arrangement. The Roman Catholic Church did not join in the agreement and often set up mission stations within a short distance from existing Protestant missions, leading to friction and competition between them.[110] But they, as well as the Protestants – with the exception of the Pentecostal mission, which did not start school work until a number of years later – set up a network of out-schools covering the whole of the North Kavirondo District.[111]

Most of these schools, however, were of a very low academic standard – partly because, as we have seen, the missionaries' main interest, at least during the early years, was not education as such but education as a tool for the evangelization of the Africans, and partly because the missionaries were unprepared for the sudden explosion of interest in education, and were therefore forced to let people go out as teachers who themselves had had only very little schooling. In 1921 the requirement for teaching in village schools as agreed upon by the Kavirondo Mission Council, of which Friends Africa Mission was a member, was four to five years of education, and the village schools themselves offered only two years' literacy education.[112] In order to improve the situation, the Legislative Council of Kenya passed a bill in 1924 requiring every school to be placed under the control of the Director of Education, so that eventually no one would be allowed to teach unless they came up to the standard demanded by the government.[113] The same bill made it possible for mission schools to receive grants-in-aid from the government, and Friends Africa Mission, among others, accepted this offer together with the closer supervision that went along with it.[114]

This development led to a change in emphasis in Friends mission work. Whereas before, missionaries had seen evangelization as their main task, which all other branches of their work were intended to serve, the schools now assumed a more independent position in relation to other mission activities, and consumed more and more of the total resources. And while he was in favour of improving the quality of education in Friends schools, Emory Rees also points out the serious consequences which this emphasis on education might have for the Church as a whole. He says that a very serious defect is:

> the lack – almost the entire absence of intelligent and spiritual Pastoral care of the numerous young meetings. Up until now the teacher of the school has supplied a kind of pastoral care. From now on, owing to increasing stress on the educational side the teacher will be more or less withdrawn from pastoral care and we have very few to take his place.[115]

With the expansion of the Friends school programme, Rees saw a danger that the educational and religious aspects of the work would to some extent be separated, leaving the Church as the loser, with only few educated people being directly involved in evangelizing and pastoral work.

Some of the other missionaries were just as concerned as Rees about the future of the Church – not only because they saw a major part of the mission's resources in money and personnel being drawn towards purely educational pursuits and away from the pastoral care of the Church, but also because they did not trust the African Christians' ability to carry on the work. They believed that the presence of missionaries was absolutely necessary if the Church was to progress, and when the number of workers sent from America decreased during the 1920s because the economic Depression forced the Mission Board to limit its activities, they found that what they saw as a shortage of missionaries constituted a serious threat to the well-being of the African Church. From the beginning they had recognized the fact that African Christians were better able to influence other Africans to become Christians than they were themselves.

Edna Chilson, for example, praises Joseph Ngaira and Maria Mwaitsi, a couple who moved with the Chilson family from Kaimosi to Malava in 1915 and whose home life she sees as a witness to the change brought about by their Christian faith.[116] And Dr Bond says of the same couple, 'they have gotten a vision of Jesus and can far outreach us in helping these black people to Christ'.[117] Nevertheless, some of the missionaries were ambivalent in their appreciation of Africans' role in evangelization, and believed very strongly that although the African Christians' preaching and example were of great importance in spreading the Gospel, the Africans were not mature enough to carry out this work without very close missionary supervision. This difference of opinion among the missionaries can be illustrated by their reactions when, in 1911 or 1912, Yohana Amugune decided to leave the Vihiga mission station, where he had been spending most of his time since 1904, and go to his own home at Chavakali in order to establish a school and a church there, at the request of the local headman.[118] A few other Christians in Maragoli were now also living outside the mission compound, and Emory Rees rejoiced at this evidence that African Christians were becoming independent of the missionaries: 'We are looking forward to and feel that the time is approaching when being a Christian will not mean living on the mission premises and drawing wages from the mission.'[119] But not all the missionaries shared this positive interpretation. Dr Blackburn and his wife refer to the same event, but interpret it as an expression of a spirit of 'discontent and unrest' and an 'outbreak against authority', and lament that these Christian young men have gone back to their home districts without proper preparation and training.[120]

Chilson and Ford, who themselves moved to the northern areas of Kabras and Bukusu respectively, were those missionaries who most consistently tried to press the Mission Board in America to send new missionaries to Kenya. During the earlier years they described how vast areas with many inhabitants had never had the chance to hear the

Gospel, and would be lost to others – Chilson says to the Catholics or the Mohammedans – unless missionary reinforcement was sent from home,[121] thereby not only revealing their attitude towards these other groups but also implying that African Christians alone would not be able to bring the Gospel to those unreached peoples. Later, in the 1920s, when there was the great increase in membership of Friends Africa Mission described above, and when many Christians were affected by the social changes taking place during that period, these missionaries' concern was not so much how to bring the Gospel to as yet unevangelized peoples but, rather, the preservation of what had already been won. Chilson says in 1923 that 'the native mind' is 'in its adolescence stage', and he continues:

> They are feeling they know enough now to be able to walk alone almost and don't enjoy too close supervision. I fear in some districts they have been pushed along too fast in self government and they are sort of intoxicated with position and authority. It seems to me they need a *wise*, *firm*, *loving* control.... They have not sufficient Christian conscience and character upon which a Christian church can stand alone.[122]

However, no new missionaries were sent to Kenya at that stage. There were economic reasons for this, but also the American Friends Board of Foreign Missions regarded the development of a national church as a natural outcome of the missionary efforts and were not afraid, as at least some of the missionaries were, that the Africans would not be able to manage their own affairs. B. Willis Beede, the Board secretary, disagreed with Chilson on the topic of missionary control, and he wrote in response to Chilson's letter:

> The development of a self-governing native church is always fraught with dangers, but there is nothing to do but trust God and go ahead with the work.... As missionaries you are called upon to work with the native people. I doubt if you will ever succeed by exercising a control over them.[123]

And actually, despite the missionaries' scepticism concerning their abilities and maturity, the African Christians carried on their work of spreading the Gospel and establishing meetings with enthusiasm. So great was their zeal that many individual evangelists did not content themselves with simply establishing one meeting, but would move on to new areas once their work was going well. As mentioned above, one such evangelist was Daudi Lung'aho; another was Abraham Sangura who, a few years later, founded a good number of meetings in various places, especially in South Bukusu. Benjamin Wegesa describes how Abraham, when he arrived at a new place, would teach children and adults in separate groups during the day and conduct worship services in the evening. As soon as he had a group of pupils who knew how to read the Gospels and how to conduct and take part in a simple service for worship he would help them to appoint a clerk from among their number, thereby laying the foundation for a Friends meeting, and then leave them on their own to develop the meeting and the Quaker community.[124] Other evangelists in other parts of the Friends area acted similarly, thereby establishing a number of centres from which the work could spread even further. In many cases the Quakers, living around these centres, would move their homes to the area surrounding the newly established churches and schools in order to develop the Christian community. These 'mission lines' or Christian villages were especially popular in the mid-1920s but declined in importance after 1933, when the Local Native Council prohibited the creation of further villages, some of the reasons being opposition from non-Christians and difficulties in deciding what to do with 'backsliders' who had broken the rules of the Church but were living within the 'lines'.[125]

In these Christian centres African Friends were faced with the task of developing their community life in ways which were consistent with their Christian faith. From the beginning the missionaries had emphasized the importance of proper moral conduct as they saw it, based on their own experiences as evangelical Quakers from the American Midwest. They, like many other evangelical missionaries from different denominations, prohibited smoking, dancing, drinking alcohol and sexual offences, especially polygamy, and any practices that would associate the Christians with the traditional religion of their people. And the African Christians adopted these rules and enforced them strictly in their communities and congregations. Those who broke them were placed under church discipline and barred from participation in meetings for a considerable period of time, after which they were required to repent their misdeeds openly and ask for forgiveness before they could be restored to church membership.[126] At least some of the missionaries saw this discipline as an important step towards preparing the Church for the Second Coming of Christ. Jefferson and Helen Farr Ford write:

> This cleaning up of the Native Church is a cause of real thankfulness to us, for we believe God is at work preparing for a work of Grace among us that will bring many into the Kingdom, before the King comes back.[127]

The practice of church discipline was consistent with the emphasis on repentance for sins as a condition of salvation, and it served the purpose of cleansing the individual concerned as well as the whole Church. In addition to these considerations, the moral conduct required of those who became Quakers marked them off as Friends over against the Roman Catholics who, as mentioned above, were seen as a threat to the work of the Friends, and who allowed their members to drink and smoke. Alta Hoyt says of the Catholics and the Anglicans that they teach that people become Christians:

> by committing to memory certain things, being baptized, changing their names, and going through a form of worship, then they go out to live the same sort of life that they lived before, drinking beer, following immoral customs, and still they say they are christians [*sic*].[128]

Friends, on the other hand, strove to be pure Christians as they understood this, upholding strict moral standards, thereby emphasizing their identity as Quakers and, ultimately, keeping their Church prepared for the return of Christ and the establishment of his kingdom.

African Christians, however, were not content simply to take over the moral rules taught to them by the missionaries but added rules of their own, developed against the background of their traditional customs. One such custom was the prohibition against women and girls eating chicken and eggs. According to Thomas Ganira Lung'aho's biography of his father, Daudi Lung'aho, it was believed that if they did, they would not be able to have any children, or that the children they gave birth to would be deaf and dumb. Christians wanted to prove that this was not true, just as they wanted to prove in other cases – for instance through revealing the secret Tiriki circumcision rites[129] – that no harmful consequences would result from disobeying the commands handed over from the ancestors. Therefore, the courageous act of eating a chicken or an egg became a real proof of their commitment as Christians for Luyia women, as well as a conscious expression on the part of both the women themselves and their husbands of their belief in the equality of men and women in the eyes of God.[130]

Friends also attempted to raise the status of women in the new society, along with that of men, by offering education for both sexes. From the beginning, very few women had come to the schools – whether because of opposition in their homes or because the missionaries directed their efforts more vigorously towards men.[131] Eventually, however, a number of women began to attend the classes, at first mainly the wives of men who had already become Christians.[132] Later, however, larger numbers of women came to realize that the modern type of education also had advantages for them. The main advantage, perhaps, was that it enabled them to follow the men in their attempts to find a foothold in the new culture and the new religion, since for many years the majority of teaching and clerical jobs had been reserved for men. The increasing involvement of women in the new social set-up is illustrated by the fact that in 1926 the number of girls in the Friends schools in the north, among the Bukusu and the Tachoni, was higher than that of boys, although part of the explanation for this was that many of the boys and young men had gone away from the reserve to seek work with European employers.[133]

As more and more people, both men and women, benefited from missionary education, and as more and more of them became Christians, there was an increasing need for the new Church to be organized in such a way that it would be able to carry on its work according to recognized Friends principles. The very first steps towards this organization had already been taken in 1909 when Sunday afternoon prayer meetings, which had been going on for some time, were changed into meetings specifically for the Church, and an office bearer was appointed as usher and treasurer.[134] And in early 1912 a Committee on Native Church Organization, made up of missionaries, drew up a plan that at each of the five mission stations there was to be a simple organization more directly recognizable as the structure known from other Quaker meetings in other parts of the world, with a chairman, a secretary and a treasurer, and with committees appointed for specific purposes. These local organizations were to be given the primary responsibility for admitting probationers into the Church and accepting them into full membership, subject to the approval of a central body. The local bodies were also given responsibility to take care of their own church offerings, the objective being that local workers should be supported by the local church. All activities of these organizations were, however, to be under the overall direction of the missionaries 'until such time as it seems wise to have independent organizations'.[135]

A further step towards the independence of the African Church was taken with the elevation of the status of these five local bodies to that of full monthly meetings, starting with Maragoli monthly meeting, which was set up in 1917; the last one to be organized was

Kaimosi monthly meeting in March 1920.[136] By 1921 Maragoli monthly meeting had become so big that it was divided into two, forming Vihiga and Chavakali monthly meetings, which were combined in Maragoli quarterly meeting.[137] New monthly and quarterly meetings were established as church membership increased, and in 1931 the missionaries suggested that the Africans ought soon to have their own yearly meeting. Fred Hoyt wrote on behalf of the missionaries to the office of the American Friends Board of Missions, requesting that initial steps towards this end be taken before the end of 1932.[138] It was to be another fourteen years, however, before a yearly meeting was established in Kenya; but the basic structure of village, monthly and quarterly meetings was in existence long before that time.

In these meetings there were different categories of members, the most important one being that of full member of the Church. But it was no easy matter for a person to attain that status, as a probationary period of about two years' duration was required. During this time the church elders would scrutinize the spiritual and moral lives of the candidates, a procedure that dated back to the early years of missionary activity. And before being accepted as a probationary member in the first place, a person had to show evidence of repentance and a wish to live according to the moral standards required of Christians.[139] It was with good reason, therefore, that Abraham Sangura said in the quotation above that he wanted to become a Christian 'if he could get the chance';[140] and it meant that those who succeeded in becoming accepted as church members had practised a new kind of life for a long time, thereby consciously setting themselves apart from the non-Christians surrounding them.

It was not only their moral conduct, however, that distinguished the Friends from the non-Christians. Through their school education, and the greater exposure to the new world of the Europeans and Americans that went with it, they came to appreciate a number of the material things which that world had to offer, and at the same time their education gave them the opportunity to get jobs where they could earn money and thus acquire some of these things. Therefore, it became common among Christians to build better houses than those of the non-Christians, many bought bicycles, and a number of them began to engage in businesses of various kinds, often assisted by the missionaries, or to improve their methods of land cultivation – activities which made the Christians stand out as generally better off economically than those around them. Japheth Amugune tells how his father began to trade in cattle, bought a bicycle, and became the first African in Maragoli to drive a lorry and the first to build a permanent house.[141] And Emory Rees describes how, in 1925, he spent much of his time helping people to set up watermills for grinding maize into flour, and says: 'The backbone of all enterprise in the district is the Christian group, and they have received a corresponding part of the rewards of enterprise.'[142]

As we have seen, it was mainly a certain section of Africans – often relatives of those who had achieved important positions in colonial society, or people who were in close contact with the missionaries – who benefited most from the educational and economic opportunities offered in modern society, and they gradually distanced themselves from the close fellowship with other Christians whose involvement in this society brought them fewer economic and social advantages. Therefore, relationships within the Christian communities were becoming increasingly strained, as some members pursued their individual careers at the expense of group solidarity, while those with fewer opportunities for social advancement continued to rely more on the unity of the Christian group for their social and religious needs.[143] And the greater emphasis which Friends Africa Mission as a whole came to put on education served to accelerate this development.

In the 1920s, therefore, there was great interest in Christianity among the Luyia, and Friends Africa Mission, as well as other missions, received a large number of new members. But at the same time, the Church was developing in two different directions: one section of the membership wholeheartedly embracing the modern educational and social opportunities brought to them through the activities of both missions and the colonial state; another striving to retain the unity of the Christian group in the face of the growing individualism inherent in much of modern development. This division within the Friends Church was to become significant when, from the mid-1920s onwards, enthusiasm for Christianity had reached a point where a revival atmosphere spread over large parts of the Friends Africa Mission area.

Revival in the Late 1920s

Arthur Chilson reports of the Native Prayer Conference in September 1924, a meeting where African Quakers from all parts of the Friends area came together at Lugulu for a number of days:

> the Holy Spirit graciously visited the meeting.... Confessions were made, tears shed, prayers made and hearts won to Christ.... Some said 'our hearts were made to quake', and we believe things are getting in good condition for the revival we expect.[144]

Clara Ford, daughter of Helen Farr and Jefferson Ford, gives a vivid description of the mood of the conference when she describes what happened after Arthur Chilson had spoken about obedience to God and his 'native leader' about the baptism with the Holy Spirit:

> Mr. Chilson then asked those who wanted the Holy Spirit to raise their hands, there was a holy hush on all, and slowly, one by one, hands were raised in all parts of the building. It was a time of solemn decision. Three sanctified Christians were asked to pray and then those who had raised their hands prayed, themselves. They prayed earnestly, some tearfully, until long after closing time.

And she continues, saying that on Sunday:

> We had a precious time talking of heaven and the second coming, and the meeting naturally led up to an altar call. Scores knelt for prayer by their own seats and it was like an altar meeting all over the church. There was no excitement or confusion but just a deep, quiet heart-felt working of the Holy Spirit.[145]

The missionaries here preached on the same topics as those which were in the forefront in the American revival: conversion through repentance and belief in the forgiveness of Christ, sanctification with the indwelling of the Holy Spirit, heaven as the destination of those who were saved, and the Second Coming of Christ as the prelude to the final victory over Satan. The revival methods they used were also the same as those they had seen and used in America, encouraging people to make a decision there and then to seek salvation and sanctification, and calling them to the 'altar' or 'mourners' bench', where they could pray with the assistance of the leader of the meeting. And as in America, so many people here responded to the preacher's call. Frank and Blanche Conover, the missionaries who were living at Lugulu at the time, reported that at this conference 'over one hundred spoke definitely to being saved and forty-four sought the baptism with the Holy Ghost',[146] the events which Arthur Chilson interpreted as the beginning of a revival.

During the Native Prayer Conferences in subsequent years, he was proved right. In 1925 the conference took place at Malava, and he and his wife say of it: 'The Conference was a real blessing and a time of heart searching and deepening in the things of God.'[147] But the breakthrough seems to have come in 1926, when Chilson reports:

> At the Native Prayer Conference, the prayers of years were answered and we had a real visitation from the Lord. Many confessed and found pardon for sin, many sought and received the baptism with the Holy Ghost.[148]

And he was happy that as a result of this revival there was 'a greater degree of fellow-ship co-operation and unity between the Christians of all our stations than ever before', and a growing loyalty to the mission.[149]

The fellowship and unity described by Chilson were soon to be broken, however, and the issue that was to cause this disunity was the very same spiritual experience that missionaries and African Christians had been seeking for years, and which had finally come to a great number of Luyia Friends. The year that is remembered as the decisive one by members of the Holy Spirit churches, who were at that time members of Friends Africa Mission, is 1927, when the Native Prayer Conference was held in September at Kaimosi. Kefa Ayub Mavuru, who was High Priest of the African Church of Holy Spirit until his death in 1979, says that Arthur Chilson was the missionary in charge of the conference, and that the message he chose to bring was the message of Pentecost. Chilson told the people, says Mavuru, that in order for them to be true Christians they had to be baptized with the Holy Spirit, and that before receiving this baptism they had to confess all their sins openly and pray for forgiveness. His message affected his listeners strongly. They knelt down, confessed, and asked God to forgive their sins. When this had been going on for some time, Chilson stood up and lifted his hands over the heads of the people. He prayed that they might receive baptism with the Holy Spirit. And now the meeting was seized by the Spirit. People cried, everything was shaking, and many began to speak in tongues. To show them the biblical authority for what they had just experienced, Chilson read Acts 2: 1–4:

> When the day of Pentecost had come, they were all together in one place. And suddenly a sound came from heaven like the rush of a mighty wind, and it filled all the house where they were sitting. And there appeared to

> them tongues as of fire, distributed and resting on each one of them. And they were all filled with the Holy Spirit and began to speak in other tongues, as the Spirit gave them utterance.[150]

And he pointed out that when they shook and spoke in tongues they were influenced by the same power of the Holy Spirit which had seized the disciples of Jesus on the day of Pentecost.[151]

Arthur and Edna Chilson also regarded 1927 as a special year, and saw that Native Prayer Conference as more important than all the previous ones:

> The Holy Spirit came upon us in mighty power in one of the beginning services and throughout the meetings, hearts were melted and bowed low before God. Sins hidden for years were confessed.... Difficulties between Christians were straightened up.... People were weeping and praying all over the house, some stood to speak and were so broken in spirit they could not voice their hearts desire. God was good to us and the Holy Ghost is working in our midst.... Everywhere hearts are burdened for sin and many Christians are seeking or receiving the baptism with the Holy Ghost.[152]

As the last part of this statement shows, the revival spirit was not felt only at the conferences. This is confirmed in the description by Japhet Zale Ambula, the late Archbishop of Holy Spirit Church of East Africa, of how pupils at the school at Kaimosi who were taught by Arthur Chilson also received the Spirit, in October 1927, and began to shout and speak in tongues.[153] And Chilson himself tells of the same kind of events throughout Maragoli, rejoicing at what was happening. But he realizes, he says, 'that Satan would turn this movement into "wild-fire" and thwart God's plan, if possible, and that the need for wise supervision is very essential'. He believed that 'the natives themselves know that they can not carry on the work alone', and he was worried how it would develop in the future, because he and his wife were supposed to go on furlough a few months later. The Fords were also in America on furlough at this time,[154] so very soon none of the evangelistic missionaries would be present to guide the movement. Chilson expresses his desperation at this situation: 'are these opportunities not lost – LOST FOREVER?'[155]

In this, Chilson voiced the concern he had shown earlier: that African Christians would not be able to take care of the work of the Church without missionary supervision. As before, however, B. Willis Beede, who probably represented the attitude of the American Friends

Board of Foreign Missions, expresses a much more optimistic view of the Africans' abilities in a letter to Chilson:

> It seems to me ... that the Native church is being prepared to assume larger responsibilities for its work. God is not leaving himself without workmen among the people and the incoming of the Holy Spirit is a pretty clear indication that He is getting the people ready to assume larger responsibilities.[156]

And, as we shall see later, the African Christians proved that they were able to continue and develop their churches even when no missionaries were present to guide them, although the direction they chose might not in all cases be the one that the missionaries would have wished them to take.

Arthur Chilson left Kaimosi in January 1928 on furlough, but although he had not foreseen this at the time, he was not to return to his work as a missionary under Friends Africa Mission. The American Friends Board of Missions decided not to send him back, apparently because they found his evangelical theology too revivalistic and intolerant of other ways of thinking, although economic considerations and policy changes were given as the official reasons.[157] What his reactions would have been to the Holy Spirit revival after that time is therefore not known. But by warning against the possibility that it might develop into 'wild-fire' he shows that his attitude would probably have been similar to that of Jefferson Ford who, upon his return from furlough in December 1928, was appointed to take charge of the evangelistic work in the whole Friends Africa Mission area.[158] He tried as hard as he could to stop the noisier expressions of those who had been baptized with the Holy Spirit,[159] an endeavour in which he had the co-operation of Alta and Fred Hoyt who, before his return, had already tried to 'check' the 'fanaticism'.[160]

Ford soon decided to arrange special three-day prayer meetings once every three months in the various districts in order to promote unity.[161] This was probably an attempt at accommodating the already established practice of those involved in the Holy Spirit revival of holding a prayer meeting at Mbale once a month, on the 18th, in order to pray for unity,[162] while the change to quarterly and longer-lasting meetings may have been necessitated by Ford's wish to be present at all prayer meetings. Judging from his correspondence, his efforts apparently met with some success, although by now a number of people were holding separate meetings, 'refusing to have fellowship with others in the church'. He describes how some of the problems were solved, and a number of those who believed in the noisy manifestations of the Holy Spirit were brought back into the fold:

> the Lord has blessedly helped some of the leaders of this movement to see their mistakes and confess them, and a good degree of harmony and unity seems to be manifest. A letter this week from one of the leaders is full of expressions of thankfulness and joy at the restored fellowship.[163]

Like Chilson, Ford attributed these beginnings of a separatist movement to the lack of missionaries: 'Had there been staff in the Mission sufficient to give proper oversight probably these tendencies would not have developed.' And he again emphasizes that through his efforts some of the separatists came back into the Friends Church:

> Our arrival put a new element into the situation.... The schismatic leaders had full confidence in us, so that when we talked the situation over with them, showing them where such customs would lead, and together prayed over it, they very humbly and meekly yielded, and took their places again in the church. So that now harmony and unity are being restored in those districts. Praise the Lord!'[164]

Kefa Mavuru confirms that the return to the Friends Church of a number of those who had joined the Holy Spirit revival was actually due to a large extent to Jefferson Ford's attempts at reconciling the two groups in the Church.[165] But there was also quite a large number of people who were not willing to give up their new practices, and when they met with opposition from missionaries and church elders, this resulted in their resignation from membership of Friends Africa Mission, or in their names being removed from the membership records.

In 1932, fifty-seven people were 'dropped from full church membership' at the recommendation of the 'Native Church' 'because of misconduct', and another nineteen were dropped from full membership at their own request.[166] And over the next two years more than 2000 people left the Church, reducing the membership of Friends Africa Mission from more than 9000 to just over 7000.[167] Even the number of pupils enrolled in the Friends schools declined sharply in the early 1930s: from about 18,000 in 1930 to approximately 13,000 in 1933;[168] but while this number began to increase again from the following year, the membership figures remained stagnant throughout the 1930s, and in 1939 there were still only about 7000 members.[169]

The split between those who joined the Holy Spirit movement and those who remained in the Friends Church eventually, to a great extent, followed the lines of the educational and social stratification which had already threatened the unity within Friends Africa Mission for some time. Japhet Zale says that at the beginning a number of leaders in Church and society were involved in the revival, but many of them withdrew from the movement and began to speak against it when it became clear to them that their involvement in open confessions and the experience of baptism with the Holy Spirit was incompatible with their positions.[170] This state of affairs is confirmed by others who joined the Holy Spirit movement during the early years, among them Kefa Mavuru; therefore, the pattern that emerged was that generally, the more economically privileged members remained within Friends Africa Mission, whereas those who joined the Holy Spirit movement were to a large extent that part of the membership who wanted to retain close relationships between people within the Christian communities, and found that these relationships were reinforced by the common experiences of open confessions of sin and being baptized with the Holy Spirit.[171]

An illustration of the importance of this stratification in deciding reactions to the revival is the fact that the effects of the new movement on the Pentecostal Church was very different from its effects among Friends. As Ezekiel Kasiera has pointed out, the evangelical theology preached by the Quaker missionaries, and especially that preached by Arthur Chilson, was not very different from the message of the Pentecostal missionaries at the neighbouring Nyang'ori mission station.[172] Having gone through a number of difficulties during its initial years, in 1924 this mission was staffed by Mr and Mrs Keller, who managed to have it affiliated with the Pentecostal Assemblies of Canada, and to organize the work more efficiently than it had been organized during the time of their predecessor, Clyde Miller.[173] Their arrival at Nyang'ori in 1924, at a time of increased interest in Christianity among the Africans in the area, with their message of the baptism with the Holy Spirit, may have been one contributing factor to the beginning of the Holy Spirit revival from precisely that year. For normally the relationship between missionaries of different mission stations was good, and there was a good deal of co-operation among them, as long as the sphere-of-influence policy was respected by all. Missionaries of Friends Africa Mission report almost every year that staff from other missions were present at their yearly missionary prayer conferences,[174] and missionaries from other missions might be invited to speak at the conferences arranged for the African Christians – as, for instance, Mr Keller did at the Friends Native Prayer Conference in 1928.[175] As a result of this positive inter-mission relationship, and of the often close relationship between African Christians across denominational boundaries, when the revival broke out it was not confined to Friends Africa Mission alone, but members of the Pentecostal mission also experienced baptism with the Holy Spirit in the late 1920s.[176]

In both churches a large proportion of the membership participated in the revival, but while in Friends Africa Mission the majority of those who received baptism with the Holy Spirit eventually separated from the parent Church, causing a drastic decrease in membership, the effect was the opposite in the Pentecostal Church: the revival brought in a large number of new members who remained in fellowship with the Church.[177] This difference may be explained as a consequence of the different evangelizing methods employed by the two churches and the resulting differences in the African congregations. Friends Africa Mission operated the four departments described above – the evangelistic, the educational, the industrial and the medical – and all four were seen as legitimate missionary endeavours serving the overall purpose of evangelizing the Africans and building up a strong, self-reliant church. In the Pentecostal Church, however, the mission's sole emphasis had been its evangelistic activities, and only very little educational work had been done until the arrival of Mr and Mrs Keller.[178] And while among the Friends the Africans' demand for education had, over the years, caused the educational department to receive more and more of the missionaries' attention and more of the total funds of the mission, no such development had taken place in the Pentecostal Church. Therefore, this church did not see the split between the educational and religious aspects of its work which Friends Africa Mission experienced in the 1920s, with the resulting split in the membership between those who had become heavily involved in the modern world and those who emphasized the building up of the Christian community. Among the Pentecostals, the Christian community was still relatively unbroken in the 1920s; therefore, when the revival came, it did not cause disunity. On the contrary, it served in this Church to reinforce the already existing unity, leading to a great increase in membership in the 1930s.[179]

The Aftermath of the Revival

In Friends Africa Mission, the separation between those who remained in the mission Church and those who joined the revival was painful for both parties. The split, however, was an important factor contributing to the general atmosphere of strain within Friends Africa Mission in the 1930s. With those who had the greatest enthusiasm for the purely religious aspects of Christianity gone from the membership, those who remained had to find a way of continuing the various activities of the Church despite the vastly decreased number of members and the loss of unity in the congregations. But other factors also contributed to the difficulties of Friends Africa Mission during this decade. One was the economic Depression of the 1920s and the 1930s, which affected Quakers both in America and in Kenya, and resulted in a sharp decline in mission finances. Also, the life of the Church was affected by strong theological controversies between fundamentalists and 'modernists' among the missionaries as well as among the mission supporters in America.

With the departure of Arthur Chilson in 1928, probably the most uncompromisingly revivalist missionary was out of the picture. But for a long time revivalist views continued to be the only acceptable theology among the majority of missionaries, and therefore also among the African Christians, who for many years were hardly exposed to any other teachings. Actually, by this time a few so-called 'modernist' missionaries had made an appearance in Friends Africa Mission, the first being Lewis and Ruthanna Moon, who arrived in 1920. But so intolerant was the attitude of the evangelical missionaries towards such views – the most important accusation being that they did not accept the verbal inspiration of the Bible – that within less than a year the Moons were made to feel very unwelcome among the other missionaries, with the result that they gave in their letter of resignation to the American Friends Board of Foreign Missions and left Kenya the same year.[180] Later, missionaries came who did not share the fundamentalist views of those already there, among them Margaret Parker and Elizabeth Haviland, who arrived in 1924 and 1927 respectively, and Edith and Bryan Michener, who came in 1930.[181] But none of them was very active in evangelizing work – Elizabeth Haviland was a teacher, Margaret Parker was a nurse, and Bryan Michener was a medical doctor.[182] The missionary who was most involved in evangelization continued to be Jefferson Ford, who was appointed superintendent of evangelistic work from 1928 and continued to act in this capacity until shortly before his retirement in 1948.[183] Therefore, although the controversy between evangelicals and 'modernists' continued to be an issue in the correspondence between missionaries and the Board office in America, and between individual missionaries, at this stage hardly any attempts were made on the missionaries' side to preach a Gospel that was not thoroughly evangelical. Nevertheless, the theological controversies caused a rift between different missionaries, and their relationships deteriorated to such an extent that in 1937 a delegation from the Mission Board had to be sent to Kenya in order to restore proper working conditions in the mission.[184]

The poor relationships between missionaries and the Board's reluctance to involve any more people in the controversies, together with the lack of funds for Friends Africa Mission in the 1930s, meant that very few new missionaries were sent to Kenya during this decade, while those who were already there had to divide the work among them, and in some cases curtail their activities because of lack of money. Also, this was the time when political opposition to the colonial administration began to develop, and Africans formed opposition movements which were critical of all whites – not only those involved in the government but missionaries as well. As mentioned above, the movement which was formed among members of Friends Africa Mission, and drew its membership almost exclusively from this church, was the North Kavirondo Central Association, and the method most commonly used by this association to show its dissatisfaction was to send letters of petition to the colonial authorities in London, ignoring the local colonial administration. With the financial and human resources of the Quaker missionaries stretched to the limit, the North Kavirondo Central Association received no support from them, with the exception of Dr Bond, who wrote favourably about them to America a number of times.[185] On the contrary, not only did the organization send letters of complaint to the Colonial Office in London, they also wrote similar letters to the American Friends Board of Missions, complaining about the treatment of Africans by certain missionaries,[186] thereby giving expression to the fact that the relationship between missionaries and African Christians was strained during the 1930s.

All in all, therefore, this decade was a time when both missionaries and African Quakers tried to carry on the work which had begun earlier, but with less enthusiasm and a more sceptical attitude towards each other. The depressing atmosphere prevailing within the Friends Africa Mission did not, however, stifle activities in all its areas of operation. In the north, among the Bukusu and Tachoni peoples, African Christians were very active during these years, spreading the Gospel and school education to new places. This was to some extent a result of the opening up from 1930 of Chief Sudi's area in South Bukusu,[187] an area which the chief had reserved until then for the activities of the Roman Catholics – partly, perhaps, because Friends had made their presence felt for a shorter period than further south – so that the factors which had led there to tensions between those Christians who were more involved in modern society and those who wanted to strengthen the local Christian communities had not developed here to the same extent. Quakerism had come to the north more than ten years later than it came to the south, with the setting up of the Lugulu mission station in 1913. Apparently, the enthusiasm for both religious and educational activities which had been felt in the south during the 1920s was now paralleled by a similar enthusiasm in the north a decade later.

At the same time, the 1930s were a decade in which African Christians in the northern locations of North Kavirondo District developed a more critical attitude towards some of the activities of the missionaries and began to carry through development projects of their own, independent of missionary guidance. Both Quakers and Roman Catholics, the two dominant denominations in this area, had their main mission stations further south, and their supporters now began to complain that this meant that the missionaries also gave most of their attention to the southerners. The feeling of many in the north was that they carried a disproportionately heavy burden in financing the educational and health services in the district, although the majority of these facilities were located further south, and therefore did not benefit them. And in fact, their dissatisfaction had a sound basis, since by 1935 Bukusu Friends alone had established 135 'out-schools' as compared with 143 in the rest of the Friends Africa Mission area, but had not, despite this performance, been given any 'primary' – that is, more advanced – school by 1939, nor had the mission built a hospital in the north.[188]

Especially among the Bukusu, dissatisfaction reached such a pitch that associations were formed in which people came together with the purpose of trying to level out the imbalance, irrespective of their denominational adherence. This was a contrast to the political associations further south, such as North Kavirondo Central Association and North Kavirondo Taxpayers' Welfare Association, which, as we have seen, recruited their members along denominational lines: from among Friends and Anglicans, respectively. In 1936 leading Bukusu from various denominations formed the Kitosh Education Society,[189] which began to collect funds for the construction of schools sponsored by various denominations. In 1939 the administration decided to ban the Kitosh Education Society after accusations of misappropriation of funds. But the same people who had been behind it almost immediately, in 1940, created a new association, the Bukusu Union, with Pascal Nabwana, a Roman Catholic, as its chairman. The Bukusu Union became even more radical than the Kitosh Education Society, and started to form its own schools, independent of any missionaries or colonial administrators, as well as protesting against what they saw as cases of abuse of power by chiefs and headmen.[190]

The members of these associations were Christians who had become heavily involved in modern society, and wanted all the benefits which Christianity and the institutions started by the missions could offer. They saw a close connection between the Christian Gospel and social betterment, and worked for the promotion of both. Some of the Quaker missionaries, in their comments on the independent attitude of the Bukusu people, described it in negative terms: as selfishness and lack of support for the true aims of the Church. Fred Hoyt writes about it as follows:

> There is an undercurrent of dissatisfaction, a wanting to do things independently of the Mission and Government rulings, with a feeling that they are not getting their share of help. There is a swinging away from the old missionary spirit of helping the weaker, unreached ones, to the desire to get all the help they can for themselves, especially in higher education and in buildings.[191]

But some missionaries – among them Jefferson Ford who, as mentioned above, spent much of his time in Kenya at Lugulu – realized the importance of bringing more services to this area. At the request of African church elders he started a Bible school at Lugulu in 1943, an act which helped to satisfy Friends in this area and to give them a feeling that the missionaries still cared for their needs.[192] Also, in 1942 the four northern monthly meetings, those of Chwele, Lugulu, Kakalelwa and Malava, were organized to form the second quarterly meeting in the Friends Africa Mission area, the first having been the one established in Maragoli in the early 1920s.[193]

Crisis in the mid-1940s: Dini ya Msambwa

While the above-mentioned protest against missionaries came from church members whose aim was to improve the services provided by the missions and by the colonial government in their area, in the early 1940s another protest movement emerged among the Bukusu which did not remain within the mission churches. This was Dini ya Msambwa, a political-religious movement whose main leader was Elijah Masinde, a former member of Friends Africa Mission who had been expelled because he practised polygamy.[194] Although the movement actually seems to have started earlier,[195] it came into the open in the early 1940s, when a number of incidents took place which were directed against the colonial administration and against missionaries.[196] In late 1941 the church building at Lugulu belonging to Friends Africa Mission had been set on fire,[197] and in 1943–44 the agricultural department became the object of attack on more than one occasion, because that department especially interfered in the lives of ordinary people, with its attempts at forcing them to carry out its soil conservation programmes. Land belonging to the agricultural department was ploughed up, cattle used by it were let loose at night. Masinde refused to allow a veterinary surgeon to inject his cattle, and threatened to beat up an agricultural officer who was instructing people in the uprooting of the weed Mexican marigold; and in November 1944 the English agricultural officer's house in Kimilili was burnt down. There were other cases of open opposition to the demands made by the colonial authorities – for instance, against their recruitment of Africans to serve in the British military forces during World War II – and on a number of occasions Masinde and other leaders of the movement refused to obey the chiefs' orders. In February 1945 Masinde was charged with two cases of assault, and sent to prison. While he was serving his sentence he was declared insane and sent to Mathare Mental Hospital in Nairobi, where he remained for two years until his release in May 1947.[198]

Not all the cases of obstruction in the 1940s can be attributed with certainty to members of Dini ya Msambwa.[199] But members of this movement were sufficiently involved in anti-government activities for the authorities to suspect them, although the dissatisfaction they expressed was shared by a large proportion of the population, and also came to the surface in protests from other quarters, for instance from the Bukusu Union.[200] Elijah Masinde and other leaders of Dini ya Msambwa were able to exploit the general atmosphere of discontent, and give expression to it – not only in acts of obstruction or violence such as those mentioned above, but also in their attempts to gather the Bukusu people in a form of worship which was seen as being in keeping with the ways of the ancestors and as a refusal to follow the ways of the missionaries.

These two aspects of its activities – religious worship and acts of defiance of the foreign masters in both state and Church – were inseparable in Dini ya Msambwa, as Audrey Wipper has pointed out.[201] This was demonstrated in September 1947, when Elijah Masinde led a group of about five thousand Bukusu dressed as warriors to Chetambe, where several hundred Bukusu had lost their lives in 1895 when they tried to fight the British and stop them from taking their land. Here he performed a sacrifice in honour of those who had died, and promised his followers that the time would come when the Europeans would leave the country and Africans would have their own religion and their own government.[202]

In performing this and other sacrifices, Masinde and the members of Dini ya Msambwa followed the customs of their Bukusu ancestors, just as they did in other ways – for instance, when they offered food or drink to the departed before they took any themselves.[203] They also honoured the ancestors by planting special, traditionally well-known plants around their houses and by worshipping on Mount Elgon, the impressive mountain which had also been of importance to the Bukusu people long ago. However, the specifically religious significance of Mount Elgon seems to have been a new creation in Dini ya Msambwa, who regarded it as a holy mountain like Mount Zion in the Bible, and actually gave the name Lake Zion to a particular lake on the mountain.[204] Likewise, other practices of the Dini ya Msambwa differed from the traditional religion of the Bukusu as it had been before the advent of colonialism. One important difference was that in Dini ya Msambwa sacrifices were performed on a larger scale than before, no longer confined to the family or clan, and at specific places of worship rather than at the traditional family shrines, 'namwima' and 'wetili'. Also, Dini ya Msambwa members would sing during their religious ceremonies, just as Christians did in church, and they quoted from the Bible, used the cross as a symbol, and prayed in the name of God the Father, God the Son and God the Holy Spirit. Furthermore, they believed in a millennium where all the problems of this world would come to an end, the foreigners would have been evicted, and all their wishes would be fulfilled.[205]

In spite of taking over a number of symbols and customs from the Christian churches, however, Dini ya Msambwa remained basically a movement built on the foundations of the ancestors, only now the concept of 'ancestor' had been widened to include not only the departed Bukusu people but also the biblical ancestors.[206] There was never any suggestion that Dini ya Msambwa members regarded their movement as a Christian church. On the contrary, they were strongly opposed to the existing churches in their area which had been brought into the country from the outside.

Dini ya Msambwa showed its opposition to the foreign missionaries on 7 February 1948, when Elijah Masinde led a group of about a thousand followers to the Roman Catholic mission station at Kibabii. According to the mission diary, their purpose was to perform a sacrifice on the mission compound, and they did this, despite the missionaries' attempts to stop them, including shooting a gun into the air.[207] The Father who wrote the entry in the diary said: 'They do not seem to hear nor understand or to be able to speak on such occasions. They are not fierce, but obsessed to madness.' According to him, the group did not constitute any danger to the missionaries; but not all the priests appear to have shared this opinion, since one of them decided to report the incident to the authorities. And government reports say that the Dini ya Msambwa people told the missionaries to leave and threatened to burn the mission down, making the events appear more dangerous from a security point of view than does the description in the mission diary.[208] At any rate, the authorities regarded the situation as serious, and reacted by sending police to guard the mission.

When three days later, on 10 February, a large crowd of Dini ya Msambwa followers marched towards the police station at Malakisi, the police were already nervous. Government reports say that the aim of the group was to come to the rescue of three members who had been detained by the police,[209] and one report describes how on the previous day a meeting had been held at which members of Dini ya Msambwa had decided to go to Malakisi and fight the Europeans if any were to be found there, and they had been told not to fear police bullets, since they would turn into water and could not do them any harm.[210] Dini ya Msambwa's secretary wrote in a notebook that the group was only passing the police station on their way to hold a meeting.[211] Whatever the truth may have been, the police felt threatened, and an English Superintendent of Police who had just arrived to inspect his people in Malakisi ordered them to open fire on the crowd. According to police reports, this took place after the Dini ya Msambwa people had first attacked him personally and tried to grab his revolver. The result was that eleven of the Dini ya Msambwa people were killed and sixteen wounded.[212]

After this incident the authorities wanted to arrest Masinde, and on 16 February he was found in a hole in the ground where he had been hiding. He gave himself up to the police and was deported to Lamu on the coast, far away from his followers.[213] While he was there he distinguished himself as a football player, a fact that enhanced his prestige in the eyes of his supporters but further irritated the colonial authorities.[214] Meanwhile, on the day after his arrest a notice in the *Official Gazette* declared Dini ya Msambwa an illegal society.[215]

After these events Dini ya Msambwa's violence within the Bukusu 'reserve' seems to have died out. But there were several cases of anti-European propaganda and of arson in the Trans Nzoia and Uasin Gishu Districts in the White Highlands, and on several occasions followers of Dini ya Msambwa were arrested and charged with these offences. Its activities also spread to the eastern parts of Uganda.[216] However, the most violent episode in the history of Dini ya Msambwa took place among the Pokot people, where a man by the name of Lukas Pkech had gathered a number of followers after he himself had been influenced by the teachings of Elijah Masinde.[217] In August 1948 Lukas Pkech was jailed because of his involvement in Dini ya Msambwa, but he managed to escape from prison and hide from the authorities for more than a year. Finally, on 24 April 1950 a police party consisting of five European officers and forty Africans came face to face with Lukas and two to three hundred of his followers. It is doubtful whether the Pokot had any intention of attacking the police, but eventually the District Commissioner, who was at the head of the police group, decided that Pkech and his group seemed to be hostile; consequently he ordered the police to open fire. The Pokot were carrying spears, and it came to a battle in which three European officers and one African on the police side and between twenty and thirty of Pkech's followers were killed, including Lukas Pkech himself.[218]

After this incident police supervision of the Dini ya Msambwa was intensified. In most cases those who continued its activities gave up that aspect of the movement which consisted in open defiance of the colonial authorities and threats against all categories of white people, and to a large extent limited themselves to expressing their religious feelings in more peaceful ways. Government reports mention a number of cases in which Dini ya Msambwa members were discovered by the authorities holding their meetings, with some people being arrested because of their membership, although apparently they had not been engaged in any activities that could threaten the public order. On the whole, after 1952 government officers report a gradual quietening down in the movement's activities, and in the second half of the 1950s it does not seem to have given the authorities much cause for concern.[219] Since Elijah Masinde and other leaders, together with a good number of their followers, were in jail, the rest who were still at large had to concentrate on the survival of their movement and avoid acts which could lead to further repression by the authorities. This corresponds with Audrey Wipper's estimate that the membership of Dini ya Msambwa seems to have reached its highest point around 1948–49,[220] although she believes that all through its existence 'The core activists were probably few in number, but the movement apparently could tap, when need arose, a much wider base of ancillary support.'[221]

In May 1961 Elijah Masinde was released from prison. But Dini ya Msambwa as an organization was still proscribed, although a number of cases that came up in the courts show that both Masinde and at least some other members continued its activities. During these years, immediately prior to Kenya's national independence from colonial rule, Masinde made an attempt to ally himself with KANU, one of the two big nationalist parties; and after independence the new government, under the leadership of Jomo Kenyatta and KANU, legalized Dini ya Msambwa and granted it official registration in May 1964.[222]

However, as Gideon Were has pointed out: 'To a large extent, the social grievances which the movement highlighted are still with us and will take a long time to be eradicated.'[223] Therefore, even after independence, Masinde and some followers were dissatisfied and continued to behave aggressively towards foreign missionaries and

Ane Marie Bak Rasmussen, the author.

ABOVE. Kathleen Staudt and Ane Marie Bak Rasmussen, Aarhus, 17 May 1991. BELOW. The family in Aarthus December 1990; Zakarias, Hans Peter, Ane Marie and Joseph Mululu.

ABOVE. Memorial to Ane Marie Bak Rasmussen. BELOW. Hudson Azangu, Fr. Agapitus Muse (Mukumu-Roman Catholic Mission), Leah Ganira, the author and EAYM executive secretary Thomas Ganira at Kaimosi Mission.

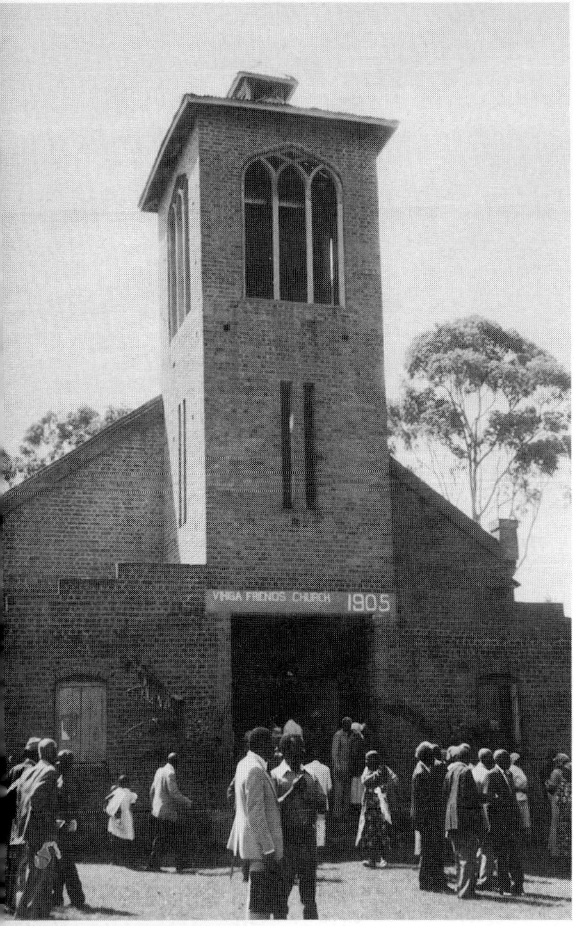

LEFT. East Africa Yearly meeting (south) Kidundu Church, January 1985.

BELOW. At the conference, Chwele August 1974.

ABOVE. Friends Church Kitale, 1987. BELOW. Harold and Everlyn Smuck, Friends Mission Board representatives to East Africa Yearly Meeting 1962-66. FUM's Associate Secretary of World Ministries 1966-81 Richmond Indiana. (Photo by AMB, Rasmussen 1985).

ABOVE. Open air Friends Women Meeting at Chwele (ERSF).

LEFT. Samusen Wekesa Lugula, Church Elder and pioneer teacher among Elgon friends, Makhonge 18 July 1991.

ABOVE. Moi Primary School, Bungona, 1987. BELOW. Seventy fifth anniversary of East Africa Yearly Meeting (Society of Friends), at Friends Bible Institute, Kaimosi on 6 November 1977. Anniversary message by Thomas G. Lung'aho.

RIGHT. Kefa Ayubu Mavuru who was High Priest of the African Church of Holy Spirit until his death at Lugala.

BELOW. Left to right: New Church at the Lugala headquarters of the African Church of Holy Spirit, 20 April 1975.

towards the authorities, even though these authorities were now African. As a result several cases came up in court and Masinde was given new prison sentences. Consequently, in 1968 Dini ya Msambwa was again proscribed, and the ban has not been lifted since.[224] During the 1970s and the 1980s Elijah Masinde was out of jail part of the time, and every time he was released he immediately resumed his activities. He held meetings with his followers, many of whom were now Pokot people, and continued his protests against everything he saw as wrong.[225] Elijah Masinde died in 1987. Large numbers of people from all walks of life, including a government minister and two members of parliament, attended his funeral and were witness to the impact of his religious and political activities even among people who had never had any formal affiliation with Dini ya Msambwa. This happened even though Dini ya Msambwa was no longer active as an organization.[226]

There are a number of important similarities, but also a number of differences, between Dini ya Msambwa and the Holy Spirit movement described above. The Holy Spirit movement gained a foothold among those members of Friends Africa Mission who had not been able to secure for themselves a place in the new political and religious establishment, and had not therefore been very much influenced by its individualistic values. On the contrary, they wanted to re-create a meaningful community where people could live in solidarity, and their religious experiences (when they received the Holy Spirit) helped precisely to strengthen their feeling of oneness and their wish to help each other – also in the ordinary, practical business of everyday life. The Holy Spirit movement had developed among the southern Luyia peoples who, by 1927, had been under the influence of Friends Africa Mission for a quarter of a century. By this time, the Bukusu had been under its influence for only fourteen years; therefore their society had not yet seen as much of the social and economic stratification which the activities of the colonial authorities, coupled with missionary education, brought with them. Consequently, the Bukusu church had not yet experienced the rift between 'modern'-orientated and community-orientated groups which had developed further south. Therefore, among Bukusu Friends the Holy Spirit revival did not meet with any significant response. On the contrary, those who were already Christians at that time concentrated their efforts on helping the missionaries to spread the Gospel to the rest of the Bukusu people.

Around the time of the outbreak of the Second World War, however, Bukusu society had come to experience the stratification which had begun earlier further south. And, as in the south, those who had contact with the Christian missions but had not been able to secure a prominent position in the new type of society now started an alternative religious movement which would allow them the freedom to express their social and religious sentiments. This was the Dini ya Msambwa.

Audrey Wipper points out that its members were not necessarily only very poor people. Rather, in many cases they were that group of people who had earlier enjoyed a certain degree of material benefit in the new society, but whose wishes for advancement had been frustrated. One reason for this could be that they had not reached a sufficiently high level of formal education to secure a prominent position in mission or government service. She says that the group which was hardest hit was those squatters who worked for European farmers in the White Highlands, who had to suffer drastic wage cuts in the late 1930s because their employers experienced financial difficulties. In some cases the squatters were even evicted from the European farms, often without a place of their own in the 'reserve' to return to because, as squatters, they had moved to the White Highlands with their whole family. Another group that was affected in a strongly negative way by the European farmers were those Bukusu who owned land just inside the 'reserve' near Kamukuywa. Here the British government decided to settle a number of British ex-soldiers after the Second World War; in order to do this they extended the area of the White Highlands and took the land away from the original owners, who in most cases were in the same position as the evicted squatters in that they had no land of their own further inside the 'reserve' where they could go to settle.[227]

Therefore, the people who joined Dini ya Msambwa seem to have been mainly those who had reaped no benefits from the colonial society and, more specifically, those who had been deprived of their former rights and now felt frustrated and unable to find a place in that society. In this respect Dini ya Msambwa was similar to the Holy Spirit movement. But just as the Holy Spirit revival had stirred no response among the Bukusu when it started around 1930, so Dini ya Msambwa met with only very little response in the southern Luyia locations. Here, those who were less successful, from the point of view of the social and religious establishment, had by this time already formed their alternative communities and therefore had no need to express any protest against a wider society that did not seriously affect them. On the contrary, as we shall see below, in the 1940s the Holy Spirit people were slowly beginning to adjust themselves to the society around them, and to some extent to appreciate its values. There was no impulse to engage in activities directed against that society.

While Dini ya Msambwa and the Holy Spirit movement recruited their followers from among similar groups of people in the northern and southern Luyia locations, respectively, they differed in their abilities to gather people into lasting new communities. Whereas the Holy Spirit movement developed into churches which are still alive today, Dini ya Msambwa did not, for the majority of those associated with it, form a permanent group to which they could belong, although a very large part of the Bukusu, and a number of other people as well, supported Elijah Masinde in the late 1940s.[228] There may be various reasons for this fact, an important one being that Dini ya Msambwa was proscribed by the authorities, and was therefore not a very attractive group for most people to join. Moreover, its aims were radically different from those of the Holy Spirit people. Whereas the religious experiences of these people resulted in the building up of small, local fellowships whose members formed alternative and, for them, meaningful communities within the wider society, the religious beliefs of Dini ya Msambwa members did not direct them towards community building in the same way. Rather, they believed that some day the Europeans would be driven out of the country, after which Africans would again live a happy life without suppression, and all their activities were aimed at provoking changes to this effect.[229]

However, as Audrey Wipper has pointed out: 'Msambwa, like many peasant movements, failed when it came to large scale mobilization and organization. Its leaders lacked the breadth of view and the ability to move from localized opposition to a mass movement on a territorial scale.'[230] Therefore it did not succeed in forming a political party but instead employed what Wipper calls 'guerilla warfare'. She shows that although the Dini ya Msambwa people may not always have attained the desired goals, their tactics did disrupt the authority system and served notice to the administration 'that time is running out'.[231] And its wider aim of changing the whole society, combined with the fact that it was proscribed, made it more difficult for Dini ya

Msambwa than for the Holy Spirit movement to form a lasting community.

The more violent activities of Dini ya Msambwa and its wider political outlook probably have to do with the fact that some of the Bukusu people – the squatters and those evicted from their former land, as described above – were more directly affected in a negative way by the presence of white people. And this heavier pressure resulted in a more violent reaction, as well as in a stronger wish to see all the foreigners leave the country. Furthermore, as John Lonsdale has pointed out, during the years after the Second World War African political associations developed a national outlook, wanting to gain influence on a country-wide level, whereas between the wars their goals had been limited to improving the local situation.[232] Dini ya Msambwa, appearing when it did, shared this new outlook in a way that the Holy Spirit movement did not, and its national goals, coupled with its members' more negative experiences under colonialism, made it natural for them to apply 'guerilla tactics' aimed at freeing the country from the presence of white people.[233]

This double form of response to the colonial situation – the more peaceful one of the Holy Spirit movement and the sometimes violent one of Dini ya Msambwa – corresponded well with the traditional Luyia (and African) outlook on the world which, as I have described above, made no distinction between secular and religious spheres. For all its political features, it must not be forgotten that Dini ya Msambwa was above all religious. Gideon Were says that 'there is no doubt whatsoever that the leadership of the sect regarded politics, especially the struggle for independence and social justice, as a paramount function of religion';[234] and B.M.W. Lusweti has pointed out in his study of Bukusu religion that Dini ya Msambwa should be looked upon as a revival of the Bukusu religion. But it was not simply a return to the forms which that religion had had before the coming of the Europeans. The enlargement of scale that had taken place in society was followed by an enlargement of scale in the religious sphere when Dini ya Msambwa took over certain elements from Christianity and integrated them into the Bukusu religion. One such element was its prayers to God the Father, God the Son and God the Holy Spirit, seeing Wele as the God of all human beings. Another was the establishment of places of worship common to all people, instead of the traditional shrines used only by individual families or clans. Assimilations of elements from other religions had taken place before – for instance from the Kalenjin, with whom the Bukusu had had close contact. The result of this was still regarded as the true Bukusu religion. Similarly, now, Dini ya Msambwa was looked upon as the old religion revived, but with a wider cosmology to suit the new situation.

Lusweti explains its protest actions as a logical consequence of its nature as the revived Bukusu religion. Traditionally, he says, Bukusu religion served as an instrument of social solidarity and kinship unity, helping to maintain the balance between individuals and between different sections of the population. And just as spiritualism had been most conspicuous in times of unrest, so now, at a time of oppression and great social change, the function of religion became that of re-creating the balance that was lost. And this could be done only through attempts at changing the existing political superstructure.[235] Dini ya Msambwa's activities, therefore, both spiritual and material, come to be seen as inseparable and as equally genuine exprcssions of a religious, millenarian movement which was, at the same time, a political protest movement.

Notes

1. I am using the most common forms of spelling in referring to the subgroups of the Luyia. They themselves use prefixes to these roots to denote persons (omu- or mu- [singular] and ba-, va-, or aba- [plural]). But as these prefixes vary slightly from one group to another, I have chosen to leave them out, especially since the forms used here are also in general use and are clearly recognizable by everyone concerned.

2. Gideon S. Were, *A History of the Abaluyia of Western Kenya c. 1500–1930*, East African Publishing House, Nairobi, 1967, pp 41 ff.; Günter Wagner, *The Bantu of Western Kenya, With Special Reference to the Vugusu and Logoli*, Oxford University Press for the International African Institute, repr. 1970, vol I, pp 22 ff. (vol I first published 1949, vol II 1956); F.E. Makila, *An Outline History of the Babukusu of Western Kenya*, Kenya Literature Bureau, Nairobi, 1978, pp 134 ff.

3. Wagner, *The Bantu of Western Kenya*, vol II, pp 19 ff., 75 ff.

4. Were, *A History of the Abaluyia*, pp 99 ff.; John Osogo, 'The Historical Traditions of the Wanga Kingdom', in *Hadith 1, Proceedings of the Annual Conference of the Historical Association of Kenya 1967*, ed. Bethwell A. Ogot, East African Publishing House, Nairobi, 1968, pp 32–46.

5. Walter H. Sangree, *Age, Prayer and Politics in Tiriki, Kenya*, Oxford University Press, London, 1966, pp 3 ff.

6. Wagner, *The Bantu of Western Kenya*, vol I, pp 53 ff.; Günter Wagner, 'The Political Organization of the Bantu of Kavirondo', in M. Fortes and E.E.

Evans-Pritchard (eds), *African Political Systems*, Oxford University Press for the International African Institute, repr. 1964, pp 197 ff. (1st edn 1940); Jan J. de Wolf, *Differentiation and Integration in Western Kenya: A Study of Religious Innovation and Social Change among the Busuku*, Mouton, The Hague/Paris, 1977, pp 127 ff.; Were, *A History of the Abaluyia*, p 155.

7. Wagner, 'The Political Organization of the Bantu of Kavirondo', pp 230 ff.; Sangree, *Age, Prayer and Politics*, pp 83 ff.

8. Wagner, *The Bantu of Western Kenya*, vol I, pp 295 ff.; Sangree, *Age, Prayer and Politics*, pp 30 ff. The Tiriki have three different groups of elders: judicial elders, ritual elders, and those too old to perform any of these duties (ibid., p 69).

9. Wagner, *The Bantu of Western Kenya*, vol I, pp 242 ff., 212, 156; Makila, *An Outline History*, pp 89 f.

10. Wagner, *The Bantu of Western Kenya*, vol I, pp 164 ff., 280.

11. 'Heart' = 'omwoyo' (Luragoli), 'kumwoyo' (Lubukusu). 'Shadow' = 'ekilili' (Luragoli), 'sisinini' (Lubukusu). 'Body' = 'ombili' (Luragoli), 'kumubili' (Lubukusu). 'Spirit' = 'ekigingi' (Luragoli), 'kumusambwa' (Lubukusu; normally, the plural form, 'kimisambwa', is used).

12. Lubukusu: 'Emakombe'.

13. Wagner, *The Bantu of Western Kenya*, vol I, pp 159 ff.; Gideon S. Were, *Essays on African Religion in Western Kenya*, East African Literature Bureau, Nairobi/Dar es Salaam/Kampala, 1977, p 20.

14. Lubukusu: 'Namwima' and 'wetili'; Luragoli: 'amagina gemisango'.

15. Wagner, *The Bantu of Western Kenya*, vol I, pp 281 ff.

16. Ezekiel M. Kasiera, 'Development of Pentecostal Christianity in Western Kenya: With Particular Reference to Maragoli, Nyang'ori, and Tiriki 1909–1942', unpublished PhD thesis, Aberdeen, 1981, pp 33 ff.

17. Were, *Essays on African Religion in Western Kenya*, pp 5 ff. Were gives the names of the Supreme Being as Were, Nyasạye, and Nasay (p 7).

18. Ibid., p 19.

19. I saw this clearly when I followed the activities of a diviner (Lubukusu: 'Omufumu'), Victorina Khakasa, for a number of days in April–May 1978.

20. Sangree, *Age, Prayer and Politics*, pp 30 ff.

21. Sangree says that the Tiriki traditionally had no conceptualization of a 'high God, Creator of all things' (ibid., pp 38 f.). Kasiera strongly disagrees, and asserts that all the Luyia peoples believed in a High God before the coming of missionaries ('Development of Pentecostal Christianity', pp 38 f.).

22. Were, *Essays on African Religion in Western Kenya*, pp 7 f.; Wagner, *The Bantu of Western Kenya*, vol I, pp 170 ff.

23. Ibid., p 170.

24. Ibid., pp 172, 290.

25. Ibid., p 177.

26. Lubukusu: 'bulosi'.

27. Wagner, *The Bantu of Western Kenya*, vol I, pp 111 ff.

28. Ibid., pp 257 ff.

29. Ibid., pp 106 ff., 245 ff.

30. John M. Lonsdale, 'A Political History of Nyanza 1883–1945', unpublished PhD thesis, Cambridge, 1964, p 23.

31. D.A. Low, 'British East Africa: The Establishment of British Rule 1895–1912', in Vincent Harlow and E.M. Chilver (eds), assisted by Alison Smith, *History of East Africa*, vol II, Clarendon Press, Oxford, 1965, repr. 1976, pp 6 ff.; Were, *A History of the Abaluyia*, pp 155 ff.

32. Ibid., pp 165 ff.; Charles W. Hobley, *Kenya: From Chartered Company to Crown Colony. Thirty Years of Exploration and Administration in British East Africa*, Frank Cass & Co., London, 2nd edn 1970 (1st edn 1929), pp 76 ff.

33. Gideon S. Were and D.A. Wilson, *East Africa through a Thousand Years: A History of the Years A.D. 1000 to the Present Day*, Evans Bros, London/Nairobi/Ibadan, 1968, pp 191 f.; Lonsdale, 'A Political History', pp 4 ff., 166; John Middleton, 'Kenya: Administration and Changes in African Life 1912–45', in Harlow and Chilver (eds), assisted by Smith, *History of East Africa*, vol II, pp 336 f.

34. Lonsdale, 'A Political History', pp 10 ff.; C.C. Wrigley, 'Kenya: The Pattern of Economic Life 1902–45', in Harlow and Chilver (eds), assisted by Smith, *History of East Africa*, vol II, pp 237, 262 f.

35. Lonsdale, 'A Political History', pp 30, 92 ff.; John M. Lonsdale, 'Political Associations in Western Kenya', in Robert I. Rotberg and Ali A. Mazrui (eds), *Protest and Power in Black Africa*, Oxford University Press, New York, 1970, p 591; Kenneth Ingham, *A History of East Africa*, Longmans, London, 3rd edn, 2nd impr., 1966 (1st edn 1962), p 309; Were, *A History of the Abaluyia*, pp 163 f., 171 ff., 177 ff.; Low, 'British East Africa', pp 46 ff.

36. Kenya National Archives: North Kavirondo District Annual Report 1925 (DC/NN.1/6).

37. Kenya National Archives: North Kavirondo District Annual Report 1936 (DC/NN.1/18).

38. Middleton, 'Kenya: Administration and Changes', pp 351 f.; Were, *A History of the Abaluyia*, p 175.

39. Kenya National Archives: North Nyanza District Annual Report 1948 (DC/NN.1/30). In 1956 the District was divided into two, the northern part being given the name of Elgon Nyanza District (Kenya National Archives, North Nyanza District Annual Report 1955 [DC/NN.1/36]).

40. Kenya National Archives, North Kavirondo District Annual Report 1923 (DC/NN.1/4).

41. Carl G. Rosberg Jr and John Nottingham, *The Myth of 'Mau Mau': Nationalism in Kenya*, Frederick A. Praeger, New York, 1966, p 162; de Wolf, *Differentiation and Integration*, p 142.

42. Rosberg and Nottingham, *The Myth of 'Mau Mau'*, p 71.

43. Lonsdale, 'A Political History', pp 10, 136.

44. Ibid., p 211; Middleton, 'Kenya: Administration and Changes', pp 353 ff.

45. Lonsdale, 'Political Associations', p 596; Were and Wilson, *East Africa through a Thousand Years*, pp 217 f.; Wrigley, 'Kenya', pp 250 f.

46. Lonsdale, 'A Political History', pp 25, 136; Lonsdale, 'Political

Associations', pp 618 ff.; John M. Lonsdale, 'European Attitudes and African Pressures: Missions and Government in Kenya between the Wars', in Bethwell A. Ogot (ed.), *Hadith 2*, East African Publishing House, Nairobi, 1970, pp 236 f.

47. Lonsdale, 'Political Associations', pp 635 ff.; John M. Lonsdale, 'Some Origins of Nationalism in East Africa', *Journal of African History*, IX, 1 (1968), pp 123 ff.; Wrigley, 'Kenya', pp 253 ff.

48. Were and Wilson, *East Africa through a Thousand Years*, pp 270 ff., Lonsdale, 'Some Origins of Nationalism', p 125.

49. Lonsdale, 'Political Associations', pp 591, 593 f.; Lonsdale, 'A Political History', pp 191 ff.

50. J.F. Lipscomb, *White Africans*, Faber & Faber, London, 1955, p 57.

51. Ibid., pp 136 f.; de Wolf, *Differentiation and Integration*, p 150.

52. Kathleen Staudt, 'Sex, Ethnic, and Class Consciousness in Western Kenya', *Comparative Politics*, January 1982, pp 149 ff.

53. Edna H. Chilson, *Ambassador of the King*, Wichita, KS, 1943, pp 17 ff., 52 ff.; Levinus K. Painter, *The Hill of Vision: The Story of the Quaker Movement in East Africa 1902–1965*, East Africa Yearly Meeting of Friends, 1966, pp 19 ff.

54. For instance, a girls' boarding school was established at Lirhanda in 1921 and one for boys at Vihiga in 1922; they were both moved to Kaimosi in 1923 (ibid., pp 52 f.).

55. Ibid., pp 24 f.

56. Friends United meeting (FUM) records: Letter from Arthur B. Chilson to Charles E. Tebbetts (American Friends Board of Foreign Missions [AFBFM] secretary), 18 April 1915.

57. Hotchkiss, *Sketches from the Dark Continent*, pp 111 ff.

58. See Alta H. Hoyt, *We Were Pioneers*, Wichita, KS, 1971, p 31.

59. Kasiera, 'Development of Pentecostal Christianity', pp 141 f.

60. Painter, *The Hill of Vision*, p 27.

61. Chilson, *Ambassador of the King*, pp 46, 61 ff.; Elizabeth H. Emerson, *Emory J. Rees, Language Pioneer: A Biographical Sketch*, American Friends Board of Missions, 1958, pp 13, 20 f.; Japheth Amugune, *A Christian Pioneer*, East Africa Yearly Meeting of Friends, 1971, p 8; Rose Adede, *Joel Litu: Pioneer African Quaker*, Pendle Hill Publications, Wallingford, PA, 1982, pp 9 ff.

62. Painter, *The Hill of Vision*, pp 36, 57, 74, 142; Adede, *Joel Litu*, pp 17 f.

63. That is to say, they were not born into Quaker families.

64. In the FUM records there are statements by most of the missionaries describing their religious experiences.

65. Chilson, *Ambassador of the King*, pp 1 ff.

66. Helen Kersey Ford and Ester Ford Andersen, *The Steps of a Good Man Are Ordered by the Lord*, Africa Inland Mission, Pearl River, NY, 1976, pp 22 f.

67. Chilson, *Ambassador of the King*, p 11.

68. FUM: Letter from Arthur Chilson, received at the Mission Board office

3 February 1921.

69. Edgar Hole and Alta Hoyt, for instance, sometimes describe elements of Luyia traditions in sympathetic terms. FUM: Article by Edgar T. Hole, 'How to be Born Successfully', 1923, tells how the behaviour of people participating in a traditional ceremony became a lesson for him in the need for Christians to be equally concerned about receiving God's blessings and serving Him. Alta Hoyt has published a collection of Luyia stories, *Bantu Folklore Tales of Long Ago*, Wichita, KS, 1951.

70. FUM: Letter from Helen Farr Ford to 'Friends', 2 April 1918.

71. Ford and Andersen, *The Steps of a Good Man*, p 48.

72. Chilson, *Ambassador of the King*, p 237.

73. Entry in Arthur B. Chilson's diary, 6 October 1924, quoted in ibid., p 156 ff.

74. Painter, *The Hill of Vision*, p 35.

75. Report for 1909 by Arthur Chilson to the Friends Africa Industrial Mission Board, quoted in Chilson, *Ambassador of the King*, p 84.

76. FUM: Letter from Arthur B. Chilson to 'Co-Workers in the Home-land', 5 October 1917.

77. FUM: A.A. and Mira Cope Bond to 'Dear people', 5 October 1918. Willis Beede of the AFBFM is reported in a letter from Fred and Alta Hoyt to Ross A. Hadley of 7 November 1919, to have said that the Board did not want the pre-millennium doctrine taught on the mission field, thereby indicating that this was the general teaching of the majority of the missionaries.

78. Roland Oliver, *The Missionary Factor in East Africa*, Longmans, London, 2nd edn, 2nd impr., 1967, pp 169 ff.; Kasiera, 'Development of Pentecostal Christianity', pp 211 ff., 262 ff.

79. The Salvation Army is reported to have opened a mission station at Malakisi in 1926 (North Kavirondo District Annual Report 1926. KNA: DC/NN.1/7), and the Seventh-Day Adventists were permitted to start work in Kabras in 1937 (North Kavirondo District Annual Report 1937. KNA: DC/NN.1/19).

80. Amugune, *A Christian Pioneer*, pp 6 f.; Thomas Ganira Lung'aho, *Daudi Lung'aho*, East Africa Yearly Meeting of Friends, n.d. (about 1970), pp 6 ff.; Painter, *The Hill of Vision*, p 32.

81. Chilson, *Ambassador of the King*, p 44.

82. Elizabeth H. Emerson, *Emory J. Rees*, pp 14 ff.; Emory J. Rees, *Milestones on the African Trail*, AFBM, Richmond, IN, 1931, pp 1 ff.

83. Chilson, *Ambassador of the King*, p 45; Painter, *The Hill of Vision*, p 24 f.

84. Oliver, *The Missionary Factor in East Africa*, pp 172 ff., 198 ff.

85. Painter, *The Hill of Vision*, p 32.

86. Ibid., p 35.

87. FUM: Annual reports from missionaries 1916–17, 1917–18, and 1919. The epidemics and the famine are also reported in North Kavirondo District Annual Reports 1917 and 1918–19 (KNA: DC/NN.1/1 and DC/NN.1/2, respectively).

88. This Sunday schedule is reported, for example, in FUM: Annual Evangelistic Report for Kaimosi 1916–1917 (written by Alta H. Hoyt), by Chilson, *Ambassador of the King*, p 14, and in FUM: Report by Jefferson and Helen Farr Ford, 14 October 1916.

89. Painter, *The Hill of Vision*, p 33.

90. Chilson, *Ambassador of the King*, pp 105 f.; FUM: Letter from Arthur B. Chilson to Ross A. Hadley, 4 March 1919; Painter, *The Hill of Vision*, p 36.

91. Ibid., p 26.

92. Emory Rees reports two such schools in Maragoli in 1912: FUM: Letter from Emory J. Rees to Charles E. Tebbetts, 6 May 1912.

93. Amugune, *A Christian Pioneer*, p 7; Lung'aho, *Daudi Lung'aho*, pp 12 f.

94. Hoyt, *We Were Pioneers*, p 31.

95. FUM: Letter from Arthur B. Chilson. Received at the AFBFM office 3 February 1921.

96. FUM: Letter from Fred N. and Alta H. Hoyt to 'Friends', 29 May 1916.

97. FUM: Report by Jefferson and Helen Farr Ford, 14 October 1916; letter from Arthur B. Chilson to AFBFM, 28 February 1915.

98. FUM: Annual Report, Maragoli Station, 1922, by Emory J. Rees.

99. FUM: Annual Report, Malava Station, 1925, by Arthur B. and Edna Chilson; Annual Report, Maragoli Station, 1925, by Emory J. Rees; Report of Evangelistic and Educational Work, Kaimosi Station, 1925, by Jefferson W. Ford.

100. Benjamin Wegesa, *A Life of Abraham Sangura, East African Friend*, AFBM, Richmond, IN, no date (mid-1950s).

101. FUM: Annual Report, Maragoli Station, 1922, by Emory J. Rees.

102. FUM: Annual Report, Maragoli Station, 1927, by Arthur B. Chilson.

103. FUM: Annual Report of FAM, 1927.

104. FUM: FAM Survey, January 1921.

105. FUM: Report of FAM, five-year period 1922–26, by Emory J. Rees.

106. FUM: Personal Report of Jefferson W. Ford, 1929.

107. In 1921 there were 55 schools, in 1926 there were 155, with 60 more among labourers at European farms (FUM: Report of FAM, five-year period 1922–26, by Emory J. Rees).

108. Painter, *The Hill of Vision*, p 30, tells of one such agreement between the FAM and the Church Missionary Society in 1905–6.

109. For example, FUM: Letter from Arthur B. Chilson to B. Willis Beede, 28 May 1923, saying that the Church of God Mission disrespected the sphere-of-influence policy.

110. Missionaries of the FAM frequently complain in their correspondence about the activities of the Catholics, especially at Lirhanda, where the proximity of the Roman Catholic mission station at Mukumu was felt to interfere with the Friends' work (FUM: Annual Report, Maragoli and Lirhanda Stations, 1911, by Edgar T. Hole; letter from Arthur B. Chilson to AFBFM, 28 February 1915).

111. The North Kavirondo District Annual Reports in KNA give the numbers of such schools each year.

112. Painter, *The Hill of Vision*, p 52.

113. FUM: Letter from Arthur B. Chilson to B. Willis Beede, 15 June 1924.

114. Painter, *The Hill of Vision*, p 57; Stafford Kay has carried out a thorough study of the Friends school system in Kenya: 'The Southern Abaluyia, the Friends Africa Mission, and the Development of Education in Western Kenya, 1902–1965', unpublished PhD thesis, University of Wisconsin, 1973.

115. FUM: Annual Report, Maragoli Station, 1925, by Emory J. Rees.

116. Chilson, *Ambassador of the King*, pp 101 ff.

117. FUM: Letter from A.A. and Mira C. Bond to 'Friends', 18 May 1921.

118. Amugune, *A Christian Pioneer*, p 7.

119. FUM: Maragoli Station Report, first quarter 1912, by Emory J. and Deborah G. Rees.

120. FUM: Annual Report of evangelistic and educational departments, Kaimosi, 1912, by Elisha and Virginia I. Blackburn.

121. For example, FUM: Letter from Arthur B. Chilson to AFBFM office, 28 February 1915; letter from Jefferson W. Ford to Ross A. Hadley, 13 July 1916.

122. FUM: Letter from Arthur B. Chilson to B. Willis Beede, 15 May 1923.

123. FUM: Letter from B. Willis Beede to Arthur B. Chilson, 5 July 1923.

124. Benjamin Wegesa, *A Life of Abraham Sangura*; also the author's interview with Abraham Sangura, 1 December 1977.

125. Wagner, *The Bantu of Western Kenya*, vol. II, pp 94 f., describes this development in Maragoli. The name 'lines' stems from the placing of homesteads in two rows, or lines, along a road.

126. FUM: Letter from A.A. and Mira Cope Bond to 'Friends', 12 June 1922, describes cases of church discipline in response to such practices.

127. FUM: Jefferson and Helen Farr Ford to 'Friends', 12 April 1924.

128. FUM: Letter from Alta H. Hoyt to 'Friends', 12 December 1931.

129. FUM: Letter from Chief Amiani of Tiriki to Mr and Mrs Hoyt, 24 January 1921.

130. Amugune, *A Christian Pioneer*, p 14; Lung'aho, *Daudi Lung'aho*, p 10.

131. For instance, in 1912 three schools were reported in Maragoli, two for boys and one for girls, and the girls' school held classes for only one hour per day because Emory and Deborah Rees were not able to devote more time to it (FUM: Maragoli Station Report for the first quarter of 1912, by Emory J. and Deborah G. Rees). The situation improved with the arrival at Vihiga in 1913 of Roxie Reeve, who devoted a large part of her time to the education of women (Painter, *The Hill of Vision*, p 145; FUM: Report on girls' work at Maragoli 1916–17, by Roxie Reeve).

132. FUM: Letter from Helen Farr Ford to Ross A. Hadley, 3 April 1918.

133. FUM: Annual Report, Kitosh Station, 1926, by C. Frank Conover.

134. Chilson, *Ambassador of the King*, p 81.

135. FUM: Report of Committee on Native Church Organization and Kindred Subjects, 30 January 1912.

136. FUM: FAM Survey, January 1921.

137. FUM: Annual Reports, Maragoli Station, 1921 and 1922, by Emory J. Rees.

138. FUM: Letter from Fred Hoyt to B. Willis Beede, 21 November 1931.

139. For example, FUM: Letter from Jefferson W. Ford to B. Willis Beede, 1 August 1922. In a letter from him and his wife to 'Friends' on 22 July 1926, they distinguish between four categories of relationship to the Church: full members; candidates for membership; those who were not yet candidates but believed themselves to be Christians; and finally, those who had not yet begun to serve Jesus but wished to do so henceforth.

140. Wegesa, *A Life of Abraham Sangura*.

141. Amugune, *A Christian Pioneer*, p 13 f.

142. FUM: Maragoli Station Report, 1925, by Emory J. Rees.

143. Clifford Wesley Gilpin: 'The Church and the Community: Quakers in Western Kenya, 1902–1963', unpublished PhD thesis, Columbia University, 1976, p 163.

144. FUM: Letter from Arthur and Edna Chilson to 'Friends', 6 December 1924.

145. FUM: Letter from Clara G. Ford to 'Friends', 20 October 1924. Arthur Chilson's 'native leader' was Joseph Ngaira, according to Chilson, *Ambassador of the King*, p 156.

146. FUM: Annual Report, Kitosh Station, 1924, by C. Frank and Blanche A. Conover.

147. FUM: Annual Report, Malava Station, 1925, by Edna and Arthur Chilson.

148. FUM: Report of Native Affairs Committee, 26 February 1927, by Arthur B. Chilson. This conference was held at Chavakali.

149. FUM: Personal Report of Arthur B. Chilson, 1926.

150. I quote from the Revised Standard Version of the English Bible.

151. Kefa Ayub Mavuru and Peter Ihaji: 'African Church of Holy Spirit. Historia', unpublished pamphlet distributed by the Church on the occasion of the official opening of a new church building at the Lugala headquarters of the Church on 20 April 1975; interview with Kefa Ayub Mavuru, 24 January 1975.

152. FUM: Letter from Arthur and Edna Chilson to 'Friends', 16 October 1927.

153. Speech during church service at Bukoyani headquarters of Holy Spirit Church of East Africa on 18 January 1975, and interview with him on 16 June 1975.

154. Ford and Andersen, *The Steps of a Good Man*, pp 85 ff.

155. FUM: Annual Report, Maragoli Station, 1927.

156. FUM: Letter from B. Willis Beede to Arthur Chilson, 16 December 1927.

157. FUM: Letter from Errol T. Elliott (new Board secretary) to Arthur B. Chilson, 13 September 1932. In 1933 Arthur and Edna Chilson were sent as pioneer missionaries to Urundi by a new mission board set up by Kansas

Yearly Meeting (Chilson, *Ambassador of the King*, pp 179 ff.).

158. FUM: Letter from Jefferson and Helen Farr Ford to 'Friends', 27 February 1929.

159. Ezekiel Kasiera has pointed out ('Development of Pentecostal Christianity', pp 340 ff.) that Chilson's theological language was similar to that used by Pentecostals, whereas Ford's was more in line with the Holiness revival in America, which did not emphasize speaking in tongues as a sign of having received the Holy Spirit, as did the Pentecostals. As early as 1902, bringing a caravan of porters to Kaimosi through the then dangerous area of Nyang'ori, Chilson writes about his joy after being assured of God's protection: 'Well, I had a time. I shouted and sang and praised God out there alone, except for the wondering natives around in the bush' (quoted in Chilson, *Ambassador of the King*, p 33). This shows that noisy expressions of religious sentiments were not strange to him, and his prayers from as early as 1909 (ibid., p 84) for an outpouring of the Holy Spirit confirm Kasiera's observation that his theology was close to the Pentecostal position. I agree also that the specific Pentecostal vocabulary seems to have been absent from Ford's theological language, whereas Kasiera's statement that Chilson did not emphasize baptism in the Holy Spirit before 1924 ('Development of Pentecostal Christianity', p 341) is not supported by his own diary, and reports in which this phenomenon is mentioned a number of times – for instance very clearly in 1909, as mentioned above.

160. FUM: Letter from Fred Hoyt to B. Willis Beede, 4 June 1928.

161. FUM: Letter from Jefferson and Helen Farr Ford to B. Willis Beede, 1 April 1929.

162. I have heard the meetings of the 18th at Mbale mentioned a number of times, for example in a speech by Japhet Zale Ambula during a church service at the Bukoyani headquarters of his Holy Spirit Church of East Africa on 18 January 1975, and they were also mentioned to Ezekiel Kasiera in interviews ('Development of Pentecostal Christianity', pp 371 ff.).

163. FUM: Letter from Jefferson and Helen Farr Ford to 'Friends', 8 February 1929.

164. FUM: Letter from Jefferson and Helen Farr Ford to 'Friends', 27 February 1929.

165. Interview with Kefa Ayub Mavuru, 24 January 1975.

166. FUM: Minutes of Annual Meeting, FAM, held at Kaimosi, 29 December 1932. Among those who left at their own request was Petro Tsimonjero, who was to become the second High Priest of the African Church of Holy Spirit after the death of Kefa Mavuru.

167. FUM: Report of the AFBM to the Five Years Meeting of 1935.

168. Kay, 'The Southern Abaluyia', p 213, quoting the AFBM Annual Reports 1930–34.

169. John Allen Rowe, 'Kaimosi: An Essay in Missionary History', unpublished MSc thesis, University of Wisconsin, 1958, p 79, quotes statistical tables in the AFBM Eleventh Annual Report, 1939–40, appendix, which gives the number of members in 1939 as 7065.

170. Speech by Japhet Zale Ambula, 18 January 1975, and interview with him, 16 June 1975; Kasiera, 'Development of Pentecostal Christianity', p 375.

171. Gilpin, 'The Church and the Community', pp 199 ff.

172. Kasiera, 'Development of Pentecostal Christianity', pp 338 ff.

173. Ibid., pp 262 ff.

174. For example, FUM: Letter from Jefferson W. Ford to Ross A. Hadley, 16 July 1920.

175. FUM: Letter from Alta Hoyt to 'Friends', 11 October 1928.

176. Kasiera, 'Development of Pentecostal Christianity', pp 364 ff. It is not clear to what extent the Holy Spirit movement among Friends and Pentecostals was connected with a similar movement among members of the Anglican Church. Here, Dini ya Roho (The Religion of the Spirit, in Kiswahili) was formed in 1934 after violent clashes between members of the Luo ethnic group, who supported the movement, and Luyia people, who were opposed to it, resulting in several deaths (Hans-Jürgen Greschat: 'Dini ya Roho' in Hans-Jürgen Greschat and Hermann Jungraithmayr [eds], *Wort und Religion. Kalima na Dini*, Evangelisches Missionsverlag, Stuttgart, 1969, pp 265 ff; Michael G. Whisson, *Economic and Social Change among the Kenya Luo*, Christian Council of Kenya, Nairobi, no date, p 119 ff.). According to Lonsdale ('A Political History', pp 359 ff.), the Anglican evangelist who brought the revival to the Luo in the first place was influenced by the Holy Spirit movement in Maragoli. And members of Holy Spirit Church of East Africa relate how in 1936, during the funeral of one of their leaders, five strangers came to them dressed in a way similar to their own, and told them about the Dini ya Roho among the Luo, after which the two groups continued to have some fellowship with each other for a number of years (interview with Japhet Zale Ambula, 13 January 1975).

177. Kasiera, 'Development of Pentecostal Christianity', pp 473 ff.

178. The Kellers began to build up an educational programme, despite a good deal of resistance from the mission board in Canada (ibid., pp 313 ff.).

179. By 1942, when David Zakayo Kivuli led a group which split from the Pentecostal Church at Nyang'ori and formed the African Israel Church Nineveh (Kasiera, 'Development of Pentecostal Christianity', pp 532 ff.; F.B. Welbourn, 'The African Israel Church Nineveh', in F.B. Welbourn and B.A. Ogot, *A Place to Feel at Home: A Study of Two Independent Churches in Western Kenya*, Oxford University Press, London, 1966, pp 73 ff.), the educational programme initiated by the Kellers from the mid-1920s, and the resulting divisions between well-educated and less educated members, may have been one contributing factor to the split, as it had been among Friends ten to fifteen years earlier.

180. FUM: Letter from Lewis C. Moon to Ross A. Hadley, 12 July 1920.

181. Painter, *The Hill of Vision*, pp 57, 144 f. A letter from B. Willis Beede to Arthur Chilson on 12 October 1927, (FUM) shows that the missionaries had tried to question Margaret Parker and Elizabeth Haviland concerning their theological views, but they had refused to answer – a response of which Beede approves. In 1930 Jefferson Ford wrote to the Home Office against the

Micheners' arrival because they did not, he says, believe in the full inspiration of the Bible (FUM: Letter from Jefferson Ford to B. Willis Beede, 31 July 1930).

182. Painter, *The Hill of Vision*, pp 57, 75 f.

183. Ford and Andersen, *The Steps of a Good Man*, p 96; FUM: Correspondence between Jefferson Ford and the AFB(F)M.

184. FUM: Letter from A.A. Bond to Merle Davis, administrative secretary of the AFBM, 24 October 1938.

185. For example, FUM: Letter from A.A. Bond to Merle Davis, 1 December 1935.

186. FUM: Letter from Andrew Jumba, President of North Kavirondo Central Association, and the Committee of NKCA, to 'The Committee of Friends Mission Board America', 8 July 1934.

187. FUM: Letter from Jefferson W. Ford to Alta Jewell, AFBM, 20 September 1930.

188. FUM: Report of the Evangelistic Department, 1935, by Jefferson W. Ford; FUM: Letter from A.A. Bond to Merle L. Davis, 16 February 1939.

189. Kitosh was the name which the colonial administration used for the Bukusu.

190. De Wolf, *Differentiation and Integration*, pp 147 ff., 178 f.

191. FUM: Evangelistic Report of the North District for 1939, by Fred N. Hoyt.

192. In 1949, after Ford's departure from Kenya, the Bible school was moved to Kaimosi where it reopened in 1950. This move was opposed by Bukusu Quakers, who had wanted to retain the Bible school in their area (FUM: Evangelistic Report, 1949, by Leonard E. Wines).

193. FUM: Annual Report of the Evangelistic Department, 1942, by Jefferson W. Ford. In 1943 a third quarterly meeting was created in the central part of the FAM area, making a south, a central, and a north quarterly meeting (FUM: Annual Report of the Evangelistic Department, 1943, by Jefferson W. Ford).

194. 'Dini ya Msambwa' means, approximately, 'Religion of the ancestors' or 'Religion of the ancestral customs', 'Msambwa' being a Swahili-ized form of a Lubukusu word based on the stem '-sambwa'. 'Kumusambwa' (plural 'kimisambwa') stands for the ancestral customs, and 'omusambwa' (plural 'basambwa') denotes a person, and means 'ancestor'. This reference to the ancestors should not be understood in too narrow a sense, though. Audrey Wipper (*Rural Rebels: A Study of Two Protest Movements in Kenya*, Oxford University Press, Nairobi, 1977, p 149) believes that the central place given to God, 'Wele' in Lubukusu, in Dini ya Msambwa's message indicates that the 'Msambwa' in its name – or 'Musambwa', as it is sometimes written – should be interpreted as the creator-spirit, or the Supreme Being. She does not want to press this point too far, however, and says that to many members it may simply mean 'ancestor spirits'. Jan J. de Wolf, in his discussion of Wipper's book, says that he thinks it unlikely that the 'Msambwa' can mean the Supreme Being. He thinks it more useful to interpret the word on the basis of the

meaning of 'kumusambwa' which he understands as 'ancestral power' (Jan J. de Wolf, 'Dini ya Msambwa: Militant Protest or Millenarian Promise?', *Canadian Journal of African Studies* 17, 2, 1983, p 273). Perhaps Gideon S. Were comes closest to the members' own interpretation of the name when he writes: 'To many of its adherents the D.Y.M. appears to have been a genuine attempt to find an alternative religion consonant with the teachings of the Bible and the traditions of the people' (Were, 'Dini ya Musambwa: A Reassessment', in his *Essays on African Religion in Western Kenya*, p 33). And he quotes the North Nyanza District Commissioner: 'Why the name "Musambwa" was given to it is that theirs was an attempt to return to the teachings of the Bible in its literal sense, and as both Moses and Abraham are described as having offered sacrifices, the same practice, which is a Kitosh (Babukusu) custom, was adopted and so the name' (KNA: DC/NN.10/1/5, quoted in Were: 'Dini ya Musambwa: A Reassessment', p 24). Were therefore shows that the ancestors in question are to be seen not only as those Bukusu who have died but also as the biblical ancestors; consequently, 'Dini ya Musambwa' comes to mean the true religion based on the practices of both types of ancestors.

195. The vice-president, Benjamin Wekuke, claimed that he was the real founder, and that the movement had started in 1937 (Wipper, *Rural Rebels*, p 124).

196. Audrey Wipper says that its first open appearance was around 1943 (ibid., p 126).

197. FUM: Annual Report of the Evangelistic Department, 1941, by Jefferson W. Ford. Audrey Wipper mistakenly places this incident in the years 1943–44 (*Rural Rebels*, p 337).

198. Ibid., pp 336 ff.

199. Ibid., pp 346 f. (note 1). The same point is made by Were in 'Dini ya Musambwa: A Reassessment', p 25.

200. Wipper, *Rural Rebels*, pp 175 ff. Although there were some links between members of Dini ya Msambwa and the Bukusu Union – seen, for instance, in the fact that Pascal Nabwana publicly defended Elijah Masinde – they were, as Wipper shows (ibid., pp 188 ff.), two different responses to the colonial situation, the Bukusu Union being less extreme in its methods than Dini ya Msambwa and, as mentioned above, recruiting its members from the supporters of mission churches rather than opposing them as the Dini ya Msambwa did. Although de Wolf attempts in his later criticism of Wipper's book ('Dini ya Msambwa: Militant Protest or Millenarian Promise?', pp 271 f.) to show that she describes the connections between the two organizations as being closer than they actually were, he does use terms similar to hers when he says: 'The Bukusu Union also welcomed the political ideas of Elijah Masinde' (de Wolf, *Differentiation and Integration*, p 152); and he adds, like Wipper, that in spite of this the administration was unable to find any evidence to support their suspicion that the Bukusu Union was behind some of the Dini ya Msambwa activities. A similar view of the relationship between the two bodies is expressed by Were ('Dini ya Msambwa: A Reassessment', pp 29 f.).

201. Wipper demonstrates the close connection between the two in several places in *Rural Rebels*, e.g. p 199; and also very clearly in her response to Jan J. de Wolf's criticism in 'Lofty Visions and Militant Action: A Reply to Jan de Wolf', *Canadian Journal of African Studies* 17, 2, 1983, pp 277 ff.

202. Wipper, *Rural Rebels*, pp 142 f. Were, 'Dini ya Musambwa: A Reassessment', p 24. For the 1895 war see Were, *A History of the Abaluyia*, pp 166 f.

203. I have personally seen Elijah Masinde pouring a few drops of beer on the floor of a house before drinking, on 21 May 1976. For traditional parallels see Wagner, *The Bantu of Western Kenya*, pp 278 f.

204. Wipper, *Rural Rebels*, pp 137 ff.

205. Ibid.; Were, 'Interaction of African Religion with Christianity in Western Kenya' in his *Essays on African Religion in Western Kenya*, pp 62 ff.; B.M.W. Lusweti, 'An Approach to the Study of the Bukusu Religion', *Journal of the Historical Association of Kenya* 2, 2, 1974, p 245; also noted in a report on Dini ya Msambwa by W.R.B. Pugh, Superintendent of Police, Nyanza Province, on 15 March 1948 (KNA: DC/NN.10/1/5).

206. Wipper, *Rural Rebels*, pp 366 ff.

207. Kibabii mission diary for 7 February 1948.

208. KNA: North Nyanza District Annual Report 1948 (DC/NN.1/30); *Report of the Commission of Inquiry into the Affray at Kolloa, Baringo*, Government Printer, Nairobi, 1950, p 2.

209. Ibid.

210. KNA: DC/NN.10/1/5, quoted by Were, 'Dini ya Musambwa: A Reassessment', p 28. Audrey Wipper also mentions their belief that bullets would not harm them (*Rural Rebels*, p 184).

211. Ibid.

212. *Report of the Commission of Inquiry into the Affray at Kolloa, Baringo*, p 2.

213. KNA: North Nyanza District Annual Report 1948; *Report of the Commission of Inquiry into the Affray at Kolloa, Baringo*, p 3.

214. Were, 'Dini ya Musambwa: A Reassessment', p 28, based on KNA: DC/NN.10/1/5.

215. *Report of the Commission of Inquiry into the Affray at Kolloa, Baringo*, p 3. The Bukusu Union was proscribed together with it, although Pascal Nabwana had to be released from jail due to lack of evidence against him (Wipper, *Rural Rebels*, p 189).

216. KNA: North Nyanza District Annual Report 1948; *Report of the Commission of Inquiry into the Affray at Kolloa, Baringo*, p 3 f.

217. Among the Pokot, the movement was called Dini ya Msango (Wipper, *Rural Rebels*, p 209).

218. *Report of the Commission of Inquiry into the Affray at Kolloa, Baringo*, pp 4 ff.; the number of deaths on Pkech's side is given as twenty by B.E. Kipkorir ('The Kolloa Affray, Kenya 1950', *Transafrican Journal of History* 2, 2, 1972, p 114) and as twenty-eight by Audrey Wipper (*Rural Rebels*, p 214, quoting

Official Government Press Office Handout No. 248, Nairobi, 12 September 1951).

219. KNA: North Nyanza District Annual Reports 1951–59 (DC/NN.1/33–39).

220. Wipper, *Rural Rebels*, p 222.

221. Ibid., p 224.

222. Ibid., pp 341 f. KANU means 'Kenya African National Union'.

223. Were, 'Dini ya Musambwa: A Reassessment', p 47.

224. Wipper, *Rural Rebels*, pp 342 ff.; James Bandi Shimanyula, *Elijah Masinde and the Dini ya Musambwa*, Transafrica Book Distributors, Nairobi, 1978, pp 24 ff., describes Masinde's relationships with the authorities between 1964 and 1978.

225. I once saw Elijah Masinde holding a meeting with a group of Pokot followers when I came to visit him in his home at Maeni on 1 April 1978.

226. *The Weekly Review*, Nairobi, 19 June 1987, pp 14 f.

227. Wipper, *Rural Rebels*, pp 170 f., 227 ff., 295 f.

228. Ibid., pp 221 ff.

229. Robert Buijtenhuijs, in his discussion of Dini ya Msambwa, sees it as a 'counter-society' in line with what he, borrowing an expression from South Africa, calls Zionist churches, that is, churches of basically the same type as those that grew out of the Holy Spirit movement. Like the members of these churches, he says, Dini ya Msambwa members had experienced the colonial situation not first and foremost as political and economic oppression, but more as social and cultural upheaval, and their response was, accordingly, not to form political associations aiming at the conquest of political power, but rather to form 'counter-societies' in which they tried to 'escape' from a hostile environment (Robert Buijtenhuijs, 'Dini ya Msambwa: Rural Rebellion or Counter-society?' in W.M.J. van Binsbergen and M. Schoffeleers (eds), *Theoretical Explorations in African Religion*, Routledge & Kegan Paul, London, 1985, p 323). In so far as the term 'counter-society' can be used to describe Dini ya Msambwa, it must be understood in an active, outward-going sense. It is true that its members wanted to 'escape' from a hostile environment and, to that end, tried to set up an alternative community. But their 'escape' did not consist of passive withdrawal as that term might seem to imply. On the contrary, their protest was to a large extent expressed in outward-going activities, and often even in acts of violence. And when we take into account the basis of support for Dini ya Msambwa among those frustrated in modern society – often those who were economically underprivileged – we see that Dini ya Msambwa fits into Buijtenhuijs's own theory that those who experienced the colonial situation as political and economic oppression responded by forming political associations. The aim of Dini ya Msambwa was political: namely, to form a 'counter-society' encompassing not only the Bukusu area but the whole of Kenya from which all Europeans would have been driven out and where Africans would, once again, be masters of their own destiny. The term 'counter-society' seems, therefore, to take on a wider meaning than that suggested by Buijtenhuijs. On the one hand, it is appropriate for describing

the counter-establishment nature of Dini ya Msambwa, as well as that of the Holy Spirit movement. But on the other, it seems to me that if escapism is taken to be an important characteristic of a 'counter-society', then the political – or potentially political – importance of these religious movements does not receive sufficient emphasis.

230. Wipper, *Rural Rebels*, p 266.

231. Ibid., p 265. Wipper's use of the term 'guerilla warfare' is disputed by Buijtenhuijs ('Dini ya Msambwa', pp 326 f.) and by de Wolf ('Dini ya Msambwa: Militant Protest or Millenarian Promise?' pp 266 f.) who both find that it implies more violence than there actually was. However, even if the term is perhaps too strong, the fact that Dini ya Msambwa's tactics did include the use of some forms of violence must not be overlooked.

232. Lonsdale, 'Some Origins of Nationalism in East Africa', p 125.

233. While Dini ya Msambwa's national goals, shared with many other Kenyans at the time, to some extent confirm Wipper's statement that 'there is a rough correlation between the type of response and the historical period' (*Rural Rebels*, p 117), I believe, with Buijtenhuijs and de Wolf, that this point cannot be taken to support a general theory that militant prophetic movements succeed political reform movements chronologically. Wipper herself admits that the two types of responses sometimes occur simultaneously, and Buijtenhuijs and de Wolf stress this last point. In Buijtenhuijs's words: 'millenarian or prophetic movements and political parties should not be seen as different, succeeding phases in an on-going process of political protest, as Wipper is tempted to do, but rather as different, contemporary responses' ('Dini ya Msambwa', p 323). Jan J. de Wolf says ('Dini ya Msambwa: Militant Protest or Millenarian Promise?', p 266) that North Kavirondo Central Association and Dini ya Msambwa appeared among two different sections of the Luyia. They cannot therefore be used, he says, as Wipper uses them, to show that militant protest succeeds political reform movements. Instead he compares the Bukusu Union, as an example of a political reform movement, and Dini ya Msambwa (both among the Bukusu), and believes that they should be seen as alternate responses occurring at the same time.

234. Were, 'Interaction of African Religion with Christianity in Western Kenya', p 66.

235. Lusweti, 'An Approach to the Study of the Bukusu Religion', pp 243 ff.

3

The Church under African Leadership

The Establishment of East Africa Yearly Meeting of Friends

Dini ya Msambwa posed a serious threat to the mission churches, including Friends Africa Mission, in the northern locations of North Kavirondo District during the 1940s and early 1950s, although its activities did not result in a lasting loss of large numbers of members, as the Holy Spirit revival had.[1] As in the 1920s, however, now crisis and progress went hand in hand. This must be seen in the light of social developments during the 1940s, which were similar in some ways to those of the 1920s. As described above, the experiences of many Luyia during and after the First World War had given them a wider outlook; as a result, the elders and the ancestors lost much of their authority, and many people turned to the mission churches instead, and became Christians. The Second World War was likewise a time of great changes for the Luyia peoples, as well as other peoples in Kenya. Many men were conscripted for service in the British army, and others went out of the 'reserve' to work – either because they were forced to participate in government projects or voluntarily – leaving the women at home to try to meet government demands for increased agricultural production to feed the troops.[2] And in a sequence similar to the one in the 1920s, this new phase of accelerated change in the lives of the Luyia peoples, with the accompanying further breakdown in the old authority system, resulted in a new influx of members to the churches in North Kavirondo, and also to the Friends Church. While membership here in 1939 had stood at approximately 7000, as we saw above, it had increased to nearly 17,000 by 1949.[3]

And after many years of discussing what would be the best time to grant the Quakers in Kenya their own yearly meeting, the American

Friends Board of Foreign Missions now decided, against the background of the growth in membership, that the time was ripe for this development.[4] The regular procedure for setting up a new yearly meeting was followed when the Mission Board sent an application to the Five Years Meeting of American Friends in session in October 1945. The Five Years Meeting accepted the application and recommended that the Board of Missions send one or two Friends from America to attend the sessions in Kenya and carry a minute from the Five Years Meeting giving authority to the new yearly meeting.[5] This was done, and on 18 November 1946 the East Africa Yearly Meeting of Friends was officially established, with Joel Litu from Maragoli as its first Presiding Clerk, Benjamin Ngaira from Idakho as Recording Clerk, and Petro Wanyama from Tachoni as Treasurer.[6] At this time a number of Friends had migrated to Uganda; therefore the name 'East Africa Yearly Meeting' was decided upon rather than 'Kenya Yearly Meeting'.[7] However, the laws of Kenya did not allow African churches to hold property in the colony, so what was transferred from America at this stage was the responsibility for the religious work of the Church, whereas transfer of administration and property did not take place until the early 1960s.[8]

On the whole, therefore, the 1940s were an encouraging period, and one of progress for the Friends Church in Kenya. And what many Luyia found particularly important in the Christian churches at this time (as in the two previous decades) was the educational opportunities they had to offer. But now, due to the increasingly national outlook of many people, school education took on an even greater significance than before as a means of achieving a good position in wider society, and prosperity among the Luyia during the war meant that they had more money to invest in extending educational facilities. This prosperity was created through higher prices for their agricultural products and higher wages for labour. In Friends Africa Mission, members' contributions to both Church and school increased strongly in the early 1940s, and a large number of new schools were established. [9] This heavy emphasis on education led again to a further split between well-educated and less educated Christians which not only resulted in the formation of Dini ya Msambwa, in the same way as the similar developments in the 1920s had led to the rise of the Holy Spirit movement, but also existed also among those who remained in the Quaker Church. This tendency was reinforced by the government's agricultural policies after the war which, as described above, benefited the already better-educated, well-off farmers at the expense of less educated members of society who were not able to turn the new measures to their advantage.

The added enthusiasm for education, as well as the general view of it as an integral part of the Church,[10] is reflected in the fact that during the early 1940s schoolchildren, both boys and girls, showed renewed interest in becoming church members. After a few years during which this trend had been observed, Jefferson Ford wrote in 1945 that 'harvest time' had come. Friends Africa Mission now had about 33,000 pupils in its schools, and hundreds of those were coming forward at monthly meetings, 'seeking salvation'.[11]

Another group of people who came to the Church in greater numbers at this time was the women. As early as 1939 Dr Bond had noted that although the number of new members was about average, the number of men and boys was lower, while more women and girls joined the Church. But in spite of their interest in membership they took a less active part in church affairs than before; as a result, the business and activities of the meetings were concentrated in the hands of a group of elderly men – a fact which Dr Bond found unfortunate.[12] During the 1940s women's groups were organized in most of the monthly meetings, even though the missionaries regretted that they were not able to give sufficient attention to the women's work. One reason was that the missionaries, just like the African church leaders, gave higher priority to educational work, so that Helen Kersey Ford, for example, was able to meet women only in the monthly meetings during her periods of vacation from teaching at the Girls' School at Kaimosi, and other female missionaries also, to a great extent, concentrated their efforts around the activities taking place at the mission stations.[13]

Even among the female members of the Friends church, therefore, a split occurred at this time, when a number of young women were able to receive school education, which gave them the opportunity to take an active part in modern society. Female farmers, however, were often left with a great workload when their husbands went away from home in search of work, and although they were eager to become church members they did not receive very much attention either from the missionaries or from the African church leaders, who saw the educational role of the Church as the most important aspect of its work. In economic terms, these women, many of whom had little or no school education and no prominent positions in society, were among the group of people who were mainly left out of the progress experienced by many better-off farmers after the Second World War.[14]

During the 1950s church membership continued to grow, with the exception of 1952, when a decrease in the number of members was reported.[15] And, as in the 1940s, the growth was seen especially among women and young people.[16] No dramatic fall in male membership is reported, however. But doubts among the missionaries, as well as among the African church leaders, as to what the transfer of authority for the religious aspects of the work to East Africa Yearly Meeting entailed seem to have led to misunderstandings between them, and to dissatisfaction on the part of a number of the Africans with what was going on in the Church. Many missionaries apparently continued to act much as before, while the new leaders of the yearly meeting wanted a greater degree of independence and expected more responsibility to be placed on their shoulders.

One problem arose in 1949, when Friends Bible Institute was transferred from Lugulu to Kaimosi after the departure of Jefferson Ford. The missionaries' rationale for this was that since most of the mission's institutions were situated at Kaimosi and most of the missionaries lived there, it would be easier to find part-time teachers to help in the Bible school work. The decision was taken by the missionaries together with a 'representative committee' from the yearly meeting because, as Leonard E. Wines, the missionary now in charge of the evangelistic department of the mission, writes: 'It is our policy to make the bible Institute an indigenous part of the Yearly Meeting, as far as possible, and not an institution thrust upon it by America.' He continues: 'In carrying out this policy we asked the various Monthly Meetings to help financially with the preparation for the opening of the Bible Institute. The response has been very good except for the Monthly Meetings in the north.'[17] And this was exactly where the problem lay. As we have seen, during the late 1930s Bukusu Friends had been dissatisfied with the services they received from Friends Africa Mission, who concentrated a large part of their work in the southern Luyia locations; therefore, the setting up of the Bible Institute at Lugulu had helped to assure them that the missionaries still cared about their needs. Consequently, when it was removed to Kaimosi there was strong opposition among Bukusu Friends.

Another issue that created a cleavage between the northern and southern parts of the Friends Church, as well as between Africans and missionaries, was the question of the location of the mission's more advanced schools. Since the early 1920s the only two such schools, one for boys and one for girls, had both been at Kaimosi.[18] But in 1949 the Beecher Report, the work of a government committee, recommended that a number of intermediate schools be upgraded to secondary school status, and among those to be upgraded was the Boys' School at Kaimosi. By now, however, the dissatisfaction in the northern locations with the concentration of institutions at Kaimosi had become such that Bukusu Friends demanded that the school must be moved to their area, and the unrest created by the activities of Dini ya Msambwa made the government support this demand.

The colonial administrators felt, like the Bukusu Quakers themselves, that Friends Africa Mission had not given sufficient attention to this area, and that in order to avoid the violence of the previous years it would be necessary to bring more services to the Bukusu to satisfy their demands. At the same time, financial problems made the American Friends Board of Missions consider the possibility of giving up the plan of establishing a secondary school in any of its areas of operation altogether. This created unrest in the southern Luyia locations because Friends wanted a secondary school in their area, but also insisted that it should remain under Friends sponsorship. After some years of intense debate the American Friends Board of Missions managed to raise sufficient funds in 1953, and despite much opposition from the people in the south it gave in to the government demand and decided to move the Boys' School from Kaimosi to Kamusinga in the north. They also agreed to employ an English headmaster and a number of English teachers so that the new school would fit more easily into the country's education system. The school was opened in January 1957,[19] but the questions arising in connection with setting up the boys' secondary school had made southern and northern Luyia Friends stand sharply against each other, both wishing to have the planned school in their area. At the same time, the controversies surrounding this issue had given rise to much dissatisfaction with the missionaries and the Mission Board among African Friends in both south and north.

From the point of view of at least some of the missionaries, the disagreements between themselves and the African members of the Church were a sign that the Africans were becoming too independent and refusing to follow the missionaries' decisions. Leonard Wines writes:

> We are in the midst of an Africa experiencing growing pains. Old restrictions and controls are broken down and liberty without control marks much of the present tendency. The moral let-down in Africa since the war has been terrific. Church leaders deplore the situation, and older missionaries in service say, 'It never used to be this way.' With immorality unleashed, and the Africans' ever increasing feeling of self-sufficiency over-balancing good judgment, Christian missions need to strive hard to establish a continuing work before their presence is unwanted.

He attributes this state of affairs to his belief that 'Africa's moral consciousness is still for the most part undeveloped'. The problem, therefore, as he sees it, lies in the negative influence of the members' traditional background: 'in this part of Africa there is the struggle to rise above the former condition of darkness, ignorance and poverty, and to acquire a life equal to the European standard.' And he believes that a 'lack of close supervision of their business procedures' is to blame for the 'spiritual slump' he sees in the yearly meeting.[20]

Leonard Wines, therefore, disliked much of what he saw going on in the yearly meeting, and he believed that the remedy would be closer supervision by the missionaries. On the other hand, the disagreements between Kenyan Friends and the missions on the issues of the Bible school and the boys' secondary school showed that Africans were not willing simply to give in to the wishes of the missionaries or the Mission Board. They wanted to form their own Church, even though different sections of members did not always agree as to what would be the best course of action. And their dissatisfaction when they were not taken seriously by the mission authorities – who in some cases simply attributed their opposition to a 'moral let-down' – was reflected in a lack of interest in a church where members' viewpoints were not heard. As a result, the number of registered members decreased, as reported in 1952. Even church attendance fell to about half of the membership, a situation which was the reverse of the earlier one, when the number of people coming to meetings had normally been a good deal higher than the actual membership figure.[21]

In 1952 John Retherford arrived in Kaimosi to take over from Leonard Wines as Superintendent of the Evangelistic Department.[22] His theological views, like those of Wines, were strongly evangelical, but he appears to have been more optimistic than Wines about the potential of the Kenyan Church and its leadership. He reports a steady progress in the number of members during the early 1950s, with the biggest growth still taking place in the women's and young people's departments, and he writes that there is a 'high type of leadership' in the yearly meeting.[23] His more positive evaluation of the yearly meeting may be due to the fact that some of the most controversial issues between African Christians and the mission were now out of the way, so that Africans were again willing to join the Church and take part in its activities.

The tension was released to a large extent because renewed interest in the Church in Kenya among American Quakers at this time enabled the American Friends Board of Missions to increase its support for East Africa Yearly Meeting in terms of both money and personnel. We have seen that in 1953 the Board managed to raise funds to finance the setting up of the new boys' secondary school, and in the same year, in the midst of the controversies in East Africa Yearly Meeting surrounding the school issue, and in particular the question of where to locate the new secondary school, the Mission Board sent a delegation to Kenya consisting of its Executive Secretary, Charles Lampman, the Executive Secretary of the Five Years Meeting, Errol T. Elliott, and two British Friends educators, to look into the future plans for the mission's educational work and to make recommendations for arrangements that would improve the relationship between the missions and African Christians. As a result of their recommendations it was decided to create a United Executive Committee, including a subordinate committee on education, with participants from both Friends Africa Mission and East Africa Yearly Meeting, thereby giving the African Friends greater influence on decisions regarding their Church.[24]

This closer co-operation with African members of the Church made it necessary for the missionaries to have greater freedom than before to make decisions without first consulting the Board, and for this purpose it was decided to set up the post of Executive Secretary of the mission, so that one missionary would be responsible for co-ordinating all activities. The person chosen to take up this new post was Fred Reeve, who arrived in Kenya in 1954 with the following instructions from the American Friends Board of Missions:

> Friends mission work in Kenya has been going on for more than fifty years. It is time to make definite plans for the work to be taken over by East Africa Yearly Meeting. Give the matter careful study and send us your considered judgment on how quickly this can be accomplished and by what means.

According to Reeve: 'A brief survey ... indicated that much preparation and development would be necessary before such a move would be made successfully.' He found that the work had been kept going only by the 'tireless effort and selfless devotion of dedicated yearly meeting leaders and missionaries' during a time when there was a loss of interest and support on the part of American Friends – first because of decreased financial resources during the Great Depression, and then because of diverted attention during the war years.[25]

Now, however, the new eagerness among American Friends to support the Church in Kenya meant that they began to send much more money and personnel. More than thirty new missionaries and their spouses arrived during the 1950s,[26] many of them teachers. A number came under an arrangement with British Friends, who supplied a large proportion of the educators needed to oversee the development of the Friends schools, as well as to teach in the several intermediate and secondary schools that were created during this decade and the next.[27] These efforts by Quakers in both Britain and America were recognized by the government of Kenya, which stepped up its financial subsidies for overseas staff as well as buildings and equipment for the schools.[28] All in all, therefore, there was a great expansion in educational services in the 1950s, an important factor contributing to the renewed interest on the part of the Luyia in Church and school and, therefore, to a steady increase in membership of East Africa Yearly Meeting during this decade.

The Influence of Later Missionaries

While the provision of secondary school education was the top priority for East Africa Yearly Meeting, as well as for Friends Africa Mission in the 1950s, there was also a renewed emphasis on practical training. The mission's industrial department had continued over the years to play its role in performing the practical jobs needed in the mission, in training young people in various skills, and in generating an income. Fred Hoyt had been in charge of this department for more than thirty years, until his retirement in 1946,[29] and the work continued after his departure. But the Luyia's eagerness for academic education had gradually forced the Quaker missionaries to develop this aspect of their work to such an extent that it came to receive a very large proportion of the mission's total resources, as described above, in the process reducing the industrial work to a less prominent position on their list of priorities. Now, however, with more funds available for the Kenyan Church, and in keeping with government attempts to create an economically sound African middle class, there was renewed interest on the part of Friends Africa Mission in helping to train Africans in practical skills. At the same time there was an urge to meet the increasing demand for such skills in the mission – for instance, in connection with the great amount of construction work needed for the expansion of its activities.

One example of 'on-the-job training' in building was the construction of a tuberculosis ward for Kaimosi Hospital and houses for convalescent patients carried out by the participants in an international work camp for about two years from 1956 to 1958. The German doctor in charge of the hospital at the time, Horst Rothe, developed the idea of having recovering tuberculosis patients stay in special houses in the hospital compound which were to be surrounded by garden plots. Here the patients could work, and thereby serve the dual purpose of getting exercise and growing crops that could be given to the mission in order to cover part of their hospital fees. It was decided to build these houses with the help of an international work camp. Young Africans taking part in it were living and working side by side with young men from America, England and Denmark. This experiment had not been tried before in the history of Friends Africa Mission, but after an initial period of opposition from some of the missionaries it worked out satisfactorily.[30]

Two areas particularly received the attention of some of the new missionaries who arrived during the 1950s: the business area and the agricultural area. Fred Reeve helped to establish a number of Maragoli Quakers in various business enterprises. The agricultural programme, run by Rodney Morris from 1955, gave assistance to African farmers. Morris introduced a programme aimed at improving the good production rate of African farmers through the use of hybrid maize and fertilizers and improved cultivation methods, and this excited great interest from the farmers because of the substantially higher yields they could get from their land. The higher volume of produce from the farms resulted in improved incomes – not only for the farmers themselves but also for the Church, since the agricultural services were seen as part of its stewardship programme, and farmers were encouraged to set aside a portion of their fields as 'the Lord's Acre'. The intention was that the income from the harvest of this part should be given to support the Church. From the early 1960s Rodney Morris, together with a number of assistants in what was now called the Rural Service Programme, gave instructions in all parts of the yearly meeting. These instructions were not only about improved agricultural methods but also concerned the ideas underlying the Lord's Acre programme, how to deal with health problems, and basic principles of accountancy which would make it easier for the meetings to control their finances, and to see that the proper amounts were sent to the quarterly meetings and the yearly meeting. In 1965 Sven Rasmussen, a horticulturist, and his wife Inga were sent by Danish Friends with support from the Danish Ministry of Foreign Affairs to work in this programme; Rasmussen emphasized the importance of growing vegetables and made sure that better seeds were made available to African farmers.[31]

During the 1950s and 1960s, therefore, the missionaries who came to take care of these new projects were, generally, of a different type from the old ones. While many of the former missionaries had been willing and able to take on a number of different kinds of work, often without much specialized training, these newcomers were professional people, each specializing in their own field. Allan Bradley, an Englishman who became the first headmaster of Friends Secondary School Kamusinga, illustrates the difference between the two types of missionary when he compares himself to many of those Americans whom he found in Kenya on his arrival:

> The reason why American Friends were at Kaimosi and elsewhere was fundamentally evangelical; they wanted to be 'missionaries', and they saw themselves as bringing their message through their work. The professional aspect of their work was sometimes of secondary importance, and in the past several people had found themselves undertaking responsibilities for which they did not have very appropriate inclinations or qualifications. This was in no way to their discredit; the jobs had to be done by the people who were available. The reason, on the other hand, why I had come to Kenya was that I was a professional person who was also a Friend, and that I was happy to exercise my profession amongst Friends in Kenya at a time when I could be useful. My purpose was never evangelical, and it was embarrassing to me to accept the description 'missionary'.[32]

While not all the other missionaries might agree with Bradley's last sentence, his observations do underline an important difference in missionary outlook. Apart from a few exceptions, all these new people, like the old missionaries, were Friends, and followed Friends' principles as they understood them.[33] But their purpose was not first and foremost evangelistic, as it had been in the past. They wanted to contribute to Kenyan society's development towards greater participation in the modern world by training Kenyan Friends to take up full responsibilities as members of that society.

This clearer distinction between evangelistic and professional work on the part of the missionaries only served to emphasize the tendencies which had been developing among Kenyan Friends since the 1920s. We have seen that in 1925 Emory Rees had warned that the heavy emphasis on education was leading to a state of affairs where teachers would be more or less withdrawn from pastoral work, leaving the meetings almost without any 'intelligent and spiritual' pastoral care.[34] Already at that time, therefore, African church workers were beginning to specialize – some dealing mainly with teaching, others mainly with the spiritual welfare of the meetings. As the government became more and more involved in providing and supervising educational facilities, and as the Luyia people themselves devoted an increasing amount of money to the establishment of schools, this division between educational and pastoral work, begun in the 1920s, continued through the 1930s and 1940s, and in 1953 John Retherford wrote: 'There is cause for concern over the Spiritual decline on the part of many of our teachers',[35] thereby illustrating the teachers' own view of themselves as being first and foremost educators rather than spiritual leaders. Some years later, in 1966, Fred Reeve observed that younger teachers were inclined to view their work as a job with a definite salary, and many were not fired with the evangelistic fervour characteristic of teachers a decade or more earlier. He found, though, that despite this change in attitude, they gave 'much honest and faithful service'.[36] Therefore, African teachers, like their European and American counterparts, were beginning to regard themselves mainly as professional people who, although in many cases still taking part in the meetings and their leadership, left most of the pastoral work to other people.

Into this situation in 1954 came a new missionary couple, Herbert and Beatrice Kimball, to take over the leadership of Friends Bible Institute. They were both trained theologians: he had served as a pastor of a Friends church in America; she specialized in Christian education.[37] They were, therefore, well equipped to take over the running of the Bible school after Leonard Wines. And in employing Herbert Kimball as Principal of the Bible Institute the American Friends Board of Missions took one more step towards specialization of the missionaries: Wines had served as both General Superintendent of East Africa Yearly Meeting, in his capacity as head of the Evangelistic Department of Friends Africa Mission, and at the same time as Principal of the Bible Institute. When he left, these two functions were separated, John Retherford became General Superintendent, and the Bible school was headed for an interim period by a missionary, Dorothy Pitman, who was already working at the Girls' Boarding School, together with two of the Bible school teachers, Jeremiah Mugofu and Benjamin Wegesa.[38] And now, with the coming of the Kimballs, the posts of General Superintendent and Principal of the Bible Institute became permanently separated.

This separation was made without a clear definition of the limits of each person's responsibilities. Apparently, the Mission Board had expected Retherford and Kimball to work together in the task of training and developing the pastoral leaders of the yearly meeting. In practice, however, their relationship became far from smooth, partly due to the unsolved question of who was given the final authority to determine matters related to the running of the Bible school. But underlying their difficulties in co-operating with each other was a fundamental difference in theological views. As has been described above, all evangelistic missions – and the majority of their missionaries, too – had hitherto been under the influence of the nineteenth-century revival in the United States and the resulting fundamentalist evangelical theology in many American Quaker meetings, and John Retherford was no exception to this rule. But Herbert and Beatrice Kimball held very different theological views. Rather than emphasizing the Second Coming of Christ and the importance of preparing oneself for the judgement to come, through conversion and subsequent good works in a sanctified life, the Kimballs told their listeners repeatedly: we shall not wait for a Second Coming. Jesus has already come and is living among us, and the important thing to do, since we do not know what will happen after death, is not to focus attention on a judgement taking place then but to concentrate on living this present life in active love towards other people. They emphasized that God is not a God of revenge, who wants sinners to suffer in hell, but the loving Father of all who forgives sinners and cannot throw them into everlasting fire. They did not, like the previous missionaries, speak much about Christ's atoning death, but more about his humanity, and on a number of occasions Herbert Kimball refused to pray in the name of Jesus, apparently because such prayers seemed to him to imply a direct identification of Jesus with God, and not to take seriously the fact that he had become man.[39]

The Kimballs' theological teachings and the vigour with which they were sometimes presented, both at the Bible Institute and out in the numerous meetings they visited, were prompted not only by their opposition to the evangelical theology of former missionaries but also by their wish to impart to the Africans more of what they understood as the specific teachings characteristic of Friends. They found on their arrival in Kenya that what was taught to newcomers in the Church was selected Bible verses, such as Psalm 23 and the Ten Commandments, and also the Apostles' Creed. For them the latter was completely contrary to the Quaker principle of refusing to be bound by specific creeds in order to remain open to the leadings of the Light within. And they found no attempt to bring Friends' testimonies, illustrated through the complete lack of a Peace Committee in any of the monthly meetings and the low number of Service Committees trying to bring help beyond their own communities.[40]

Their emphasis on the present life rather than the life to come, and their wish for people to take an active part in society in love towards each other, was well suited to the other trends within Friends Africa Mission and East Africa Yearly Meeting of Friends at this time, as we have seen, since so much effort was being made to offer and receive training that was relevant to the needs of modern society. And for this reason – together with the fact that they travelled out to all parts of the Friends Church in East Africa, and consciously made closer contacts with the African Christians than most other missionaries – Herbert and Beatrice Kimball made a big impact on the Kenyan Church.[41] Many older people were shocked at their teachings,[42] but a number of people belonging to the younger generation, especially those who attended the Bible Institute under their leadership, were strongly influenced by their views.

However, their theological views were too different from those of most other missionaries for them to be accepted, and the disagreements between Herbert Kimball and John Retherford over the question of who had the authority to decide the training of yearly meeting leaders became so serious that the two of them, and Fred Reeve as Executive Secretary of the mission, became engaged in copious correspondence with the American Friends Board of Missions in order to try to get help from there to sort out their differences.[43] Although Retherford left Kenya in 1956,[44] the atmosphere between Herbert

Kimball and other missionaries had become such that it was difficult for them to co-operate. And eventually, in 1961, the Kimballs had to leave Kenya, even though East Africa Yearly Meeting of Friends took a much more positive view of their work.[45]

Two of the teachers at Friends Bible Institute – first Elisha Wakube, and from 1962 Joseph Kakai – acted as principals of the school until another missionary could be sent from America to take up this work.[46] The missionary who came in 1962 was Harold Smuck, and his original appointment was Principal of the Bible Institute. However, he soon became so heavily involved in administrative duties that another missionary had to be found for the work at the Bible school. And now a British Friend came to take over as Principal: Eric Wyatt, who held the position from 1964 until 1968.[47] After him came another American missionary until 1971, and shortly after he had left the position of Principal was finally handed over permanently to a Kenyan Friend, Josiah Embegu.[48]

Administration and Property in African Hands

The high level of activity in the Friends Church during the 1950s had to do not only with the massive support from the American Friends Board of Missions and other outside agencies but also with the fact that Africans were now becoming more and more involved in determining the affairs of their Church at all levels. In late 1955 the Board of East Africa Yearly Meeting decided to create the post of Administrative Secretary, and they appointed Benjamin Ngaira, a well-educated man who belonged to the younger generation, to take up the new post from January 1956.[49] Before this, Ngaira had already been Presiding Clerk of the yearly meeting for six years,[50] and his involvement in its leadership was an indication that at this time the Kenyan Quakers wanted leaders who understood modern society and could help their members adjust to it.[51] When Benjamin Ngaira fell ill in 1958, the yearly meeting appointed another young man who, like him, had attended the famous Alliance High School in Kikuyu, Thomas Ganira Lung'aho, from Isukha, as the new Administrative Secretary.[52] These new administrative leaders were able to ensure that East Africa Yearly Meeting made a place for itself and took part in the developments leading up to Kenya's political independence from Britain in 1963. They were therefore in full agreement with a large part of the yearly meeting members who wanted the Church to go wholeheartedly into the provision of education and other services which would enable its members to become fully integrated into modern society, and in this, as we have seen, they had the support of the American Friends Board of Missions.

Then, in 1961, in accordance with new government policies, East Africa Yearly Meeting was granted the right to hold property in Kenya.[53] And shortly afterwards, in 1962, the American Friends Board of Missions decided to hand over all land and property titles to East Africa Yearly Meeting. Fred Reeve, as Mission Board representative, suggested that Thomas Lung'aho should take over a newly created position as Assistant Administrative Secretary of Friends Africa Mission under himself, in order to create continuity and ease the transition from mission to yearly meeting ownership.[54] When this happened, Jotham Standa, a Tachoni, took over Lung'aho's former position as Secretary to the yearly meeting.[55]

Now things moved quickly towards national control, with all assets belonging to the Friends Church. Instead of remaining in the position of Principal of Friends Bible Institute, as he had intended on his arrival in Kenya, Harold Smuck soon became co-secretary with Lung'aho of Friends Africa Mission when Fred Reeve left in early 1963. In order for East Africa Yearly Meeting of Friends to hold property in Kenya it would have to be registered with the government, and have a properly recognized constitution. During 1963, therefore, Smuck helped to develop a constitution which was to take effect from 1 October 1963, and a few days earlier, on 28 September the first meeting took place of the new Permanent Board of the yearly meeting, reconstituted in such a way that it would be able to take over all the property formerly belonging to the American Friends Board of Missions. Before that, on 21 September, Friends Africa Mission had held its last meeting and dissolved itself, leaving individual missionaries – or 'overseas workers', as they came to be called – to become members of East Africa Yearly Meeting, and in this way take part in the affairs of the Kenyan Church. The formal handing over of all property to the yearly meeting trustees took place on 9 February 1964.[56]

The new constitution of East Africa Yearly Meeting provided for two executive committees: one for 'institutions and Projects' to handle the matters formerly taken care of by Friends Africa Mission, and one for 'Church Programme' to deal with the directly religious aspects of the work; the latter had been under yearly meeting control since

1946. At the first meeting of the reconstituted yearly meeting Board it was decided that Thomas Lung'aho should be Executive Secretary to the first committee, and Jotham Standa Executive Secretary to the latter, with Harold Smuck as Co-Secretary to both committees.[57] This arrangement soon proved inconvenient, however, and from late 1964, after Standa had resigned and taken up a government post, and the constitution had been revised, the yearly meeting had only one executive committee, with Thomas Lung'aho as its Executive Secretary.[58] The work formerly taken care of by the executive committee on 'Church Programme' was handed over to a General Superintendent from October 1964. The person who was chosen for this position was Charles Wakhisi, a Bukusu who had previously served as pastor of Nairobi, Kabete and Thika monthly meetings.[59]

Shortly before this attainment of independence from the American Friends Board of Missions, the number of members of East Africa Yearly Meeting of Friends was about 31,000.[60] In Kenya, as in all other branches of the Society of Friends, the most important organizational level is the monthly meeting. It is here that membership is registered. In 1961 there were sixty-four monthly meetings, and they sent representatives to fourteen quarterly meetings whose main purpose, according to Benjamin Ngaira, was 'to nurture the spiritual well being of the monthly meetings'.[61] Each monthly meeting is divided into a number of preparative meetings, in Kenya called village meetings, and at the other end of the organizational structure is the yearly meeting assembly to which members come from all parts of East Africa Yearly Meeting, and the business of which is carried out by representatives from the constituent quarterly meetings. Each organizational level is administered by a Presiding Clerk, a Recording Clerk, and a Treasurer; in addition, each of the monthly meetings has one or more pastors who care for the spiritual life of their members. The majority of them perform their pastoral duties on a voluntary basis, only perhaps sometimes receiving a certain amount of money as a sign of appreciation for their performance of specific tasks – for example, preaching in one of the larger meetings or conducting a funeral service[62] – but a few are full-time pastors who receive a definite salary. This may be the case in areas where a specific need has been identified – for instance, in the larger towns and cities. In 1961 there were nine full-time pastors and also three superintendents who acted as supervisors of the pastoral work of the yearly meeting.

The business of the yearly meeting as such is conducted by a Permanent, or General, Board, which at independence was made up of forty-one members representing their respective quarterly meetings. All types of matters of concern to the entire yearly meeting may be taken up here, both those related to the spiritual work and those which have to do with the institutions run by East Africa Yearly Meeting. The Board's decisions are carried out by the Executive Committee and its employees in co-operation with a number of standing committees.[63] Also at monthly meeting level a good deal of the business is conducted by committees. Herbert Kimball mentions that in the late 1950s there was a Committee of Elders, a Committee on Finance, and a Nominating Committee in all the monthly meetings, while a Sunday School Committee existed in about three-quarters of them and a Ministers' Committee, a Building Committee, an Education Committee and a Service Committee in a smaller number. He observed, as mentioned before, that no monthly meeting had a local Peace Committee.[64]

At independence the members of East Africa Yearly Meeting took up the work formerly carried out by the American Friends Board of Missions with enthusiasm, and a number of new projects were started during the first few years after 1963. Some of these, as well as some of the old ones, although still partly financed from outside sources, put a heavy strain on the financial resources of East Africa Yearly Meeting at times. Nevertheless, their contribution to the life of the Quaker Church in Kenya, and to its outreach towards other people, was considered so important that they were continued despite the economic difficulties involved. The old projects included Kaimosi Hospital, the health centre at Lugulu (later to be elevated to the status of a full hospital), Friends Bible Institute, and the Agricultural and Industrial Departments. An important project outside western Kenya was Friends Centre Ofafa, in Nairobi. Those Luyia Friends who left their home areas in order to earn money by working on the farms owned by Europeans, or in the cities, took their church along with them, and continued to hold meetings for worship and business wherever they went. In Nairobi, in particular, there was a large Quaker meeting where, in the mid-1950s, about four hundred people would come together for worship every Sunday, although they did not have their own church building. British Friends at that time, in the midst of the state of emergency implemented in 1952 because of the Mau Mau struggle, decided to start a community centre in the Ofafa housing estate. It was opened in 1954, and it provides social, educational and recreational activities for the people of the neighbourhood. Besides, the pastor for Quakers in Nairobi and surrounding areas came to live there, and its premises were used as a Friends meeting house.[65]

One of the new projects begun after 1963 is the Lugari Rural Christian Training Centre, set up in 1964 by East Africa Yearly Meeting of Friends in co-operation with the Christian Council of Kenya and the Department of Lands and Settlement of the Kenyan government. At around this time a number of Maragoli and other southern Luyia families migrated to the north, where the new government could provide them with more land than they had had in their original home areas. And with the establishment of the Rural Christian Training Centre it became possible for Friends to serve their needs by arranging courses in agriculture and dairy management, and by appointing a Friends pastor to assist in gathering many of the settlers into a number of new meetings. As early as 1965 a monthly meeting could be opened here, consisting of about twenty village meetings. Other projects are the Turkana Friends Centre at Kalokol in northern Kenya, whose main activities, besides the establishment of Quaker meetings in a new area, are a village polytechnic and an orphanage, and a second Friends Centre in Nairobi which housed the offices of the Africa Section of Friends World Committee for Consultation, besides providing room for weekly meetings for worship and for an international centre. Another project that was being planned at the time of independence, and was launched around 1971, was Friends College at Kaimosi, which offers courses for young people in accountancy, secretarial duties, and so on. Also launched in 1970–71 was Partnership for Productivity, which was started by an American Quaker businessman in close co-operation with Friends United Meeting and East Africa Yearly Meeting to give counsel and loans to people starting or improving small businesses. And in addition, a number of urban meeting houses were built at around this time with financial aid from American Friends: in Eldoret, Kitale, Nairobi, Mombasa, Nakuru, Kericho, Bungoma, and in Kampala in Uganda. Quakers in Kakamega built one some years later on a completely local initiative.[66]

Most of the work of running the day-to-day activities of the village, monthly and quarterly meetings, and even the yearly meeting, was (and is) carried out on a voluntary basis, with only a few of the pastors, the superintendents, and staff members employed by the yearly meeting Board receiving a salary for their work. In this, Kenyan Friends follow the traditions of world Quakerism of being, essentially, a lay movement. Nevertheless, a good deal of money was required for keeping up this work, and to finance the above-mentioned projects. Apart from outside aid from the American Friends Board of Missions, British Friends and other sources, which was still substantial in the 1960s and 1970s, income for the Church was generated through members' contributions. All members were expected to pay a fixed annual amount to the Church, and at each worship meeting a free-will offering was taken. A third major source of income was the money contributed by those who had pledged their support for the Lord's Acre programme.[67]

The 1960s, however, were not only a time when new projects were started and the operation of old ones was continued, it was also a decade of devolution of responsibility for one of the institutions which had been of vital importance for the life and growth of the Quaker Church in Kenya: the Friends school system. East Africa Yearly Meeting, like all other churches in the country, following the wishes of the independent Kenyan government, transferred the whole of their primary education programme to government supervision and control. The official transfer took place on 1 July 1965, but even before that the Friends secondary schools and the Teacher Training College at Kaimosi had set up boards of governors to administer them directly under government supervision. East Africa Yearly Meeting, however, did not lose complete control of its schools under these new arrangements. Each denomination continued to sponsor the schools which were formerly theirs – which in practice meant that they had the right to ensure that the schools were managed according to the principles of that particular Church. Furthermore, after Kenya had achieved national independence a number of self-help secondary schools were set up on the initiative of their local communities, often in close collaboration with the churches, the so-called 'Harambee' secondary schools; and most of these remained outside official control, although some of the more successful ones were later granted government subsidies. In this way Friends continued to be involved in the creation and running of a number of schools.[68]

The practical arrangements surrounding the handing over of the primary schools of East Africa Yearly Meeting, as well as those belonging to other denominations, to state control were managed by the Christian Churches' Educational Association in whose care all

Protestant churches placed their schools in the early 1960s as a transitional step before finally surrendering the administrative responsibilities to the government.[69] This co-operation was symptomatic of ecumenical relations as they had developed over time. As we have seen, now and then the Quakers had experienced problems with other churches when these others seemed to encroach on the territory traditionally belonging to Friends, and to recruit members from among their potential followers. Generally, however, they had enjoyed peaceful relations with other Protestant denominations. In 1924 the Kenya Missionary Council had been created, and Friends Africa Mission had joined that organization and co-operated fully in its programmes over the years. In 1943, when the Christian Council of Kenya was formed to take over from the Kenya Missionary Council, Friends transferred their membership to that organization, and in 1962–63 Thomas Lung'aho served as its chairman.[70] The Christian Churches' Educational Association was one of the co-operative structures set up by this council.

At local level also the smooth relationships between churches were palpable – for instance, when Thomas Lung'aho relates that members of 'sister churches' were present at the yearly meeting sessions in 1961, 'and even some Catholics!'[71] This last point shows an important development, since Friends had earlier seen Roman Catholics as some of their worst enemies, hardly to be regarded as Christians at all. In addition, as early as the 1950s the tensions that had existed between Quakers and the Holy Spirit people ever since the break between them in the years following 1927 had become so relaxed that in 1957 Fred Reeve could report that Friends had allowed some of the Holy Spirit people to build a school on a plot belonging to one of the monthly meetings, although legally it was still a Friends school because of government rules against African churches holding property.[72]

So, a decade after gaining independence from the American Friends Board of Missions, East Africa Yearly Meeting was living in harmony with other churches, and actively involved in running a number of projects aimed at serving both their own Church and the wider society around them. Within the Quaker church itself, however, tensions were rising. On the one hand, as Clifford Gilpin has observed, the eagerness with which church leaders engaged in development projects aimed at improving members' performance in the fields of education, farming and business, although they were beneficial to many, also had a negative side: 'the increasing impoverishment of the mass of rural peasantry, particularly in areas such as Maragoli which were already subject to land pressure and high labor migration'.[73] A number of people were unable to take advantage of the opportunities Church and society had to offer; and, as we have seen, many were therefore left out of the development process, among them a good deal of women farmers. The tensions arising between the developing middle class and the rural poor are reflected in the fact that from the late 1950s onwards a number of members left the Quaker Church in order to join one of the African independent churches, and more specifically the Holy Spirit churches, as we shall see. On the other hand, the wish for self-determination among Kenyan Quakers did not end with the setting up of East Africa Yearly Meeting and the transfer of property to it from the American Friends Board of Missions. On the contrary, in many of its areas of operation old grievances about differences and unequal opportunities between various groups were now coming to the surface, and finally resulted in the creation of a second yearly meeting in Kenya only ten years after the Church had become independent.

A Split in 1973: Elgon Religious Society of Friends

The majority of missionaries of Friends Africa Mission had looked at Kaimosi as the natural centre of their activities. It was the first mission station to be established, and the place had been chosen because it provided good conditions for the kind of industrial work the early missionaries wanted to set up. And once a number of institutions had been started at Kaimosi – such as the industrial department, the hospital, and the girls' and boys' schools – it had seemed inevitable to many that they must be maintained. Therefore, most of the missionaries came to live at Kaimosi, and this again attracted new institutions because of the human resources already present there. An example was the Bible Institute which, as we have seen, was moved from Lugulu to Kaimosi in 1949 after Jefferson Ford's departure from Kenya, precisely because at the latter place a number of part-time workers were available who could help to teach at the school. As we have already noted, however, the removal of the Bible Institute from Lugulu had led to increased dissatisfaction with Friends Africa Mission from the Quakers in the north, as did the controversies surrounding the secondary school issue which eventually resulted in the setting up of Friends School Kamusinga in the northern area, but only after many negative feelings had been generated between northern and southern Luyia Friends.[74]

These specific problems arose as a result of the general feeling in the north since the late 1930s: that the area did not receive as many services from the American Friends Board of Missions as the people in the south did. This feeling persisted in later years, for while the Rural Service Programme, when it was set up, finally covered the whole East Africa Yearly Meeting area, other programmes started by missionaries – such as training and economic support for small-scale businesses initiated by Fred Reeve, or the vocational training given at the industrial department – mainly served the interests of the Maragoli, the Tiriki and other southern Luyia peoples. Here the scarcity of land made it imperative for a large proportion of the population to look outside traditional agriculture for a major part of their livelihood, while the lower population density in the northern areas meant that agriculture was more profitable here, and fewer people had to look elsewhere to earn a living. Reeve and other missionaries responded to the needs of the southern Quakers, but served as yet another example of how Friends missionaries, because of Kaimosi's proximity to the people in the south, understood their problems better than those of the people in the north, and therefore paid them more attention.[75]

Another consequence of the concentration on the southern areas was the fact that for many years the main language used within the Quaker Church was Luragoli. Since Emory Rees, the missionary who started the work of translating the Bible into one of the Luyia languages, had lived in Maragoli, and since the African who had translated most of the New Testament with Rees, and later the Old Testament with Jefferson Ford, was Joel Litu whose home was at Mbale in Maragoli, it was inevitable that Luragoli was the language into which the whole Bible came to be translated. But for the people in the north, Luragoli was a foreign language. Their language, although similar to Luragoli, nevertheless differed from it in many ways, and for those who were not used to hearing it there could be serious difficulties of comprehension. Connected with this language problem was the presence of a number of Maragoli teachers in the north, especially during the early years, when fervour for spreading the Gospel together with school education had been great, while at the same time only a few of those living in the area immediately south of Mount Elgon (Bukusu) had yet been converted to Christianity, and were therefore able to preach the new teachings to their own people. These Maragoli teachers were unable to make themselves understood to Bukusu people. This meant that the Friends Church first presented itself in the north as a church which was to a large extent dominated by Maragoli people and the Luragoli language. And while this fact did not present any immediate difficulties, it did in the long run cause a number of people here to feel that they had to free themselves from Maragoli 'colonialism' and have a church in which they could use their own language.[76]

Differences between individual missionaries had also contributed towards widening the gap between Luyia Friends. Jefferson Ford – who, as mentioned above, was strongly revivalist – stayed mostly at Lugulu, although as General Superintendent he served the whole Church. This meant that he had a better understanding than most missionaries of the hopes and aspirations of the northern peoples, their feeling of neglect by the mission, and their differences with southern Friends. His identification with them went so far that at the time of serious theological controversies between fundamentalist and 'modernist' missionaries in the early 1930s, when the Friends mission went through a period of serious economic difficulties, he proposed that in order to solve both the theological and economic problems the Friends Africa Mission area should be divided into two parts, the southern part continuing in the care of the American Friends Board of Missions while the northern area would be taken over by himself. Other missionaries, as well as the Board in America, were opposed to any such division of the field. But the fact that Ford suggested it illustrates not only the seriousness of the controversies between missionaries but also his feeling, like that of many people in the north, that their area constituted a special part of the Friends Church, distinct from the rest in many ways.[77] And since many people here had great veneration for Jefferson Ford, and to a great extent identified the Friends Church with him, his attitude no doubt served to reinforce this feeling among them.[78]

In later years – from around 1960, when the Mission Board began to offer scholarships for studies in America to African Quakers, and some of the Kenyan church leaders began to go overseas to attend international meetings – many in the north felt again that the majority of those chosen for these opportunities were people from the south. This reinforced their sense of being neglected by the Mission Board, and now also by their own Church leadership, whom they found no more inclined to take their interests into consideration than the missionaries had been.[79]

In the early 1940s the creation of the second Quarterly Meeting in the north had given Friends here a certain measure of independence from the south, and temporarily satisfied their wish to determine their own affairs. When the Yearly Meeting had been created in 1946 at Lugulu they again felt that they were at the centre of church activities. That feeling soon changed, however, when the head office of the new Yearly Meeting, after a few years of operating from Musingu in Idakho, ended up being located at Kaimosi.[80] And now that it had proved possible for a yearly meeting to be set up in Kenya, the northern Friends' wish for independence from the south and for more attention from America made some of them ask for a second yearly meeting to be established in their area as early as 1953.[81]

The question of a second yearly meeting was brought up a number of times in subsequent years. In 1959 and 1960, for instance, it was discussed in the Permanent Board and at the annual conferences.[82] But most of the leaders of East Africa Yearly Meeting felt that this issue ought to wait until after a large international meeting of the Friends World Committee for Consultation had been held at Kaimosi in 1961, so that Kenyan Friends could present a united church to the outside world. When northern Friends took up the question again in 1963 serious discussion of it was once more postponed, with the leadership at Kaimosi giving as the reason that it would be important to stand firm as one body precisely at the time of the transfer of administrative responsibility and property from the American Friends Board of Missions to East Africa Yearly Meeting. In each of these cases Friends in the north accepted the argument and agreed to wait until a later date before seeking to establish a separate yearly meeting. But gradually the feeling developed that southern Friends were opposed to the whole idea of a second yearly meeting, and that the reasons they had given for postponing a decision were, in fact, excuses for preventing any division, at all. Consequently, from around 1964 some northern Quakers came to the conclusion that if they wanted to reach their goal they had to work on their own, despite what they now saw as opposition from many of the East Africa Yearly Meeting leaders. As an expression of their determination they started to use the term 'Elgon Yearly Meeting of Friends', even though no such body had been officially formed by then.[83]

In 1970 East Africa Yearly Meeting decided to set up a Task Group to look into the question of how best to organize the Church. And although the issue of a second yearly meeting had not been included in its terms of reference from the beginning, it was taken up as an important topic, probably under the influence of the Task Group secretary, Elisha Wakube, who was among those Bukusu who wanted a yearly meeting in their area. After consultations with all quarterly meetings, the Task Group reported in 1971 that they had found a majority in favour of dividing the Church into two. But when that report was presented to the Permanent Board and the Executive Committee of East Africa Yearly Meeting, these bodies discarded it, saying that the Task Group had been given no mandate to look into that question.[84]

At this time, however, more and more people in the north were joining those who wished to set up a second yearly meeting, and in 1972 they appealed strongly, as they had done before, to the Mission Board in America, now renamed the Wider Ministries Commission of Friends United Meeting, asking them to support their cause. But Friends United Meeting found themselves in a dilemma. On the one hand, they wanted to be fair to all Friends in Kenya and listen sympathetically to their wishes. On the other hand, they found, as General Secretary Lorton Heusel wrote a few years later, that their direct intervention without support from both sides in the Kenyan conflict would 'put us back into the old colonialist pattern of dominating and dictating from the outside what the appropriate resolution should be'.[85] Consequently, Friends United Meeting and its Wider Ministries Commission took the official stance that they had no right to interfere in the internal affairs of a member organization. Their dealings were with the decision-making bodies of East Africa Yearly Meeting, and with its head office; therefore, all communication ought to be channelled through that office and its Executive Secretary, Thomas Ganira Lung'aho. Friends United Meeting kept to this position for a number of years, although the Elgon people pointed out to them in their correspondence that it would be impossible for them to get anything but a one-sided picture of the Kenyan situation if they maintained such a stance. The East Africa Yearly Meeting Permanent Board, its Executive Committee, and its Executive Secretary could hardly be expected to speak on behalf of those Friends who wanted to divide the yearly meeting, since they were the very bodies opposed to any such move.[86]

Having realized that appeals to East Africa Yearly Meeting and to international Quaker organizations gained no support for their cause, Friends in the north now went ahead on their own and drafted a constitution for the new yearly meeting they wanted to set up; and in October 1972 a prominent Bukusu elder, Philip Mwangale, signing himself 'Presiding Clerk, Elgon Friends Meeting', wrote to Lorton Heusel informing him that the drafting of a constitution had been completed and that a group of Friends, assisted by an advocate, were now planning to approach the Registrar of Societies in order to have their Church legally registered under Kenyan government laws.[87] They encountered no difficulties with the government, and on 19 April 1973 the new yearly meeting was officially registered under the name 'Elgon Religious Society of Friends'.[88] Philip Mwangale became its Presiding Clerk and Elisha Wakube its first General Secretary. The new body set up its head office in the premises of Friends School Kamusinga on 25 June 1973.[89]

The author of the paper entitled 'Why Elgon Broke away from Kaimosi' gives a number of reasons for the break, one of the most important being that organizational problems had arisen, due to the size of East Africa Yearly Meeting at that time (50,000 members) and the large geographical area covered by it. The large area meant that travel costs for people going to attend meetings of the governing bodies at yearly meeting level became very high, and on the whole, sheer size is seen as one factor contributing to the serious economic difficulties in which East Africa Yearly Meeting found itself at the time, forcing it to pay too much attention to financial and organizational matters and leaving too little strength for it to give sufficient attention to its main aim, that of evangelism. The author expresses the hope of the Elgon people that the establishment of the new yearly meeting will make it possible for it 'to redouble and revive its evangelistic efforts', 'to rekindle the local church', and 'to bring about the regeneration of the individual', but it is strongly emphasized that despite the fact that they had broken their organizational links with East Africa Yearly Meeting, they had no wish to separate themselves from the worldwide Society of Friends. On the contrary, they considered themselves true Quakers. The only difference is that 'Elgon Friends are no longer under Kaimosi'; they now had their own yearly meeting, just as many other yearly meetings had been set up in different parts of the world.[90]

About two months after its registration by the government, leaders of Elgon Religious Society of Friends sent a letter to East Africa Yearly Meeting of Friends officially informing them of the event.[91] However, the leaders of that body had been aware of what was going to happen, and had taken their precautions: they had already set up a commission to look into the question of reorganizing the yearly meeting. The commission came up with a report recommending that East Africa Yearly Meeting should be divided into nine regions with a degree of autonomy from Kaimosi. Each region was to have a regional office, and by 30 June 1973, only five days after Elgon Religious Society of Friends had set up their administrative headquarters at Kamusinga, the new Lugulu Region of East Africa Yearly Meeting opened its office in the old mission compound at Lugulu. But leaders of Elgon Religious Society of Friends suspected that the reorganization of East Africa Yearly Meeting was intended to frustrate their efforts to establish an independent yearly meeting in the north, and therefore did not recognize the new regions. Furthermore, they pointed out that the reorganization came too late, after the new yearly meeting in the north had already come into existence.[92]

There followed a period of bitterness between members of the two yearly meetings. Many in Elgon were disappointed at the hostile reaction from the East Africa Yearly Meeting Presiding Clerk, Hezekiah Ngoya, whose home was near Lugulu and who had been among those who had spoken out in favour of establishing a second yearly meeting in the northern area in the 1950s and early 1960s.[93] Similarly, they felt let down by its General Superintendent, Charles Wakhisi, whose home was also near Lugulu and who was, right until the time immediately prior to the official registration of Elgon Religious Society of Friends, believed by many northern Quakers to be in support of their cause, but who had eventually decided to remain within East Africa Yearly Meeting.[94]

For some, the decision as to whether to keep up membership of the old yearly meeting or to join the new one had to be made very soon after the setting up of Elgon Religious Society of Friends, when all employees of East Africa Yearly Meeting whose homes were in the north were asked to sign loyalty statements to that organization. If they did not, they would lose their membership and, by implication, their jobs. Among those whose employment was thus terminated were Elisha Wakube, who had served as Assistant Literature Secretary, and Daniel Khaoya, who had been employed as Area Superintendent.[95] These forced expulsions created bitterness among those affected, and possibly contributed further towards setting members of the two yearly meetings apart from each other.

One of the most important issues, however, became that of church property. People belonging to Elgon Religious Society of Friends continued to use the churches and church plots in their area, while members and leaders of East Africa Yearly Meeting did their utmost to prevent them from doing so. Thomas Lung'aho makes the position of East Africa Yearly Meeting clear in a letter to Elisha Wakube in April 1974:

> Since you led some Friends in Bungoma District to break away from E.A.Y.M. it meant you have no grounds to claim any share of the properties, i.e. land etc. which are held and owned by East Africa Yearly Meeting of Friends. You are not members of E.A.Y.M. therefore you have no right to use any of our properties. This has been made very clear to you many times. You should look for your own plots.

From the point of view of East Africa Yearly Meeting, Elgon Religious Society of Friends – having been formed as a result of a unilateral decision by people in the north, and not after an agreement by all parties involved – had thereby left the fellowship of East African Friends and no longer had any right to use property belonging to that fellowship. And Lung'aho warns Elgon Friends specifically against their continued use of the church plot at Chwele, saying that this is 'deliberate interference likely to cause trouble'.[96]

In the following month it is not just Thomas Lung'aho himself as Executive Secretary who writes to Elgon Friends. East Africa Yearly Meeting has now approached lawyers Kaplan & Stratton to obtain their help against members of Elgon Religious Society of Friends, who have taken over another disputed church plot at Mbakalo. The lawyers write:

> This does, of course, constitute a trespass and we must advise you that if you remain in occupation of this property or enter it again, proceedings will be taken to obtain a court order to restrain you.[97]

The threat of legal action being taken against Elgon Religious Society of Friends is repeated in August the same year by Christopher Fwamba, Region Chairman, Lugulu Region of East Africa Yearly Meeting. He states his yearly meeting's belief that they have the right to church and school plots in the north by virtue of the fact that they have created a region in Bungoma District, with its headquarters at

Lugulu. Thereby he apparently implies that East Africa Yearly Meeting also has members in the area and can, therefore, demand that the property remain in their hands. And, like Lung'aho, he warns Elgon Friends against using the church at Chwele, this time mentioning specifically their 1974 annual conference scheduled to take place there. He now uses the threat of legal action: 'Mark that if this is not observed, we shall be forced to call upon Justice to take its Course.'[98] In fact, the threats from East Africa Yearly Meeting made Elgon Religious Society of Friends change their plans and hold the annual conference in the compound of a prominent church elder and Assistant Superintendent, Andrea Chemiati, right next to Chwele church, but not use the church itself.[99]

In response to the claims by East Africa Yearly Meeting, members of Elgon Religious Society of Friends claimed in turn that the plots belonged to the local people who had donated them to the Church, and since their separation had in no way changed the fact that they were Quakers, their use of the property would still be in accordance with the original purpose. Consequently, they continued to hold meetings in the local churches and tried to bar members of East Africa Yearly Meeting from taking them over, in a few cases going so far that the situation threatened to erupt into violence.[100]

However, while the disputes sometimes resulted in police supervision of meetings conducted by Elgon Religious Society of Friends, or in a ban against their use of a specific piece of property,[101] the government authorities were by no means always on the side of East Africa Yearly Meeting against Elgon Friends. Closely related to the question of the right to use churches and plots previously belonging to East Africa Yearly Meeting was the issue of who was to sponsor the Friends schools in the northern area. In October 1973 Elgon Religious Society of Friends had requested official government permission to sponsor and manage Harambee schools,[102] and in June 1974 the Bungoma District Commissioner, E.P. Oranga, wrote very favourably about them to the Provincial Commissioner in Kakamega, saying that they had the support of 95 per cent of all Quakers in the District, that they had conducted their affairs smoothly, and that he had no objection to their being granted the right to sponsor and manage the Friends schools in the District.[103]

Meanwhile, Elgon Religious Society of Friends was also appealing to the outside world for recognition, just as it had appealed to the Kenyan government. Soon after it had been officially established it applied to Friends United Meeting for membership of that organization, and also to Friends World Committee for Consultation, as well as to ecumenical bodies such as the National Christian Council of Kenya and the All Africa Conference of Churches.[104] Actually, the Elgon leaders regarded their applications for membership of the international Quaker organizations as a mere formality, since in their own view they had never left these bodies.[105] They were still Friends, and their establishment of a second yearly meeting in Kenya only constituted a change in the administrative structure of East African Quakers which, they believed, ought not to lead to any negative repercussions as far as their relationship to the worldwide Quaker community was concerned. However, Friends United Meeting and Friends World Committee for Consultation did not view the matter in the same light as Elgon Religious Society of Friends leaders. Edwin B. Bronner, Chairman of Friends World Committee for Consultation, replied to Elgon Friends in May 1974 that it was 'clear to us that we ought not to take any action regarding your letter applying for membership at present', although they did not rule out the possibility of 'making a decision in the near future'.[106] And Friends United Meeting continued for a number of years to maintain the same stance that they had taken before the formation of Elgon Religious Society of Friends: that their official dealings must be with East Africa Yearly Meeting. And since the leaders of that body insisted that the division of the yearly meeting was a purely African problem, Friends United Meeting could not proceed with recognition of Elgon Religious Society of Friends until such time as the two yearly meetings could be reconciled, and recognition could take place with the co-operation of East Africa Yearly Meeting.[107]

Although Friends United Meeting accepted the view that a solution to the question of the two yearly meetings had to be found by Kenyans themselves, they nevertheless pressed for reconciliation between the two bodies. They now perceived their own role as that of 'enablers', ready to enable reconciliation if this could be brought about on the basis of mutual respect.[108] As early as 1974, therefore, they offered to send a visiting team to Kenya with the dual purpose of trying to understand the 'dreams and goals' of all Friends in Kenya, and of exercising a reconciliatory role. While Elgon Religious Society of Friends welcomed the idea, however, East Africa Yearly Meeting turned down the offer with reference to their conviction that this was an African problem; therefore nothing came of it at that stage.[109]

One person who figured prominently in the disputes at this time was the East Africa Yearly Meeting Executive Secretary, Thomas Ganira Lung'aho. Much of the criticism of East Africa Yearly Meeting from the Elgon Friends, both before and after the actual separation, had been directed against him. He was the top executive in East Africa Yearly Meeting, and therefore the one who had to carry out all decisions made by its Executive Committee and its Permanent Board. This made him the most visible person and therefore the target of many attacks, which at times were of a rather personal nature. He was also the person through whom most of the official communication from Friends United Meeting was channelled, and it was he who, in his correspondence with America, stood firmly by his opinion that the relationship between the two yearly meetings was an African problem to be solved by Africans themselves, and who therefore, at first, did not want any help from that quarter towards bringing them together. This did not mean, however, that Lung'aho was against any attempts to reconcile the two parties. Although he tried to keep members of Elgon Religious Society of Friends away from property which East Africa Yearly Meeting regarded as belonging to them, he was actually one of those who initiated contacts with leaders of Elgon Friends, and spoke about the need for reconciliation. In September 1975 he wrote to Philip Mwangale: 'The division which has come in our midst is not building us, but the devil has found a chance to destroy God's work … We all stand to be judged from the stand we have taken.' He expressed his happiness that Mwangale had been present at the East Africa Yearly Meeting annual conference that year, and goes on: 'Perhaps God has appointed a day when we shall talk in a spirit of love and concern.'[110] And about six months later he wrote to Elisha Wakube about the need for peace: 'As you know, I am still concerned about our relationship. Something ought to be done. It is ourselves to do that.' And he suggests that they meet, together with some other members, 'to see what God is telling us in these days'.[111]

It was not only in private letters, however, that Lung'aho spoke of the need for reconciliation. On 6 November 1977 East Africa Yearly Meeting of Friends celebrated its 75th anniversary, counted from the year 1902, when the first three missionaries had arrived. It was a happy occasion, with many Friends present, but the situation among Kenyan Quakers was reflected in the fact that no representatives of Elgon Religious Society of Friends joined in the celebrations, which took place at Kaimosi. Nevertheless, in his anniversary message outlining the achievements and the growth of the Quaker Church Thomas Lung'aho also touched on the problem of the split when he said: 'And remembering our Friends in Elgon we pray, too, that reconciliation may come between us and a God-given unity will prevail.'[112]

At that time, a reconciliation meeting had already taken place. The initiative had originated from the East Africa Yearly Meeting General Board.[113] It had been held on 10 April 1975 at Lugulu, and on 10 December 1977 the second 'consultation on reconciliation' was held at Kamusinga, again on the initiative of the Board of East Africa Yearly Meeting. But now a new development had come into the picture which allowed the second meeting to discuss the matter in ways that were more acceptable to Elgon Friends: the decision taken by the East Africa Yearly Meeting annual conference, held at Lirhanda in August 1977, to 'extend the hand of friendship and reconciliation to our sister in the Elgon Religious Society of Friends' by asking the General Board of East Africa Yearly Meeting to institute immediate steps towards legitimizing the existence of a second yearly meeting of Friends in Kenya.[114] This decision did not mean, however, that all difficulties were now out of the way, for at the consultation at Kamusinga there was a lively debate between the two sides about the question of who constituted that second yearly meeting. According to the minutes, there was agreement that the old yearly meeting was to be in the south and the new one in the north, where Elgon Religious Society of Friends and the Lugulu and Kitale Regions of East Africa Yearly Meeting were. But while Elgon Friends had hoped that East Africa Yearly Meeting's attitude would be that they now recognized Elgon Religious Society of Friends unconditionally as the second yearly meeting in the north, and members of Lugulu and Kitale Regions of East Africa Yearly Meeting would transfer their membership to Elgon Religious Society of Friends, the position of the leaders of the former group was not quite so clear-cut. On the one hand, they had come to Kamusinga in order to declare, as Assistant Presiding Clerk of East Africa Yearly Meeting Joseph Kisia said, that all faithful members of Elgon Religious Society of Friends were 'Quakers and work as Friends'.[115] But despite the recognition inherent in those words, the ten members of East Africa Yearly Meeting present at the consultation said, according to the minutes, that they were willing to recognize Elgon Religious Society of Friends only 'on condition "that the members of E.R.S.F. admit that they were wrong to take the meeting by themselves."'[116] And the consultation reached no conclusion on the question of how the proposed second yearly meeting in the north was to be formed to the satisfaction of both parties.[117]

Opposition against Elgon Friends remained strong in some quarters, especially among members of the Lugulu and Kitale Regions of East Africa Yearly Meeting, the majority of whom rejected any suggestion that they should give up their membership of that yearly meeting and join Elgon Religious Society of Friends. One example of a family who refused to do so, although their home is in the heart of the area claimed by that group, is Ex-Senior Chief Jonathan Baraza and his wife Ruth, who live in Sirisia, not far from Chwele. In spite of several incidents around the Sirisia church, which was eventually taken over by Elgon Friends, the Baraza family, supported by only a very few local people, remained staunch supporters of East Africa Yearly Meeting.[118]

In other parts of East Africa Yearly Meeting, however, there was clearly a change of attitude, many members now being in favour of reaching a peaceful settlement with Elgon Friends. And when Harold Smuck came to Kenya at the beginning of 1978 in his capacity as Associate General Secretary of Friends United Meeting in charge of its Wider Ministries Commission, this softening in the attitudes of Kenyan Friends was expressed in the recommendation from East Africa Yearly Meeting's General Board that he should accept an invitation from Elgon Friends to meet them. As a result, a meeting was arranged in Bungoma on 14 February 1978 between a number of representatives from Elgon Religious Society of Friends and Harold Smuck, accompanied by Hezekiah Ngoya as Presiding Clerk of East Africa Yearly Meeting and by Thomas Lung'aho as its Executive Secretary.[119] As Smuck points out, this was the first official meeting between himself and leaders of Elgon Religious Society of Friends, and although no important conclusions were reached, the fact that the meeting took place at all was an indication that Friends United Meeting might be willing to review its relationship with Elgon Friends once such a move was no longer opposed by East Africa Yearly Meeting.

One of the constructive ideas brought forward at the Bungoma meeting was the suggestion by Jeremiah Lusweti, Chairman of the Permanent Board of Elgon Religious Society of Friends, that in order for Kenyan Friends to develop peaceful relationships they might set up a 'Kenya Friends Council' which would consist of both the yearly meetings and meet at regular intervals to discuss topics of relevance to all. He saw this as a realistic step towards the reconciliation for which American Friends had pressed in their correspondence.[120] Smuck gave no promises at the meeting because, as he said, 'we do not see any value in making a new friend and throwing out an old one'. But the fact that he had come, and two important representatives of East Africa Yearly Meeting had come with him, clearly gave members of Elgon Religious Society of Friends the assurance that they had now come one more step closer to recognition by both East Africa Yearly Meeting and Friends United Meeting. And in a letter to Smuck a few days later Lusweti requested permission for two representatives from Elgon Religious Society of Friends to attend the Triennial Conference of Friends United Meeting that was to take place the following June; he also asked Smuck to take up Elgon Friends' application for membership of Friends United Meeting at the forthcoming Board meeting.[121] In fact, Elisha Wakube, who went to America shortly after the Bungoma meeting, was welcome to attend the Triennial sessions, albeit in a private capacity.[122] But it was to be some years yet before Friends United Meeting would give official recognition to Elgon Religious Society of Friends, and accept it as a member.

The Division into Four Yearly Meetings

Meanwhile, new developments in other areas shifted the focus of attention to some extent. The annual conference's decision in 1977 to create two yearly meetings had been based on the understanding that this would mean on the one hand a new yearly meeting in the north, and on the other the remaining parts of East Africa Yearly Meeting. However, a number of people in the 'central' area, made up mainly of the Lirhanda and Malava Regions, were beginning to feel that these proposals ignored their existence and interests. During the period of time leading up to the 1979 annual conference to be held at Kidundu in South Maragoli, plans were under way in some circles to place the headquarters of the southern yearly meeting at Vihiga once the north had become independent. But other people, among them many from the central area, were opposed to the thought of moving the offices from Kaimosi to Vihiga, and thereby enhancing the already strong Maragoli influence in the Church.[123]

As a result, during the annual conference at Kidundu in August 1979, a new suggestion came up: to divide East Africa Yearly Meeting into three rather than only two yearly meetings, to be in the north, the central area, and the south, with their administrative offices to be located at Lugulu, Kakamega and Vihiga respectively. A number of meetings of the General Board took place during the conference to discuss this matter, and the Board decided to present the proposal to the assembled group on the last day of the conference, when it was approved by acclamation by the 5000-odd people present. According to what was now the decision of the yearly meeting, the old administrative set-up was to continue until the end of the year, after which the three new yearly meetings should begin to function. The Kaimosi offices were no longer to belong to any one of the yearly meetings but were to become the centre for a new central council. The council would take care of interests common to all of them, such as the supervision of institutions and programmes; it would also deal with their relationships to ecumenical bodies, as well as international Quaker organizations. A planning committee was set up to see that these decisions were implemented.[124]

Apparently, however, not everyone was enthusiastic about what had been decided at the conference, and a number of things happened which complicated the smooth implementation of the plans and made some of the people who had been involved in making the decision change their minds. One was the strong opposition of the Tiriki people against their inclusion in the proposed southern yearly meeting with headquarters at Vihiga. This opposition was voiced only four days after the annual conference in a strongly worded letter to the East Africa Yearly Meeting Presiding Clerk, Hezekiah Ngoya. They wrote that Kaimosi Region would not join any such southern yearly meeting but would continue to regard itself as the original East Africa Yearly Meeting, with its headquarters at Kaimosi. If, however, others were prepared to go ahead and implement the Kidundu decision, the Kaimosi Region in turn was prepared to establish another yearly meeting which would, likewise, have its offices at Kaimosi.[125]

Despite this threat to form their own yearly meeting if necessary, the Tiriki people therefore preferred East Africa Yearly Meeting to remain one united group, and in this they were supported by many in Lirhanda and Malava Regions. Some members here wrote to the central office at Kaimosi, distancing themselves from the Kidundu decision, and the people in these regions did not press for its implementation, which would have resulted in the establishment of a new 'central' yearly meeting in their area. The prospect of a Quaker

Church divided into a number of different groups was probably not very appealing to them, and this might very well have been the outcome if the three yearly meetings agreed upon at Kidundu had been established. As we have seen, there was the very real possibility of yet another yearly meeting being formed in Tiriki, and in the north there was already a problem, since the suggested northern yearly meeting would not include those many Quakers who were members of Elgon Religious Society of Friends, with the result that in that area there would be two yearly meetings existing side by side. In addition, there was the question as to where city meetings were to belong. At the Kidundu meeting Nairobi Region, which also included the meetings in a number of other cities such as Mombasa and Nakuru, had been assigned to the southern yearly meeting. But many city Friends did not like that arrangement, since their original homes were in all parts of the area covered by the Quaker Church, and many of them did not feel any particular attachment to the southern group. Consequently, they, too, sent letters protesting against the plans to divide the yearly meeting into three parts.[126]

Therefore, the officers and employees of East Africa Yearly Meeting took no steps towards the implementation of the Kidundu decision. And a new factor was added to the situation a few months after the conference when there was an attempt by a group of younger people, led by Jack Jumba Chunguli from South Maragoli, to impose a new General Secretary and register with the government a new set of office-bearers of the yearly meeting who were not the ones nominated at Kidundu. They succeeded in having police evict Thomas Lung'aho from his house and his office at Kaimosi, but the old yearly meeting leadership took the case to court. It went up to the High Court, and here it was ordered that the representatives to the annual conference at Kidundu should come together again to determine who were legally the leaders of the yearly meeting. Therefore, a one-day conference was held on 8 March 1980, and on that occasion a fresh election of office-bearers of East Africa Yearly Meeting took place. Furthermore, after a court injunction had caused his office to be closed for some time during 1980, Lung'aho was allowed to resume his work as General Secretary.

However, the new Presiding Clerk, Tadayo Oudo, who was from the Kitale area, was – like the previous Clerk, Ngoya – among those who wanted a single, united East Africa Yearly Meeting. It looked, therefore, as if no immediate action would be taken to divide the yearly meeting. But – as Solomon Adagala, who was prominent among the supporters of a southern yearly meeting, explained – the large majority of people in South Maragoli, and most in North Maragoli, were unwilling to accept the outcome of the one-day conference, doubting whether the people who met there were actually the same as those who had attended the Kidundu conference. These people were not in favour of the unconstitutional action taken by the group led by Chunguli, but they wanted to uphold the Kidundu decision; consequently, they decided to go ahead and prepare for the creation of the southern yearly meeting that had been agreed upon there. They felt that those who were really breaking up the Church were those who had changed their minds and decided not to follow the agreements made at the 1979 conference, whereas they themselves represented the real opinion of the representatives to that conference. They began almost immediately to function along the lines of a yearly meeting, holding annual conferences in both 1980 and 1981; and they managed to become legally registered with the Registrar of Societies on 12 November 1981, with Joseph Kisia as Presiding Clerk and Solomon Adagala as General Secretary. As a logical consequence of their claim to represent the true East Africa Yearly Meeting they maintained that name, calling themselves East Africa Yearly Meeting of Friends (South), just as they kept the constitution of the mother yearly meeting, with only minor changes.[127]

At the time of the formation of this new yearly meeting, its members still did not recognize Elgon Religious Society of Friends as a legitimate Quaker yearly meeting, and to this they agreed with the majority of what was left of the original East Africa Yearly Meeting of Friends who, however, did not recognize the new southern yearly meeting either. But when a large number of Quakers from all over the world gathered at Kaimosi in August 1982 for an international conference and a Triennial Meeting of Friends World Committee for Consultation, things began to change. At the insistence of the international Quaker community, Friends from all the three yearly meetings now existing in Kenya were present in Kaimosi, and the visitors from America, Europe, and so on, went as guests to attend local meetings in all of them, and to stay in private homes.[128] The personal contacts established on these occasions confirmed to the visitors that the members of Elgon Religious Society of Friends, as well as those of East Africa Yearly Meeting of Friends (South), were indeed Quakers, that they were legitimate yearly meetings, and that there was no reason to continue barring their participation in the international Friends organizations. Consequently, the Friends World Committee for Consultation admitted them into membership towards the end of that same year, and the General Board of Friends United Meeting decided to recommend to the representatives to its Triennial Meeting, due to take place in 1984, that both of them be accepted as members. Those American Quakers who had taken part in the Kaimosi meeting were active, upon their return home, in convincing others of the legitimacy of the two new yearly meetings in Kenya, thereby paving the way for their recognition by members of Friends United Meeting.[129]

And the co-operation – although not without difficulties – of the three yearly meetings in Kenya in making arrangements for the Friends World Committee for Consultation conference at Kaimosi, coupled with the growing international recognition of the two new yearly meetings occasioned by that same conference, caused some Friends in Kenya to begin to reconsider their attitudes towards each other. One decisive step was taken when, very soon after the meeting, East Africa Yearly Meeting of Friends (South) decided to recognize Elgon Religious Society of Friends as a true Quaker yearly meeting,[130] since when the two have often stood together, supporting each other in the face of opposition from members of East Africa Yearly Meeting.

At around the same time the Kenyan government, represented by the Provincial Commissioner for Western Province, Mr J.K. Kobia, became involved in the conflicts between Quakers. The Provincial Commissioner says in a press release that the government decided to step in – in an attempt to reconcile the Quakers 'in the interest of peace and security in the Church and the Country'.[131] He therefore invited leaders from all three groups to a number of meetings in his office, and they now had to sit together and discuss their differences in his presence as a neutral person who was interested only in preserving peace in the area and in finding out which yearly meeting was sponsor of schools and responsible for the running of other institutions in the various parts of his Province. And these reconciliation meetings resulted in bringing the parties involved further towards recognition of each other and towards discovering how to divide the area between them.[132]

By February 1984 the discussions in the presence of the Provincial Commissioner had reached a stage where the Quaker negotiators felt that they would now be able to continue their talks on their own, and after the setting up of an interim committee consisting of ten members from each of the three yearly meetings, charged with the responsibility of setting up a central council as a body of co-operation between them, the Provincial Commissioner agreed to let them do the work alone. A constitution drafting committee was also set up, with three members from each yearly meeting, which was to draw up a constitution for the central council while at the same time respecting and upholding the constitutions of each individual yearly meeting. The constitution drafting committee was to be responsible to the interim committee, and its recommendations were to be approved by that body.[133]

In fact, many members of East Africa Yearly Meeting – prominent among them Ezekiel Wanyonyi from the Kitale area – still did not agree that there was a need to recognize the two new yearly meetings. They saw the Quaker Church in Kenya as one, and wanted to preserve that unity by upholding one undivided East Africa Yearly Meeting of Friends. And if changes were to come, and new yearly meetings were to be set up, it must, in their opinion, happen after everyone had agreed on the matter – and not, as in the case of Elgon Religious Society of Friends and East Africa Yearly Meeting of Friends (South), after a unilateral decision and a break away from the mother yearly meeting.[134] And because of that attitude from many leaders in East Africa Yearly Meeting, they decided not to take part in the work of the interim and constitution drafting committees which, therefore, came to consist mainly of representatives from Elgon Religious Society of Friends and East Africa Yearly Meeting of Friends (South), with Thomas Lung'aho often being the only representative from East Africa Yearly Meeting.[135]

Nevertheless, the constitution drafting committee continued its work, and managed within a relatively short time to draw up a constitution for the proposed central body of Quakers, which was given the name 'Friends Church in Kenya'. The draft constitution was presented to the interim committee in May 1984 and accepted, making it possible for Kenyan Quakers to demonstrate to the Triennial Meeting of Friends United Meeting – which was to take place in Orange, California, two months later – that they were now able to work together.

This was the meeting which was expected to adopt the recommendation of the Friends United Meeting General Board that Elgon Religious Society of Friends and East Africa Yearly Meeting of Friends (South) should be accepted as members. And, like the two new yearly meetings, East Africa Yearly Meeting of Friends, which was already a member, sent a number of representatives to the Triennial, where they decided, although most of them were not in favour of granting any recognition to the other two, not to oppose their acceptance into membership of Friends United Meeting. This seems to have been mainly because of a realization on their part that their protests would be fruitless and that a public demonstration of their internal disagreements would serve no purpose. Therefore, on 14 July 1984, Elgon Religious Society of Friends and East Africa Yearly Meeting of Friends (South) became official members of Friends United Meeting, and this happened without any dissenting voices being heard.[136]

Upon their return home, however, leaders of East Africa Yearly Meeting found serious disagreements among themselves because of what had happened in America. Towards the end of the meeting in California, Thomas Lung'aho had been asked to stand up and speak on behalf of East Africa Yearly Meeting about the inclusion of the other two groups into Friends United Meeting. This he had done, emphasizing its importance for the unity of Friends in Kenya and expressing the hope that they would go home and co-operate in building a strong Quaker Church. His words angered a number of the officers of East Africa Yearly Meeting, and whereas these officers said nothing while they were in America, they attacked him strongly when they came back to Kenya. Lung'aho's strongest critic became Ezekiel Wanyonyi, Presiding Clerk of East Africa Yearly Meeting since the annual conference in August 1984. He and the General Board decided a few months later to adopt the government retirement age of fifty-five for yearly meeting employees, thereby apparently hoping to force the retirement of Lung'aho and a few other employees who were above that age. In October 1984 they were served with a notice to vacate their offices by the end of that year, and on 31 December Ezekiel Wanyonyi came, with an escort of two policemen, to force Lung'aho out of his office. However, Lung'aho had the support of many Tiriki people around Kaimosi, who were even prepared to put up a physical fight in his defence. He himself argued that his sudden dismissal was an act of revenge rather than a matter of well-considered policy, and that the decision had been taken so fast that matters like pension and other terminal benefits had not been considered at all, nor had he been given sufficient time to hand over his office to his successor. The result was that for the time being he remained in his office as General Secretary of East Africa Yearly Meeting.[137]

Meanwhile, the members of the constitution drafting and interim committees continued their work after the return of the representatives to the Triennial in America. Although a draft constitution had been completed before the meeting in the USA, the question of demarcating the exact geographical boundaries between the yearly meetings, which the government saw as essential for the preservation of peace, had not yet been settled. But eventually the committees agreed on this matter as well. An application went to the Registrar General's office, and finally, on 22 May 1986, Friends Church in Kenya received its official certificate of registration from the Kenyan government. The three constituent yearly meetings were East Africa Yearly Meeting of Friends, Elgon Religious Society of Friends, and East Africa Yearly Meeting of Friends (South); and its offices of Presiding Clerk, Recording Clerk, Treasurer and their deputies were distributed evenly between members of the three yearly meetings. The headquarters of the new organization were located at Kaimosi.[138]

Even while the work on the Friends Church in Kenya constitution was in progress, however, it had been clear to those who participated in the drafting and the interim committees that Nairobi Regional Meeting – which, as we have seen, included Friends living in and around Nakuru as well as those in Mombasa – held a special place in the Quaker community. Since Friends in the cities were people who had come there in search of employment, their original homes were, in almost all cases, within the area of one or other of the three existing yearly meetings. Therefore, in order to prevent splits in the city meetings along the lines of yearly meeting membership, the committee members had already, at an early stage, indicated their willingness to work towards the creation of an independent Nairobi yearly meeting which would include all city congregations. Although the Nairobi people themselves would have preferred the one united East Africa Yearly Meeting to continue, that solution was an acceptable alternative in view of the fact that the old yearly meeting no longer existed.[139]

According to the Friends Church in Kenya constitution, Nairobi had been placed under East Africa Yearly Meeting of Friends (South), and talks between Nairobi Region and leaders of the southern group started very soon after the formal recognition of Friends Church in Kenya, resulting in a formal application being sent by East Africa Yearly Meeting (South) to a meeting on 16 December 1986 of the Kenya Friends Church Council as the executive body of Friends Church in Kenya, requesting its approval of a yearly meeting in

Nairobi. The Council welcomed the application, and agreed to let the parties involved go ahead and take the necessary steps towards the official creation of the new yearly meeting. As a result, on 26 April 1987 the first Triennial Meeting of Friends Church in Kenya, a meeting of representatives from all the constituent yearly meetings which is its highest authority, recognized the newly created Nairobi Yearly Meeting, and received it as a member. It also recommended that the Friends United Meeting Triennial to be held in North Carolina, USA, the following month should receive it into membership, and following this recommendation it was accepted by Friends United Meeting. But before that, on 3 May 1987, the inaugural meeting had been held in Nairobi, opening the way for the new yearly meeting to begin to function as such.[140]

Questions Outstanding in 1987

While Nairobi Yearly Meeting came into being peacefully, without controversy, the situation in some other areas was far from clear. Those who were left in East Africa Yearly Meeting after the boundaries between the three groups had been drawn up decided in 1985 – before the official registration of Friends Church in Kenya – to remove all those among their officers and employees who, according to the new arrangement, belonged to the area of one of the other yearly meetings. This was approved by the provincial administration. A number of people were affected by this; one of them was Ezekiel Wanyonyi, Presiding Clerk of East Africa Yearly Meeting, whose home was in the Kitale area. Another was Charles Wakhisi, Associate Secretary for its Missions Commission. Also affected was George Kamwesa who, as Director of the Friends' Theological Education by Extension programme, was based at Friends Bible Institute in Kaimosi. The latter two had homes close to Lugulu.[141]

Following the new boundaries, all areas in the north, including Kitale and Lugulu, were to belong to Elgon Religious Society of Friends,[142] but those expelled from their work at Kaimosi, as well as many others – especially around Kitale, where many people from various parts of the country had come to settle – were strongly opposed to any such idea. They saw Elgon Religious Society of Friends as a tribal Bukusu organization, unable to embrace the variety of ethnic groups represented there. And they disapproved, as before, of the way in which it had been formed, without the acceptance of the total Quaker community. Ezekiel Wanyonyi, as well as many others in this group, had been in favour of one undivided East Africa Yearly Meeting, but now that had proved impossible. He and a very large number of the Friends around Kitale, as well as a number at Lugulu and other places in the north, felt that the only acceptable alternative would be to create a new yearly meeting in Kitale, and they therefore began to take steps towards organizing such a meeting.[143] Like the members of East Africa Yearly Meeting of Friends (South) (when it was formed), they (in Kitale) wanted to see their new meeting as a continuation of the old East Africa Yearly Meeting, divided up only for practical reasons; consequently they called their organization East Africa Yearly Meeting of Friends – North (Quakers). Although it was not officially registered, it enjoyed a good deal of support from government authorities, illustrated by the fact that it was allowed to hold annual conferences in both 1986 and 1987 and, on the whole, to function just like any other yearly meeting. Ezekiel Wanyonyi acted as its Presiding Clerk and George Kamwesa as its General Secretary.[144]

On the other hand, members of Elgon Religious Society of Friends argued that the Friends Church in Kenya constitution had given them the whole of the northern area, and that the only proper arrangement, therefore, would be for all Friends in the north to join them and become members of their organization.[145] An illustration of their strengthened position was the fact that they had now finally managed to get permission to move their administrative office from Kamusinga to the old mission plot at Lugulu. This took place after many years of dispute with East Africa Yearly Meeting, sometimes even in the courts, regarding the right of ownership to that symbolically important place.[146] Consequently, many refused to give any kind of recognition to the already functioning yearly meeting around Kitale, and there were further examples of quarrels between the two groups regarding the right to use certain church plots and buildings. When members of the Kitale group tried, with a certain amount of understanding from members of East Africa Yearly Meeting of Friends (South), to be allowed into meetings of the Kenya Friends Church Council, Elgon leaders threatened to walk out of the Council, with the result that the Kitale people had to remain outside.[147]

By 1987, however, a few attempts were being made to accommodate the Kitale group within the Quaker community and to reach a solution that could be satisfactory to all concerned. As mentioned above, they met with some degree of understanding from East Africa Yearly

Meeting of Friends (South), and in early 1987 a group of members of Kenya Friends Church Council, made up of certain leaders from the southern yearly meeting and from Elgon Religious Society of Friends, visited Kitale and held talks with the people there. One important difficulty discussed at this meeting was the question of boundaries. While the Council group argued that there could be no settlement without boundaries between the yearly meetings, the Kitale people, some of whose supporters lived within the areas of other yearly meetings, maintained that the Church should be free and should not be limited by geographical boundaries. Consequently, nothing conclusive came out of this meeting.[148]

Another group whose situation was unsettled by the end of 1987 was the remaining part of East Africa Yearly Meeting. When those who belonged to other yearly meetings had been forced to retire to their own areas in 1985, this exercise included, as we have seen, the East Africa Yearly Meeting Presiding Clerk. In order to fill the vacuum, Peter Dembede Mmeyi from Tiriki was chosen in an acting capacity, and he was nominated Presiding Clerk in the normal way at the annual conference in 1985 and again in 1986.[149] He had not been among those involved in the preparations for setting up Friends Church in Kenya, and he was sceptical of that organization – not least of the idea that it was to take over the supervision of many of the institutions at Kaimosi, and of the plans to place its headquarters there. As far as he was concerned, since Kaimosi was still within the East Africa Yearly Meeting area, the institutions there belonged to it as before, and those who had decided to withdraw and form new yearly meetings on their own had no more right to decide over anything in Kaimosi.

At first, however, Dembede appears to have accepted the new state of affairs. But shortly before the first Triennial Meeting of Friends Church in Kenya in April 1987, a problem arose when he became aware of plans by that organization to add the word 'Central' to the name of East Africa Yearly Meeting of Friends, and move its headquarters to Kakamega. In his view, these changes implied that East Africa Yearly Meeting would no longer be recognized as the one original yearly meeting in Kenya but only as one among others, a position that was totally unacceptable to him.[150] And in fact, those involved in setting up Friends Church in Kenya had exactly the intention to which Dembede was opposed. Solomon Adagala says: 'We should have deregistered the East Africa Yearly Meeting and replaced it with Friends Church in Kenya.' And it was only due to the urgency of getting the new organization started, he says, that they had omitted at that stage to deal with the question of the old East Africa Yearly Meeting.[151] They saw Friends Church in Kenya as the unifying body which would hold all Friends together in much the same way as Friends Africa Mission and, after it, East Africa Yearly Meeting had done. Consequently, no yearly meeting should in the future be able to claim that it was more original than any of the others.

When Dembede became aware of this threat – as he saw it – to East Africa Yearly Meeting, and when he discovered that Thomas Lung'aho, who was still its Executive Secretary, was on the side of those who saw Friends Church in Kenya as the successor to the old East Africa Yearly Meeting, he immediately called a meeting of a number of members of its General Board. The meeting decided that because of what they saw as disloyal actions on the part of Thomas Lung'aho, he should be dismissed from his work with immediate effect.[152] Not long afterwards, however, on 16 May 1987, another meeting of the General Board of East Africa Yearly Meeting declared its trust in Lung'aho but dismissed Dembede as Presiding Clerk because of his action against Lung'aho, his critical attitude to Friends Church in Kenya, and because they found that he was fomenting disunity among Friends in general. At the same meeting it was confirmed that the official name of the yearly meeting ought to be East Africa Yearly Meeting of Friends (Central), and that its headquarters should be moved to Kakamega as soon as possible.[153]

Dembede's answer was to appeal to the High Court for an injunction preventing Lung'aho from acting as General Secretary, and the Court ruled that he was not to go to the office until matters were sorted out.[154] In mid-1987, therefore, East Africa Yearly Meeting found itself in serious difficulties. The Presiding Clerk had been suspended, and it did not have a functioning General Secretary. The Board, as well as the ordinary members, were split into a pro-Dembede and a pro-Lung'aho group, the former consisting mainly of Tiriki people from around Kaimosi who had the support of many immigrants to the settlement scheme near Lugari, the latter having its main basis of support in the Lirhanda and Chebuyusi Regions. And when preparations for the annual conference were to be made, the split between the two groups meant that the yearly meeting was unable even to agree where to hold the meeting. This situation worried the authorities, so the District Commissioner appointed a commission to see to it that the annual conference was held and new officers chosen as required by the Societies Act under which the yearly meeting was registered. Those who became members of that commission were people who were loyal to Lung'aho, its chairman being James Ashihundu, and the annual conference was held in September at Chebuyusi in Bunyala location. The conference nominated the new officers as required, and Ashihundu became the new Presiding Clerk.[155]

Therefore, this group, which was the one that wanted an East Africa Yearly Meeting (Central), was now beginning to function properly, although the injunction against Lung'aho had not yet been lifted. Dembede had tried to prevent the annual conference at Chebuyusi from taking place, but when he did not succeed, he and his supporters took the view that the East Africa Yearly Meeting (Central) was yet another group that had broken away from the original East Africa Yearly Meeting which they themselves still represented. That group continued to regard Dembede as their legitimate Presiding Clerk, and they went ahead with their activities as a yearly meeting based in the offices in Kaimosi, in spite of having no government recognition and often being barred by the authorities from holding their meetings, including their proposed annual conference in December 1987, which was stopped by the local District Officer.[156]

Yet another group in the central area whose situation was unclear by the end of 1987 were the Kabras people from around Malava. They found themselves to some extent left out of the events that were taking place. While there had been thoughts, before the Kidundu annual conference in 1979, of dividing East Africa Yearly Meeting into a northern and a southern part, some had felt that Malava should be included in the northern region. When the decision had been reached at Kidundu to divide the yearly meeting into three rather than only two parts, Malava had come to belong to the proposed central yearly meeting.[157] But later, when various factions within East Africa Yearly Meeting began to split it up into even more groups, many of the Malava people apparently felt that the best solution for them would be to belong to neither the northern group centred at Kitale nor the central group but to have their own independent yearly meeting. They sent an application for a Malava yearly meeting to the Kenya Friends Church Council meeting on 16 December 1986, but the Council was not in favour of the proposal, and it was dismissed at that stage. By the end of 1987 the situation at Malava was still unsettled. Some members took part in the activities of the pro-Lung'aho group within East Africa Yearly Meeting, but many still wanted a yearly meeting of their own.[158]

The many disagreements and divisions, and the lack of a clear settlement in many places, have made a number of people lose interest in the Friends Church. Ezekiel Wanyonyi, for example, describes how these problems have made his own children reluctant to take part in church affairs. George Kamwesa says that some decided to go to other churches, or simply to go to no church at all, and Jeremiah Mugofu, General Superintendent of East Africa Yearly Meeting, says that the disagreements threaten to spoil the spiritual value of the Church.[159] Despite such problems, however, the Quaker community has continued to grow. Behind the newly established groups in almost all cases there had been a wish by the local population in an area for more participation in the affairs of their church, often coupled with the wish to free themselves from structures which they felt restrictive in that context. Once the divisions had taken place, therefore, the new groups generally met with an enthusiastic response from their members, who went actively into efforts to spread the influence of their meeting to other people and to consolidate what had been won. Consequently, there was a steady growth in membership of the Society of Friends through the 1970s and the 1980s, and in 1987 the total membership was about 175–200,000.[160]

Notes

1. Jefferson Ford, in his report on how the Lugulu church was set on fire on 17 December 1941, attributes this case of arson to 'the forces of evil' which are not pleased with the spread of the Gospel, and he writes that Lugulu was the sixth mission station in the district to be attacked by incendiaries (FUM: Annual Report of the Evangelistic Department, 1941). In 1943 Ford writes that since the Lugulu church was burnt, attendance has become distinctly lower (FUM: Annual Report of the Evangelistic Department, 1943). In 1946 he describes what he sees as a serious attempt by the Roman Catholic Church to 'Swamp' the country and 'Choke out' Protestantism. He continues,

> Another phase of opposition to the gospel, especially in the north, comes from some young men who have returned to Kitosh area since the war full of antiwhite propaganda, which they have imbibed. They have succeeded in collecting a certain number of followers and are trying to fill the country with political and social insubordination. Even a few who have been elders

> in the church, have been carried away by them, but there is a substantial body of elders who have been able to see the fallacy of their activities, especially as they associate much immorality with their activities and are trying to revive some of the old pagan customs. (FUM: Report of the Evangelistic Department for 1946).

In March 1948 he writes to the Board office in America, telling them why he and his wife are still staying at Lugulu despite the fact that they have been retired: the 'fanatical activities of a politico-religious group' have made the provincial Superintendent of Police issue orders that they must stay on until matters have cooled down (FUM: Letter from Jefferson W. Ford to Merle L. Davis, 1 March 1948). And a few days later he writes to Dr Bond, giving a short description of 'misambwa' and saying that 'Elija' had written him some 'very crazy' letters when he was in the mental hospital, and that in November 1947 there had been vandalism at the Lugulu mission station, which was 'part of the same' (FUM: Letter from Jefferson W. Ford to Dr Bond, 8 March 1948).

2. KNA: North Kavirondo District Annual Report, 1943 (DC/NN.1/25) says that in 1942 55.07 per cent of the 'able-bodied' men were out at work, *exclusive* of those in military service. From 1943, however, the number of those performing forced labour and military duties declined somewhat.

3. FUM: Evangelistic Report, 1949, by Leonard E. Wines, gives the number as 16,829. Increase in membership of the Anglican Church among the Luyia is described by Watson A.O. Omulokoli, 'The Historical Development of the Anglican Church among Abaluyia 1905–1955', unpublished PhD thesis, University of Aberdeen, 1981, pp 330 f.

4. As shown above, the first suggestion by the missionaries of a yearly meeting in Africa was found in a letter to the AFBM written on their behalf by Fred Hoyt in 1931. Further requests were made before the Five Years Meetings in America in 1935 and 1940 (Levinus K. Painter, *The Hill of Vision: The Story of the Quaker Movement in East Africa 1902–1965*, East Africa Yearly Meeting of Friends, 1966, p 67).

5. FUM: Minutes of the Executive Committee meeting of the AFBM, 26 November 1945.

6. FUM: Report of the Evangelistic Department, 1946, by J.W. Ford; Painter, *The Hill of Vision*, pp 68 f.; Rose Adede, *Joel Litu: Pioneer African Quaker*, Pendle Hill Publications, Wallingford, PA, 1982, p 20.

7. Painter, *The Hill of Vision*, p 69. Later, others migrated to Tanganyika, spreading the Friends Church to that area also (ibid.).

8. FUM: Letter from Merle L. Davis to Fred N. Hoyt, 23 November 1945; Painter, *The Hill of Vision*, p 131.

9. Stafford Kay, 'The Southern Abaluyia, the Friends Africa Mission, and the Development of Education in Western Kenya, 1902–1965', unpublished PhD thesis, University of Wisconsin, 1973, pp 229 ff., referring to the so-called Beecher Report: Kenya Colony and Protectorate, *African Education in Kenya*, Nairobi, 1949, pp 5 ff., and to the AFBM Annual Reports 1942–44.

The same point is made by John Allen Rowe, 'Kaimosi: An Essay in Missionary History', unpublished MSc thesis, University of Wisconsin, 1958, p 156, who writes that the amount given by African Quakers for education swelled from $6000 in 1939 to almost $20,000 in 1946, while their contributions to meeting rose from $2000 in 1939 to $20,000 in 1946 (ibid., p 163). Rowe takes these numbers from the AFBM Annual Reports, 1939–46, and he believes that the improved economic conditions of Kenyan Friends at this time was an important factor contributing to 'a relaxation in the attitude of disillusionment with all things Western' and, therefore, to the greater interest in joining the Church.

10. By far the majority of the schools were run by missions. Not until 1934 had District Education Boards been set up by the government to manage secular primary schools (Allan Bradley, *One Man's Education: An Autobiographical Scrap-book*, Ebor Press, York, 1987, p 40).

11. FUM: Annual Report of the Evangelistic Department of the Friends Africa Mission, 1945, by Jefferson W. Ford; Annual Report of the Evangelistic Department, 1943, also by Ford. The number of pupils is taken from Painter, *The Hill of Vision*, p 61, who gives the following approximate numbers of pupils in Friends schools: 1933: 10,000, 1938: 20,400; 1945: 32,900; 1952: 38,300.

12. FUM: Report of the South District, 1939, by A.A. Bond. In 1937 the Fords, on a trip to South Africa, had noted that at a Zulu mission there were more women than men in the congregations. This surprised them, says Helen Kersey Ford, 'as ours were the opposite'. (Helen Kersey Ford and Ester Ford Andersen, *The Steps of a Good Man Are Ordered by the Lord*, African Inland Mission, Pearl River, NY, 1976, p 113).

13. FUM: Annual Report of Evangelistic Department, 1942, by Jefferson W. Ford. Ford writes here, though, that Alta Hoyt has kept up weekly women's meetings at Kaimosi. Progress in the number of women's groups is reported in FUM: Report of Women's Work in the F.A.M. field, 1944, by Helen K. Ford, and the similar report in 1945.

14. This point is observed by Clifford Wesley Gilpin, 'The Church and the Community: Quakers in Western Kenya, 1902–1963', unpublished PhD thesis, Columbia University, 1976, p 282.

15. FUM: Report of Evangelistic Department, 1952.

16. FUM: Annual Reports of the Evangelistic Department, 1953, 1955, 1961. In the reports for the years 1957 and 1958, women's meetings are described as lively and active.

17. FUM: Evangelistic Report, 1949, by Leonard E. Wines.

18. See Alta H. Hoyt, *We Were Pioneers*, Wichita, KS, 1971, p31.

19. Bradley, *One Man's Education*, pp 39 ff., 51 ff., 79 ff.; Kay, 'The Southern Abaluyia', pp 251 ff.

20. FUM: Evangelistic Report, 1950, by Leonard E. Wines.

21. FUM: Minutes of annual meeting, F.A.M., 8–11 January 1952.

22. FUM: A telegram from John and Julia Retherford to the AFBM on 23 October 1952 tells that they have now arrived at Kaimosi. And in a letter to

the AFBM of 9 January 1953 John Retherford says that he has taken over his duties and responsibilities as Yearly Meeting Superintendent.

23. FUM: Report of Evangelistic Department of Friends Africa Mission, 1953, by John M. Retherford. He gives the numbers of members as about 20,000 in 1953 and 26,800 in 1954 (ibid., and the similar report for 1954).

24. Kay, 'The Southern Abaluyia', pp 225 ff.; Fred Reeve, 'Education for the New Day', in Painter, *The Hill of Vision*, p 121.

25. Ibid., p 116.

26. Painter, *The Hill of Vision*, pp 141 ff. About the same number came during the 1960s.

27. In 1959, Chavakali Secondary School for boys was opened, the Girls' Boarding School at Kaimosi became a secondary school in 1961; Lugulu Intermediate Girls' School was started in 1958, and became a secondary school in 1963 (Fred Reeve, 'Recent Developments in Education', in Painter, *The Hill of Vision*, p 127.).

28. Ibid., p 123.

29. Hoyt, *We Were Pioneers*, p 139.

30. Painter, *The Hill of Vision*, p 79; information from Sven Rasmussen, the Danish participant in the work camp, on 12 March 1989, and from Joseph Wasike Mululu; also Douglas and Dorothy Steere, *Friends Work in Africa*, Friends Home Service Committee, London, 1955, pp 40 f.

31. Painter, *The Hill of Vision*, pp 94, 144; information from Sven Rasmussen, 12 March 1989; from Joseph Wasike Mululu; Gilpin, 'The Church and the Community', pp 299 f., quoting FUM: Report of Stewardship Adviser, 1963–64, by Rodney Morris. On pp 290 ff. Gilpin mentions a number of development projects initiated by Friends.

32. Bradley, *One Man's Education*, p 74.

33. During the 1950s and 1960s there were examples of a few people belonging to other denominations being accepted by the AFBM for service in Kenya (Painter, *The Hill of Vision*, pp 141 ff.).

34. FUM: Annual Report, Maragoli Station, 1925, by Emory J. Rees.

35. FUM: Report of Evangelistic Department of Friends Africa Mission, 1953, by John M. Retherford.

36. Reeve, 'Education for the New Day', pp 121 f.

37. FUM: Herbert and Beatrice Kimball (a description of their careers) (no date). The Friends church where Herbert Kimball had served was Farmington, under New York Yearly Meeting, which was less evangelical in theology than many belonging to the Five Years Meeting and which eventually, in 1955, decided to unite with the Hicksite New York Yearly Meeting to form one body with both pastoral and non-pastoral meetings (Errol T. Elliott, *Quakers on the American Frontiers: A History of the Westward Migrations, Settlements, and Developments of Friends on the American Continent*, Friends United Press, Richmond, IN, 1969, pp 338 f.).

38. Painter, *The Hill of Vision*, p 112; Christina H. Jones, *American Friends in World Missions*, American Friends Board of Missions, Richmond, IN, 1946, p 203.

39. Talk with Herbert and Beatrice Kimball, 17 April 1985; interview with Abraham Sangura, 1 December 1977; information from Benjamin Wegesa on 3 March 1985, and from Joseph Wasike Mululu; both served for a number of years as interpreters for Herbert Kimball; FUM: Letter from Charles A. Lampman to Herbert Kimball, 26 May 1955.

40. FUM: 'A Concern about the Church, East Africa Yearly Meeting of Friends', by Herbert Kimball (no date).

41. Information from Joseph Wasike Mululu; FUM: 'Revival in Bukusu', a description by the Kimballs of a two-week evangelization campaign in the north in 1958; letter from Thomas G. Lung'aho, Administrative Secretary of East Africa Yearly Meeting, to the Administrative Secretary of AFBM, 20 January 1959.

42. Interview with Rabecca Nasibwondi, 16 February 1978.

43. FUM: Letter from Herbert Kimball to Fred Reeve and Charles Lampman, 4 March 1955; letter from Charles A. Lampman to Herbert Kimball, 26 May 1955; letter from John M. Retherford to Charles Lampman, 3 March 1955; letter from Fred Reeve to Charles Lampman, 14 March 1955.

44. Painter, *The Hill of Vision*, p 145.

45. FUM: Letter from Sumner Mills and Norman E. Young, Chairman and Secretary of the AFBM, respectively, to Herbert and Beatrice Kimball, 14 April 1961; letter from Benjamin S. Ngaira, Presiding Clerk of East Africa Yearly Meeting, to Charles Lampman, 25 August 1955; memorandum from Fred Reeve to R. Ernest Lamb, acting secretary of the AFBM, 11 March 1957, referring to Benjamin Ngaira, who felt that the situation appeared much worse in America than it actually was in Kenya; the letter from Thomas G. Lung'aho to the Administrative Secretary, AFBM, 20 January 1959, expresses the appreciation of the Permanent Board of East Africa Yearly Meeting for the services of Herbert and Beatrice Kimball.

46. Painter, *The Hill of Vision*, p 113; unpublished autobiography of Elisha Wakube, no date (around 1964).

47. Painter, *The Hill of Vision*, p 114.

48. Harold Smuck, *Friends in East Africa*, Friends United Press, Richmond, IN, 1987, p 58. And information from Josiah Embegu, who was still Principal of Friends Bible Institute when I last saw him in December 1987.

49. FUM: Letter from Benjamin S. Ngaira to Charles Lampman, 25 August 1955; letter from Fred Reeve to Charles Lampman, 8 January 1956.

50. Painter, *The Hill of Vision*, p 140.

51. The AFBM approved of this move and promised to pay a part of Benjamin Ngaira's salary during the initial period, but from 1957 East Africa Yearly Meeting took over the responsibility of paying his entire salary (FUM: Letter from Charles A. Lampman to Jotham L. Standa, 16 November 1955; Painter, *The Hill of Vision*, p 105). Painter's use of the example of the Mission Board paying half of Ngaira's salary to show that 'the African church was slow in assuming the responsibility of financing its own work' is hardly justified in view of the fact that the AFBM had paid it only since April 1956.

52. FUM: Report of East Africa Yearly Meeting of Friends, 1958, by

Thomas G. Lung'aho. Painter, *The Hill of Vision*, p 58, says that Benjamin Ngaira went to Alliance High School in 1932. Thomas Lung'aho attended the same school for four years from 1937 (Harold V. Smuck, 'Thomas G. Lung'aho: East African Quaker Educator and Administrator', in Leonard S. Kenworthy (ed.), *Living in the Light*, Friends General Conference and Quaker Publications, Kennet Square, PA, 1985, vol II, pp 160–73).

53. FUM: Annual Report from East Africa Yearly Meeting of Friends, 1961, by Thomas G. Lung'aho.

54. Smuck, *Friends in East Africa*, p 10.

55. Ibid., p 13.

56. Ibid., pp 10 ff.; FUM: Letter from Charles F. Thomas, Chairman of Executive Council, the Five Years Meeting of Friends, to Filemona Indire, Chairman of the Permanent Board, East Africa Yearly Meeting of Friends, 29 January 1964; Painter, *The Hill of Vision*, p 131, quoting FUM: Annual Report for 1964, by Thomas Lung'aho.

57. FUM: Minutes of the First Meeting of the East Africa Yearly Meeting Permanent Board held at Kaimosi on Saturday 28 September 1963; Smuck, *Friends in East Africa*, p 169.

58. Ibid., pp 25 f.

59. FUM: East Africa Yearly Meeting News Notes, 1 October 1964.

60. FUM: Annual Report from East Africa Yearly Meeting of Friends, 1961, by Thomas G. Lung'aho. He says that the records show 30,741 members, but that the actual number is higher because three monthly meetings have not sent their reports.

61. FUM: Report of the Yearly Meeting of Friends in East Africa, 1957, by Benjamin S. Ngaira.

62. I have observed this practice on a number of occasions.

63. Constitution of East Africa Yearly Meeting of Friends (as first adopted in 1963); FUM: Annual Report from East Africa Yearly Meeting of Friends, 1961, by Thomas G. Lung'aho; Chart giving the organizational structure of EAYM, by Herbert Kimball.

64. FUM: 'A Concern about the Church, East Africa Yearly Meeting of Friends', by Kimball.

65. Painter, *The Hill of Vision*, p 82 and 114; Douglas and Dorothy Steere, *Friends Work in Africa*, p 41; David B. Barrett, George K. Mambo, Janice McLaughlin and Malcolm J. McVeigh (eds), *Kenya Churches Handbook: The Development of Kenyan Christianity, 1498–1973*, p 266.

66. *East Africa Yearly Meeting of Friends*, pamphlet published by Friends United Meeting, no date; Smuck, *Friends in East Africa*, pp 28 ff., 40 ff.

67. Ibid.; Painter, *The Hill of Vision*, p 66; FUM: 'A Concern about the Church, East Africa Yearly Meeting of Friends', by Herbert Kimball. The fixed annual amount is called, in Lubukusu, 'sianwa', meaning 'gift', and the word used for the free-will offering is 'esadaka', from 'sadaka' in Kiswahili.

68. Painter, *The Hill of Vision*, pp 125 ff.; Thomas Farrelly, 'Religious Education in the Schools', in Barrett et al., *Kenya Churches Handbook*, pp 50 f. 'Harambee' is Kiswahili and means, approximately, 'Let us pull together'.

69. Painter, *The Hill of Vision*, p 126.

70. Ibid., pp 98 f.

71. FUM: Annual Report from East Africa Yearly Meeting of Friends, 1961, by Thomas G. Lung'aho.

72. FUM: Letter from Fred Reeve to R. Ernest Lamb, 11 March 1957. Reeve uses the name 'Holy Ghost Church'.

73. Gilpin, 'The Church and the Community', p 312.

74. The 'north' in this context covers the areas inhabited mainly by the Bukusu and the Tachoni.

75. Gilpin has described the different economic developments in the northern and southern parts of the Friends Africa Mission area, and the response from the missionaries in 'The Church and the Community', pp 175 ff., 283 ff.

76. Language is mentioned as one reason for the northern people eventually to set up their own yearly meeting in: 'Why Elgon Broke away from Kaimosi', paper dated 27 October 1973 (no author mentioned; probably written by Elisha Wakube, who was General Secretary of the newly established Elgon Religious Society of Friends at that time). The term 'colonialism' to describe the relationship between Maragoli Quakers and Friends in the north has been used by Harold Smuck in *Friends in East Africa*, p 80.

Actually, during the 1970s an ecumenical group of church leaders, including most of the Protestant denominations in the area and also Roman Catholics, began to translate the New Testament into Lubukusu. This work resulted in the publication in 1984 of the Gospel of Matthew, *Chilomo Chindayi nga Chaandikwa ne Matayo*; and in 1986 of the letters of John, *Chibarua Chitaru cha Yohana*, both published by the Bible Society of Kenya, Nairobi.

77. FUM: Letter from J.W. and Helen Ford to the Secretary and Members of the American Friends Board of Missions, 21 May 1931; letter from Errol T. Elliott to Jefferson W. Ford, 1 September 1931; Ford seems to have expected that in the event of such a division the more evangelical yearly meetings in America, Oregon and perhaps Kansas, too, would help to finance the work in the northern area, as is evident in a letter written by Fred Hoyt as early as 1928 which mentions that Ford had already discussed such plans with Arthur Chilson before the latter left Kenya (FUM: Letter from Fred Hoyt to B. Willis Beede, 18 August 1928).

78. This veneration for Jefferson Ford was expressed in many of my interviews with elders in the north, e.g. by Temeteo Wanjala on 24 September 1977; by Jacobo Sukura on 5 December 1977; by Petro Wanyama on 7 December 1977; by Rabecca Nasibwondi on 16 February 1978; and by Andrea Chemiati and Yohana Wafula on 17 February 1978.

79. Although he was himself a member of the Executive Committee of East African Yearly Meeting, Zebedee N. Muchocho, a Bukusu, mentions these complaints, among others, in a letter to 'All Leaders, East Africa Yearly Meeting' (with copies to 'The Overseas Friends Organizations at large'), 2 September 1977. The same complaints are also referred to by the Presiding Clerk of EAYM, Hezekiah Ngoya, in a letter to 'Friends Everywhere', 29 March 1975, although he does not agree with the allegation.

80. FUM: Report of East Africa Yearly Meeting of Friends, 1958, by Thomas G. Lung'aho.

81. The wish for a second yearly meeting was expressed mainly by the Bukusu. Differences between the Bukusu and the Tachoni peoples, such as those mentioned by missionaries around 1940 (FUM: Friends Africa Mission. Report of North District Churches, 1940, by F.N. Hoyt; FUM: Annual Report of the Evangelistic Department, 1941, by Jefferson W. Ford), made a number of Tachoni distance themselves from the increasing feeling among the Bukusu that they needed a yearly meeting of their own. Some Tachoni joined them, however, and also took up leading positions once the new yearly meeting was established. 'Why Elgon Broke away from Kaimosi' mentions that their concern was brought to the attention of the annual conference in August 1953.

82. Thomas G. Lung'aho writes in FUM: East Africa Yearly Meeting of Friends, Report for 1959: 'I cannot close this report without mentioning the demand by Friends in Elgon Nyanza to split the Y.M. A move which should be studied very carefully.' And in 1960 a group of Friends from the north approached the American Friends Board of Missions giving reasons for their wish for a second yearly meeting, mainly the need for more educational opportunities in that area, especially for women (Letter from Yohana Wafula, Joseph Wasike and Elisha Wakube on behalf of 'Friends in the north' to the Administrative Secretary, The American Friends Board of Missions, 20 August 1960).

83. 'Why Elgon Broke away from Kaimosi'. Elisha Wakube uses this term in 'A Christmas Message to Friends Everywhere', 22 December 1964.

84. 'Why Elgon Broke away from Kaimosi'; letter from Hezekiah W. Ngoya to 'Friends Everywhere', 29 March 1975.

85. Letter from Lorton G. Heusel to Joseph Kakai, who had for some years earlier acted as Principal of Friends Bible Institute but was now in America, 6 December 1976.

86. For example, letter from Harold V. Smuck to Elisha Wakube, 28 September 1972; letter from Elisha M. Wakube to Harold V. Smuck, 7 October 1972; letter from Elisha M. Wakube to Lorton Heusel, 9 October 1972; letter from Harold V. Smuck to Elisha M. Wakube, 17 October 1972. The position taken by Friends United Meeting is also described by Harold Smuck in *Friends in East Africa*, p 81. He points out, however, that it was his practice to 'maintain quiet informal contacts' (ibid., p 69).

87. Letter from Philip Mwangale to Lorton Heusel, 22 October 1972.

88. Republic of Kenya. The Societies Rules, 1968 (Rule 4): Certificate of Registration No. 6418, Elgon Religious Society of Friends, 19 April 1973.

89. 'Why Elgon Broke away from Kaimosi'.

90. Ibid.

91. Letter from Philip Mwangale, Presiding Clerk, and William Yiminyi, Secretary, ERSF, to the Executive Secretary, EAYM, 11 June 1973.

92. 'Why Elgon Broke away from Kaimosi'; Smuck, *Friends in East Africa*, p 73.

93. Letter from Hezekiah Ngoya to Ben Wekesa, also from the north and

in favour of a second yearly meeting, 20 August 1960; Hezekiah Ngoya explained in my interview with him on 10 May 1978 that he had changed his opinion after he became Presiding Clerk of EAYM in 1962 and began, in that capacity, to take part in ecumenical meetings. The example of the strength of other churches, precisely because they had continued to uphold their original unity and had not split into subgroups, had shown him, he said, how destructive division could be, and made him come out in favour of one united EAYM.

94. Letter from Charles Wakhisi to North Friends Meeting, 3 July 1970. Elgon Friends' disappointment with Ngoya and Wakhisi is expressed in 'Why Elgon Broke away from Kaimosi'.

95. Ibid.; and letter from Thomas G. Lung'aho to Leslie Nash, Hospital Administrator, Friends Hospital, 27 June 1974, saying that the Executive Committee had decided to interview hospital employees from Bungoma to ascertain where they belonged.

96. Letter from Thomas G. Lung'aho to Elisha M. Wakube, 8 April 1974.

97. Letter from Kaplan & Stratton, Advocates, to the Secretary, ERSF, 30 May 1974.

98. Letter from Christopher M. Fwamba to General Secretary, ERSF, 8 August 1974.

99. I was present at the ERSF annual conference in 1974.

100. Letter from Philip Mwangale, Presiding Clerk, and William Yiminyi, Secretary, ERSF, to the Executive Secretary, EAYM, 11 June 1973; speech by Philip Mwangale at meeting between Harold Smuck and leaders of ERSF in Bungoma, 14 February 1978; interview with Hezekiah Ngoya, 10 May 1978. Ngoya told how he and Lung'aho once felt threatened by a group of ERSF elders at Chwele.

101. Ibid.; interview with Temeteo Wanjala, 24 September 1977.

102. Letter from Mrs P.W. Macharia for Permanent Secretary, Ministry of Education, to General Secretary, Elgon Yearly Meeting, through Provincial Education Officer, Western Province, 6 March 1974, referring to a letter from Elisha Wakube to the Minister for Education dated 24 October 1973.

103. Letter from E.P. Oranga, District Commissioner, Bungoma, to Provincial Commissioner, Western Province, 3 June 1974.

104. Elisha M. Wakube, 'Elgon Religious Society of Friends', paper dated 29 August 1975. ERSF leaders expressed their intention of sending a formal application for membership to FUM in the letter from Philip Mwangale and William Yiminyi to the Executive Secretary, EAYM, 11 June 1973. And on 7 July 1973 Elisha Wakube sent a letter to William Barton, General Secretary, FWCC, enquiring how to join that organization.

105. The first 'Elgon Yearly Meeting Epistle' sent to 'Friends Everywhere' after the Inaugural Conference of ERSF at Lugulu from 10 to 12 August 1973, their first annual meeting, says: 'We remain affiliated to the Friends United Meeting and will participate fully in all the activities of Quakers all over the world.'

106. Letter from Edwin B. Bronner to Elisha M. Wakube, 28 May 1974,

referring to Wakube's letter of 7 July 1973.

107. Letter from Lorton G. Heusel, writing at the direction of the FUM Executive Committee, to Elisha M. Wakube, 3 April 1974.

108. Letter from Lorton G. Heusel to Joseph Kakai, 6 December 1976.

109. Letter from Lorton G. Heusel to Elisha M. Wakube, 3 April 1974; letter from Lorton G. Heusel, again writing at the direction of the FUM Executive Committee, to the Executive Committee of EAYM, 3 April 1974.

110. Letter from Thomas G. Lung'aho to Philip Mwangale, 26 September 1975.

111. Letter from Thomas G. Lung'aho to Elisha M. Wakube, 4 March 1976.

112. '1902–1977. Seventy Fifth Anniversary of East Africa Yearly Meeting (Society of Friends). Anniversary Message, Kaimosi, (Tiriki), Kenya, 6–11–1977', by Thomas G. Lung'aho. I was present at that celebration.

113. The sources sometimes use the term 'General' Board, sometimes 'Permanent' Board, to describe the top decision-making body of EAYM between the annual conferences.

114. Seth Musisi, 'Kenya – East African [sic] Yearly Meeting of Friends Holds 32nd Session', *AACC Newsletter*, vol 3, no 10, September 1977, p 4.

115. Quoted in the minutes from the meeting: '2nd Consultation on Reconciliation of East Africa Yearly Meeting of Friends and Elgon Religious Society of Friends, Kamusinga, 10th December, 1977'.

116. Ibid. There were allegations that the minutes did not give a verbatim description of the discussions but were biased in favour of ERSF (my interview with Hezekiah Ngoya, 10 May 1978). Actually, this view may be supported by the fact that the minutes were signed by the meeting secretary, Elisha M. Wakube, but not by its chairman, Samweli Imbuye, who represented EAYM.

117. Hezekiah Ngoya explained in my interview with him on 10 May 1978, that at that time there were three main opinions within EAYM about the question of having two yearly meetings: (1) that there were only a few Friends belonging to EAYM in Bungoma District and around Kitale, and the question should therefore be solved by their joining ERSF; (2) that EAYM and ERSF must both break down, after which a new constitution for a second yearly meeting composed of members from both could be drawn up (this argument was brought forward mainly by members of Kitale and Lugulu Regions of EAYM); (3) his own opinion: that Friends in Kenya ought to remain united in only one yearly meeting.

118. Talks with Jonathan and Mrs Ruth Baraza on several occasions, e.g. 31 October 1987.

119. Smuck, *Friends in East Africa*, pp 82 f. I was present at that meeting.

120. My own notes from the meeting, which took place at Bungoma Tourist Hotel.

121. Letter from G. Jeremiah Lusweti to Harold Smuck, 20 February 1978.

122. Smuck, *Friends in East Africa*, p 86.

123. Interview with Solomon Adagala, now General Secretary of EAYM (South), on 20 February 1985; Smuck, *Friends in East Africa*, pp 90 f.

124. Ibid.; and by interviews with Thomas Ganira Lung'aho and Solomon Adagala on 29 January 1985 and 20 February 1985, respectively; also letter from Thomas G. Lung'aho to the Representatives at the 34th session of EAYM, 26 August 1979, the same day that the Board's proposals were approved by the representatives.

125. Letter from Reuben M. Sasia, Chairman, Kaimosi Friends Region, EAYM, to The Presiding Clerk, EAYM, 30 August 1979.

126. Interview with Thomas Ganira Lung'aho, 29 January 1985; Smuck, *Friends in East Africa*, pp 94 ff.

127. Interviews with Solomon Adagala, 20 February 1985; with Thomas Ganira Lung'aho, 29 January 1985; and with John Majani, Administrative Secretary of EAYM (South), 28 February 1985; Smuck, *Friends in East Africa*, pp 93 ff.; Republic of Kenya. The Societies Rules, 1968 (Rule 4): Certificate of Registration No. 10990, East Africa Yearly Meeting of Friends (South) Society, 12 November 1981; Constitution of East Africa Yearly Meeting of Friends (Quakers) – South.

128. I took part in the annual conference of ERSF at Chwele on 14 and 15 August 1982, at which many of the overseas visitors were present, and I visited the FWCC meeting in Kaimosi on 16 August 1982.

129. Information from Jeremiah Lusweti on 20 January 1985.

130. Interview with Solomon Adagala, 20 February 1985.

131. Press Release by J.K. Kobia, Provincial Commissioner, Western Province (no date).

132. Many Quaker leaders see this government involvement as a great help in their reconciliation efforts. This opinion was expressed by, among others, Jeremiah Lusweti on 20 January and 25 February 1985; by Elisha Wakube on 19 January 1985; by Solomon Adagala on 20 February 1985; by Thomas Ganira Lung'aho on 29 January and 28 February 1985; and by Alexander Ndemaki, General Secretary of ERSF, on 26 February 1985.

133. Interviews with Thomas Ganira Lung'aho on 29 January 1985; and with Jeremiah Lusweti on 20 January 1985.

134. Interviews with Ezekiel Wanyonyi, at that time Presiding Clerk of EAYM, on 21 February 1985; and with George Kamwesa, who was Director of the Friends Theological Education by Extension programme, on 28 January 1985.

135. In my interview with him on 28 February 1985 Lung'aho explained that he had come to believe that true unity among Kenyan Quakers could come about only if the two new yearly meetings were recognized as such, and their independence respected. Only then would it be possible to create a new structure of co-operation between the three yearly meetings which could bring peace to all of them.

136. Interviews with Elisha Wakube on 19 January 1985; with Jeremiah Lusweti on 20 January and 25 February 1985; and with Thomas Ganira Lung'aho on 29 January 1985; Smuck, *Friends in East Africa*, pp 102 f.; the official minute from the FUM Triennial session, 14 July 1984, was read by Filemona Indire on 27 January 1985 at Kidundu church on the occasion of

the official celebration by EAYM (South) of its acceptance into membership of FUM, at which meeting I was present.

137. Interviews with Thomas Lung'aho, 29 January 1985 and 28 February 1985. The first of these interviews took place in his office at Kaimosi, a clear indication that his opponents had not succeeded in evicting him. Also interviews with Elisha Wakube, 19 January 1985; with Jeremiah Lusweti, 20 January 1985; with Charles Wakhisi, 24 January 1985; with George Kamwesa, 28 January 1985; and with Ezekiel Wanyonyi, 21 February 1985. Kamwesa claimed that Tiriki people supported Lung'aho because his mother came from that ethnic group.

138. Republic of Kenya. The Societies Rules, 1968 (Rule 4): Certificate of Registration No. 13113 for Friends Church in Kenya, dated 22 May 1986; Constitution of Friends Church in Kenya, points nos 3 and 6; the FCK headed notepaper lists the officers of the Church, two from each constituent yearly meeting.

139. Interview with Jeremiah Lusweti on 25 February 1985; and with Solomon Adagala on 13 December 1987; letter from Zibion Kikuyu, Presiding Clerk, Nairobi Quarterly Meeting of Friends, to the Provincial Commissioner, Western Province, 2 April 1985.

140. Constitution of Friends Church in Kenya, point no. 15(a); interview with Solomon Adagala on 13 December 1987; Minutes of the Eighth Meeting of Kenya Friends Church Council, 16 December 1986. 'History of Friends Church in Kenya', by Elisha M. Wakube, Kenya Friends Church Council Secretary, written for the occasion of its first Triennial, 26 April 1987; interview with Jeremiah Lusweti on 20 October 1987; and with Thomas Ganira Lung'aho on 16 November 1987; Minute of the 42nd session of East Africa Yearly Meeting (Quakers) held at Chebuyusi High School 3–6 September 1987; invitation card for the inaugural meeting of Nairobi Yearly Meeting, 3 May 1987.

141. Interview with George Kamwesa (expelled from Kaimosi by 30 September 1985) on 28 November 1987; and with Peter Dembede Mmeyi, who was nominated Presiding Clerk of EAYM in 1985 and 1986, on 11 December 1987.

142. Friends Church in Kenya Constitution, point no. 15(b).

143. Interviews with Ezekiel Wanyonyi on 21 February 1985 and 24 November 1987; and with George Kamwesa on 28 November 1987.

144. Interviews with George Kamwesa on 28 November 1987 and 3 December 1987; and with Ezekiel Wanyonyi on 24 November 1987; also interview with Jeremiah Lusweti on 20 October 1987; Minutes of the Eighth Meeting of Kenya Friends Church Council on 16 December 1986; the name 'East Africa Yearly Meeting of Friends – North (Quakers)' is used on several papers sent out by that group as well as in its rubber stamp.

145. For example, interview with Jeremiah Lusweti and Alexander Ndemaki on 8 December 1987.

146. Elisha Wakube described in my interview with him on 19 January 1985 how, about a year earlier, there had been serious disagreements between mem-

bers of ERSF and EAYM over the right to use the church and the office at Lugulu, with both parties placing padlocks on the doors to keep the others out. He said that ERSF had decided to have the official celebration of their acceptance into membership of FUM at Lugulu Girls' High School on 12–16 December 1984. On 11 December Ezekiel Wanyonyi had managed to get a court injunction from the High Court in Nairobi to stop ERSF from meeting at Lugulu. However, the local Assistant Chief and District Officer had assured them that they could go ahead. Therefore, they had held their celebration as planned. EYAM subsequently wanted to cite ERSF for contempt of court. But according to Jeremiah Lusweti and Thomas Lung'aho, the Provincial Commissioner, during a meeting on 25 February 1985, advised Ezekiel Wanyonyi to withdraw the case, since in his view it was obvious that the former FAM property at Lugulu must now belong to ERSF (my interviews with Jeremiah Lusweti, 25 February 1985; and with Thomas Lung'aho, 28 February 1985). By 1987 ERSF was using the Lugulu property without encountering any further difficulties, and I visited their office there several times between October and December 1987.

147. Interview with Solomon Adagala on 13 December 1987; with George Kamwesa on 9 December 1987; and with Ezekiel Wanyonyi on 24 November 1987, where he described how he was turned away – by force, as he saw it – from a meeting at Nang'eni in Bungoma District. He said that on the whole he did not feel quite safe in that area.

148. Interview with George Kamwesa, 9 December 1987; and with Solomon Adagala, 13 December 1987. Adagala described how even people from around Kimilili, at the heart of the ERSF area, claimed to belong to the Kitale group, thereby complicating the question of boundaries. As mentioned above, there were other pockets of Friends, such as the small group supporting Ex-Senior Chief Jonathan Baraza at Sirisia, who refused to respect the boundaries and join ERSF.

149. Interview with Peter Dembede Mmeyi on 11 December 1987; and with Thomas Ganira Lung'aho on 16 November 1987.

150. In 1987 there were two versions of the Friends Church in the Kenyan constitution, one consisting of twenty clauses and one of fifteen. The fifteen-clause one added the word 'Central' to the name of EAYM and placed its headquarters in Kakamega, whereas the twenty-clause one omitted the word 'Central' and spoke of Kaimosi as the headquarters of EAYM. When the FCK constitution was first handed over to a group of representatives of EAYM (including Dembede) in May 1986, it was the twenty-clause version. Dembede apparently accepted it, probably because it maintained Kaimosi as the headquarters not only for FCK but also for EAYM. When, however, in early 1987, he became aware of the existence of the other version of the constitution, the fifteen-clause one, its addition of the word 'Central' and its change of headquarters for EAYM to Kakamega were completely unacceptable to him. At the same time he discovered that Thomas Lung'aho had known about the existence of both versions all along, and this caused him seriously to doubt Lung'aho's sincerity (my interview with him on 11 December 1987).

It appears that the version which Dembede discovered at a later stage, consisting of fifteen clauses, was the original draft constitution which was first sent to the office of the Registrar General. The changes in the other version, consisting of twenty clauses, which left out the word 'Central' and mentioned Kaimosi as the headquarters of EAYM, seem to have been necessitated by the fact that legally, the yearly meeting in the central area was East Africa Yearly Meeting, without the word 'Central' being added to its name. And according to its registration certificate its headquarters were at Kaimosi. Therefore, these legal facts had to be included in the official version of the Friends Church in Kenya constitution, probably on the understanding that the wishes of the constitution drafting committee could be included in an amended constitution later, when the necessary legal changes in the EAYM constitution had been made.

151. Interview with Solomon Adagala, 13 December 1987. Adagala, as well as Jeremiah Lusweti, in my interview with him and Alexander Ndemaki on 8 December 1987, admitted that those who created FCK did so without sufficient consultations with ordinary members; therefore, many did not understand it, and they had a duty to explain the ideas behind it.

152. Interview with Peter Dembede Mmeyi on 11 December 1987 and with Thomas Ganira Lung'aho on 16 November 1987; also with Jeremiah Lusweti on 20 October 1987 and with Jeremiah Mugofu, General Superintendent of EAYM, on 1 December 1987.

153. Minutes from 'East Africa Yearly Meeting of Friends (Central)' General Board meeting, 16 May 1987; interview with Jeremiah Mugofu on 1 December 1987.

154. My interviews with Thomas Ganira Lung'aho on 16 November 1987 (which took place in Kakamega, since he was barred from going to the Kaimosi office) and with Jeremiah Lusweti on 20 October 1987; letter from the District Commissioner, Kakamega District, Mr N.K. Mberia, to 'All Regional Chairmen, E.A.Y.M. of Friends Regions', 14 August 1987.

155. Ibid.; Minute of 42nd session of East Africa Yearly Meeting (Quakers) held at Chebuyusi High School, 3–6 September 1987; the geographical distribution of members of the two groups may be seen from the minutes of 'East Africa Yearly Meeting of Friends (Central)' General Board meeting, 16 May 1987.

156. Interview with Peter Dembede Mmeyi on 11 December 1987; 'Programme. 42nd Session of East Africa Yearly Meeting of the Religious Society of Friends (Quakers) 3–6 December, 1987 at Kaimosi Friends Church'.

157. Interview with Solomon Adagala on 13 December 1987.

158. Ibid.; Minutes of the Eighth Meeting of Kenya Friends Church Council, 16 December 1986; letter from Hon. S.M.B. Mudavadi, Minister for Local Government and Member of Parliament for Vihiga, to Herbert Asava, Chairman of Kenya Friends Church Council, 23 April 1987; some members from Malava took part in the 'East Africa Yearly Meeting (Central)' General Board meeting on 16 May 1987, an indication that they were on the side of the pro-Lung'aho group.

159. Interviews with Ezekiel Wanyonyi, 21 February 1985; with George Kamwesa, 9 December 1987; and with Jeremiah Mugofu, 1 December 1987.

160. The membership of EAYM (South) and of EAYM was, according to Republic of Kenya, The Societies Rules, 1968 (Rule 13), Annual Return, 70,111 by 31 December 1986 and 40,000 by 31 December 1987, respectively. EAYM – North (Kitale) had about 25,000 members in 1987 (interview with George Kamwesa on 28 November 1987), and the membership of ERSF is, likewise, around 25,000 (telephone interview with Jeremiah Lusweti on 14 March 1989). In 1985 Nairobi Regional Meeting, which by 1987 had become Nairobi Yearly Meeting, had about 15,000 members (letter from Zibion Kikuyu to the Provincial Commissioner, Western Province, 2 April 1985).

Conclusion

KATHLEEN STAUDT

This book analyses how Africans gradually assumed control of their Church. It is a history that begins in Britain and the United States, but develops in Kenya. It is in part the history of an idea: the idea that individuals, in direct communication with their deity, can be inspired by an inner Light. But as all historical analyses show, economic, political and social contexts shape ideas and provide unique structures around which people sustain and further elaborate their ideas. Such is the history of the Society of Friends in Kenya, a spiritual community which grew to nearly a fifth of a million people in just three-quarters of a century.

Growth on this scale is spectacular. Hard work, inspiration and good organization all help to explain these outstanding successes. But rapid growth in large-scale organizations invariably produces disagreement and conflict. And conflict, as social analysis has long theorized, has many positive consequences.[1] Yet one might wonder how and why people who share a *spiritual* community come into disagreements and even conflicts with one another.

This Conclusion is divided into three parts. First it develops theoretical perspectives through which we can understand the organization, ideas and material stakes around which Friends agreed and disagreed. It then summarizes the historical phases of the Friends' history in Kenya, utilizing this framework. Finally, it closes with the significance of this history, and poses some implications for the way Kenyan Friends build their future.

Theoretical Perspectives

Conflicts occur among those who share a spiritual community because of the tremendous stakes involved. These stakes are based on ideas and beliefs: beliefs about how people relate both to their deity and to others, both Friends and non-Friends. In this book, we have learnt about some of the theological disputes. To what extent should Friends rely on the Scriptures for spiritual guidance? Who decides whether someone is a Friend: the individual or clergy, based on standards or conditions met (and who decides these standards?)? Should a layer of clergy even be supported with salaries, or not? How much energy should Friends devote to spreading their spiritual message to others versus sustaining their own community? How much economic inequality among Friends is compatible with maintaining spiritual community? These are the kinds of issues, among many more, about which Friends disagreed.

Yet as the contextual analysis of Kenya shows, there are also *material* issues. The Friends Africa Mission began work in western Kenya with a wide-reaching agenda, one that supplemented their spiritual work with education, industrial training, and health services. People in western Kenya, hungry for educational opportunity and the economic advancement it could bring, were keenly aware of how church and school placement decisions would influence inclusion in (or exclusion from) benefits, depending on one's location.

Yet another factor is at work in understanding conflict among Friends, a factor that draws our attention to the very special relationship between religious beliefs and everyday practices that lie at the core of Quaker thinking. Most religious organizations could be classified as 'purposive' organizations, according to a conceptual scheme developed by James Q. Wilson.[2] Purposive organizations attract membership based on satisfaction derived from commitment to a set of ideas which give purpose to life. A subtype of purposive organizations draws membership based on ideas *and* transformation of everyday life behaviour. In other words, putting ideas into practice – or, as slang would have it, 'practising what you preach' – is at the heart of the transformative organization. On the surface, all religions seem to fall into this organizational subtype, but at Quakerism's central core is a personally transformative agenda. The inspiration of inner Light operates all the time, every day, and not just on a day of worship. Thus it challenges Friends to demonstrate to and expect of each other a special, inspired lifestyle. As people bring different degrees of intensity to their religion, these differences become yet another source of disagreement.

As if anticipating a community of discussion and disagreement, the Friends' organizing principles encourage openness, voice, and accountability. An egalitarian spirit prevails, as does a suspicion of hierarchy, as alluded to above with historical questions about the legitimacy of a clergy. Meetings are frequent, organized around time segments (week, month, year). Such is the nature of a democratic organization: the extent to which it is inclusive of men and women of all economic strata and regions. In the terms of economist Albert Hirschman, who writes about organizations, members exercise 'loyalty, voice, and exit'.[3] Friends exercise loyalty and voice in their meetings, but when disagreement becomes intolerable, exit occurs. And exit occurs with some frequency among Friends, whatever the historical context.

Historical Summary

The story of the Society of Friends begins with the rise of Quakerism in mid-seventeenth-century England. Quakerism was born in and rebelled against a rigid economic hierarchy where established religion was affiliated with state and monarchy. In its central and pure form, at birth, Quakerism was an egalitarian faith in which adherents communicated directly with their deity, without intermediaries: '"The inner Light' ... was seen as Christ revealing himself directly to a human being, or "the Seed" planted by God inside a person which could grow only when it was activated by the Holy Spirit' (p 3 above).

Quakers moved to other parts of the world, planting and spreading their ideas. Fertile new ground for these ideas was in the American colonies, where they initially faced intolerance and persecution. A combination of migration and economic differentiation led to differences within the Society of Friends – differences that led to disagreements, challenges to existing authority, and splits into separate organizations. The 'exit' option is part of early history. Leaders tried to forge compromises, but the Friends, who then numbered seventy thousand adherents, represented wide geographic space and economic strata by the mid nineteenth century. Separation should not be surprising. Thereafter, a religious revivalism in the United States among Friends and other denominations spurred the shift towards greater emphasis on the Scriptures, on ritual, and on a clergy. One loss in this shift away from egalitarianism towards clerical (male) hierarchy was the decline in female spiritual voice and service.

In this period of late-nineteenth-century revivalism, Friends' evangelical interests led to an interest in missionary work beyond national boundaries. In the peculiar dialectic of Quakerism, it was the more hierarchical, clerical, formalistic and scriptural version that was transplanted to western Kenya, then part of what was called the British East Africa Protectorate, in 1902. These beliefs overlapped to some extent with indigenous spiritual beliefs among the eastern Luyia peoples, but the contexts from which these missionaries came contrasted greatly from those where they settled. The eastern Luyia consisted of Logoli, Tiriki, Isukha, Idakho, Kabras, Tachoni and Bukusu peoples, all of whom had migrated from the north. They sustained themselves through cattle-raising and agricultural production at self-sufficiency levels. Languages, beliefs, and economic practices differed from north to south.

Although the British colonial officials sought to work through chiefs, leadership at the turn of the century was exercised largely through male elders. Elders derived their authority in part from their age status as closest to ancestors who were believed to influence the living. The deceased acquired a 'spirit' which could, on occasion, possess the living and provide signals to them. This idea of a spirit probably resonated well with the idea of a Holy Spirit and an inner Light, but the meaning and interpretation differ from Quakerism to indigenous thought. The ultimate religious authority among most Luyia peoples was a Supreme Being, 'all-powerful, benevolent, creator and protector of all people and creatures, and the source of all life, health, prosperity, [and] wealth' (p 30). This belief was especially strong in the north, among the Bukusu people.

Initially, the Friends Africa Mission had little success in its conversion efforts. Communication was nigh-impossible at the beginning; Swahili-speaking intermediaries were needed. In their public and personal writing, missionaries rarely discussed local cultures in sympathetic or positive terms, but rather in terms of 'darkness and evil' (p 43). Surely this patronizing and/or distancing attitude influenced behaviour, and was communicated to and understood by all.

Missionaries gradually learned the languages of eastern Luyia peoples, even translating the Bible into Luragoli, the language of the Maragoli in the south, who lived near the mission station in Kaimosi. Luragoli became a privileged language among Friends, and the south a privileged location. These early decisions about mission location and translation were to have important consequences for the non-

Luragoli speakers who lived in the central and northern regions of the Mission's 'sphere of influence' (geographic space recognized by other missions).

The broad-based agenda of the Friends Africa Mission, including schools and vocational training, began to appeal to some local people, for colonialism soon eliminated once autonomous, self-sufficient societies through taxation, location boundaries, and the stimulation of wage-related out-migration. However, only five had converted by 1906, and the Church grew to around fifty members in 1914. During World War I, economic crisis and famine motivated interest among Luyia people in their quest for new spiritual meaning. 'By now, the traditional elders and ancestors had been proved powerless when it came to solving many of the problems which people encountered as colonial subjects' (p 49).

New mission stations, important to new growth, opened, easing the way for more Africans to spread the word. Membership increased from over a thousand in the early 1920s to 4100 in 1926 and 7500 in 1929. Schools sustained the evangelization programme. Africans were better able to stimulate conversions than missionaries, a reality not always appreciated by the latter. Yet: 'The American Friends Board of Foreign Mission regarded the development of a national church as a natural outcome of the missionary efforts and were not afraid, as at least some of the missionaries were, that the Africans would not be able to manage their own affairs' (p 53).

African Friends brought enthusiasm and zeal to their work. Church members even moved near churches and schools to develop Christian villages, where they could live in ways consistent with their moral beliefs. They went beyond missionaries' moral beliefs to challenge customary injustices, such as prohibitions against females eating chicken and eggs. Within these very seeds of success were sown sources of dissension. Differentiation developed between well-off Friends, who were able to take advantage of material opportunities, and those who sought satisfaction of their needs from their religious community. Amid these strains a revival atmosphere grew.

A turning point occurred in 1927 during a prayer conference at which many were 'seized by the Spirit. People cried, everything was shaking, and many began to speak in tongues' (p 60). Many found spiritual meaning in these practices, legitimation in the Scriptures, and even encouragement from the presiding missionary, later recalled to the United States. Subsequent missionaries discouraged these practices, leading to a drop in membership and school enrolment throughout the 1930s. This dissension gave birth to the Holy Spirit movement, thereafter formalized as the Holy Spirit Church. The rift was based as much on differences in ideas as on economic differentiation and related social commitments to community versus individualism; it continues to this day.

Much scholarly attention has – rightly – been devoted to the well-documented Dini ya Msambwa Bukusu protest movement of the 1940s, led by former members of Friends Africa Mission. Scholar Gideon Were credits Dini ya Msambwa, a significant challenge and threat to colonial authorities, with the attempt to forge an alternative religion consistent with both biblical teachings and popular traditions. Some similarities exist between the Holy Spirit movement and Dini ya Msambwa, in terms of both theological aims and the economic strata from which adherents came. Yet the Holy Spirit movement persists and survives, as does the more gradual cosmological fusion in the Society of Friends. Such is not the case with Dini ya Msambwa.

During the 1940s, Friends once again saw great growth in church membership, due partly to the economic changes which resulted from World War II and people's direct and indirect participation in the war effort through conscription and agricultural production. In 1946 the American Friends Board of Foreign Missions allowed the first East Africa Yearly Meeting of Friends, a significant recognition of the size and strength of the Church. Nearly seventeen thousand people were church members. A significant number were women, but leadership was concentrated in the hands of elderly men. Even among women, there were differences between those who were able to take advantage of education and the many farmers worn down by heavy labour. Their option, however, seems to have been 'loyalty' rather than voice or exit.

In the 1950s, conflicts began to emerge over issues related to the size and scale of the Church and the exclusion some felt, given their place of residence and distance from important institutions and meetings. One example involved the location of the Friends Bible Institute. Another was the placement of schools, especially secondary schools. Finally, long-standing regional differences provoked the eventual division of a single yearly meeting into several – first between north and south, and later adding central and others.

Ironically, it was both the peculiar dialectic of Quaker theology and the development and educational agenda of the mission which sowed the seeds of these differences. How disappointing it must have been to African Friends to learn of some missionaries' views that this conflict represented a 'moral let-down'. Meanwhile, however, the American Friends Board of Missions put a leadership in place to consider the eventual transfer of authority to an independent Kenyan Society of Friends. A new type of missionary arrived in the 1950s and 1960s, more professionally orientated to the academic education, industrial and agricultural training agendas of the Friends overall spiritual and development mission. Some missionaries renewed interest and support in Quakerism's central core: reliance on the inner Light.

In 1964, the Church was formally under the control of Africans. By this time, membership had increased to around thirty-one thousand. Educational and development programmes continued and expanded to include a Friends College and business loans, among other noteworthy activities. But a church under African control did not eliminate disagreement. The Church was too large (in terms of size and geographic space), the membership was highly diverse, and the theological menu was quite wide. In 1973, the Elgon Religious Society of Friends broke away for reasons related to long-standing language differences and distance from significant Friends institutions and meetings. Naturally, property and school control became highly contentious issues. By the late 1970s, similar issues led to yet another yearly meeting to accommodate north, central and south. Yet a unity of friends exists in Kenya, despite separate meetings.

Significance and Implications

The Society of Friends in Kenya is an example of how Africans successfully adapted a spiritual belief system initially introduced from Britain and the United States to their own. The seeds of these beliefs, planted in the western Kenyan context, bore fruit that African voices increasingly shaped and developed. This book bears academic witness to the spectacular growth and stability of an idea that resonated well with those of the various Luyia peoples in the region.

Friends not only nurtured a spiritual community, but also supported education and training to Africans at a time when the British colonial support was deficient and scarce. As a relatively egalitarian organization, Friends encouraged 'voice' and sought to hold their religious institutions accountable to members' interests. Testimony to the value of this development mission is the survival and strength of these educational institutions under the government of Kenya and the spirit of dialogue within the Church. Material and spiritual missions reinforced one another. Voice is a sign of organizational health; it virtually guarantees further adaptation.

Yet Friends have also disagreed, and disagreed so much as to promote 'exit'. Separatist tendencies have been driven as much by spiritual as by material considerations. Will Friends, once divided by economic differentiation, embrace one another in the future? Are the spiritual links strong enough, and the development commitments to one another unselfish enough, for Friends and Holy Spirit members to join together once more? Regional conflicts of a more recent vintage have occurred within a still-unified church; a yearly meeting structure and a keen sense of material stakes permit such accommodation. For how long will such structures maintain ties?

'Loyalty' within the Church is strong – perhaps too strong for those who lack voice in mainstream church affairs. While women represent large numbers of loyal members, they are neither visible in church leadership nor part of its aspiring democracy. Moreover, economic inequalities render the impoverished invisibile. In this silence of loyalty, separatist and exit strategies are born. Inner Light, and an individual's capacity to act on that Light, knows no socially constructed boundaries of economy, gender or ethnicity.

The answers to these questions in the Kenya Society of Friends will be found in the Kenya context. The tradition of hard work, inspiration, and good organization among Friends will probably ensure a fruitful and productive future.

Notes

1. Lewis Coser, *The Functions of Social Conflict*, Free Press, Glencoe, IL, 1957.
2. James Q. Wilson, *Political Organization*, Basic Books, New York, 1973.
3. Albert O. Hirschman, *Exit, Voice and Loyalty: Responses to Decline in Firma*, Harvard University Press, Cambridge, MA, 1970.

Index

Act of Toleration (1689) 7
Adagala, Solomon 130, 137
Africa Section of Friends World Committee for Consultation 111
Agricultural Betterment Fund 39
agriculture
  administration 110
  colonial rule 33–4, 37–9
  Masinde attacks officials 70
  missionaries' project 102
  women's workload 96–7
Akhonya 41, 45
American Friends Board of Missions 19–21, 112, 159
  concentration on southern area 115, 116–17
  decides to establish yearly meetings 94–5
  development of local church 52–3
  overseas scholarships 116–17
  raises money for secondary school 98, 100
  support for African influence 100–1
  supports East Africa's independence 107–8
  wary of evangelism 61–2
Amugune, Japheth 58
Amugune, Yohana 41
  education 47
  first to come to mission 45
  returns home to establish church and school 52
Anglican Church Missionary Society 37
Ashihundu, James 139
Austin, Ann 7–8

Baraza, Jonathan 126
Baraza, Ruth 126
Beede, B. Willis 53
  on independence of Native Church 61–2
Bible 14–15, 16
  education and 47–8
  effect of Holy Spirit split 66
  translated into Luragoli 41, 45, 115–16, 158–9
Bible Institute 69, 108, 110
  dispute over location 97, 114, 160
  the Kimballs 104–5
  later teachers 107
Blackburn, Dr Elisha 41
  worried about independent converts 52
Bond, Dr Archie 41, 44, 52, 96
Bond, Mira 44
Bradley, Allan 103
Britain
  birth of Quakers 1–7, 157
  colonial rule 26, 32–9, 48–9, 76, 158
  freezes African boundaries 35–6
  Restoration and toleration 7
  risings against rule 71–3, 76–7
Bronner, Edwin B. 123
Bukusu people 26, 30, 36, 68–9
  Bible Institute 97
  Dini ya Msambwa movement 70–9, 160
  effect of colonial rule 76
  girls in school 56
  Holy Spirit movement 158
  religion 71–2, 78–9
  want yearly meeting in their area 118
Bukusu Union 69, 71
Bungoma District 111, 121–2

Canada (Northwest Territory) 8
Charles I, king of England 1
Charles II, king of England 8

Chavakali
monthly meetings 56–7
Chebuyusi 139
Chemiati, Andrea 122
Children of the Light 4–6
Chilson, Arthur B. 21
arrival in East Africa 39–40
Holy Spirit revivalism 58–62
message similar to Pentecostals 64
mission at Kabras 47
not returned to Africa 62, 66
sanctification 42–3, 44
sermon in Kiswahili 45
on unreached Africans 52–3
Chilson, Edna 41, 43, 61
on husband's activities 42
on newly Christian couple 52
Christian Churches' Educational Association 112–13
Christian Council of Kenya 111, 113
Christianity
ecumenical co-operation for social reforms 68–9
strains relationships among Africans 58
Chunguli, Jack Jumba 129
Church Missionary Society 44
Church of England 11, 55
Chwele
disputed property 121, 122
monthly meetings 70
Conover, Blanche 59
Conover, C. Frank 41, 59
Cromwell, Oliver 1–2, 5
Crosfield, George 12

Danish Friends 103
Dembede Mmeyi, Peter 137–9
Dini ya Msambwa 70–9, 160
effect on Quakers 94
and Holy Spirit movement 75, 76–7

East Africa Protectorate 32, 36
East Africa Yearly Meeting
acquires property and administration 107–14
becomes part of Friends Church of Kenya 134–5
bitter split with Elgon group 119–23
conflict between Lung'aho and Dembede 137–9
considers second yearly meeting for north 117–18
divides into four yearly meetings 127–35
establishment 94–5
government works for reconciliation with Elgon 131–3
Kimballs' evangelistic theology 106, 107
monthly meeting administration 109–10
property dispute with Elgon people 121–2
revolt against regional divisions 129–30
splits region into nine 120
East Africa Yearly Meeting, North 135–7
East Africa Yearly Meetings
establishment 160
north and south tensions 114–19, 160–1
reconciliation with Elgon group 123–7
education
and Bible 47–8
divides society 95–7
Elgon people run schools 122
emergence of Quaker school system 47–51
under independent Kenyan Friends 112
Kitosh Education Society 69
language and regional divides 115–16
new generation coming to church 96
north v. south tensions 97–8, 114–15
numbers fall with church split 63–4
seen as way to liberation 48–9
teachers 51, 104, 112
training for missionaries 101–3
women 55–6
Eldoret 111
Elgon Religious Society of Friends 161
becomes part of Friends Church of Kenya 134–5
bitterness in formation 119–23
conflict with Kitale group 135–7
forms independently 117, 119
government works for reconciliation with East Africa 131–3
official recognition 131
property dispute 121–2
reconciliation with East Africa 123–7, 130–1
Elliott, Errol T. 100
Embegu, Josiah 107

family and clans 27–8
Finney, Charles Grandison 14
Fisher, Mary 7–8
Ford, Clara 59
Ford, Helen Farr 43, 54
Ford, Helen Kersey 43, 96
Ford, Jefferson 41, 43, 69
  Bible Institute 97
  church discipline 54
  continues evangelism 67
  on educated young 96
  Lugulu mission 47
  northern sympathies 116
  tries to prevent separate movement 62–3
  worries about unreached Africans 52
Fox, George 2–6
Friends Africa Industrial Mission Board 20, 37, 58
  arrival 39–40
  asked to bring more services to Bukusu 98
  conversion 44–8
  dissolves itself 108
  ecumenical relations 113
  education 96
  effect of split 66–70
  Holy Spirit movement 65, 75
  Kimballs' evangelistic theology 106
  membership 50, 63–4
  missionaries 158–9
  teachers 51
  theory and agenda 156
  threat from Dini ya Msambwa 94
  training for missionaries 101–3
Friends Centre Ofafa 110–11
Friends College, Kaimosi 111
Friends Foreign Mission Association 19
Friends School Kamunsinga 114–15
Friends Theological Education by Extension 135
Friends United Meeting 18
  recognizes Elgon meeting 131
  reconciliation of Kenyan Quakers 133
  refuses to recognize Elgon group 123, 126–7
Friends World Committee for Consultation 117
  and Elgon group 123, 131
Fwamba, Christopher 121

Gilpin, Clifford 113
Gould, Thomas B. 13
Gurney, Eliza B. 13
Gurney, Joseph John 10–13, 14

Haviland, Elizabeth 66–7
Heusel, Lorton 118, 119
Hicks, Elias 12
  first split in Quakers 9–10
Hirschman, Albert 157
Hobley, C.W. 39
Hole, Edgar T. 21, 41, 44
  arrival in East Africa 39–40
  sets up school 47
  spreading missions 47
Holy Spirit movement 58–62, 158–60
  and Dini ya Msambwa 75, 76–7
  easier relationship with Quakers 113
  revivalism 58–66
  splits from Quakers 62–6
Hotchkiss, Willis R. 20–1
  arrival in East Africa 39–40
  leaves mission 41
Hoyt, Alta 47
  criticizes Anglican and Catholic discipline 55
  education 48
  worried about fanaticism 62
Hoyt, Fred 41, 101
  on bringing in services 69
  education 48
  requests yearly African meeting 57
  worried about fanaticism 62

Idakho people 26
Islam 53
Isukha people 26
  Hole mission 47

Kabras people 26, 139–40
Kaimosi 40
  becomes headquarters for Friends Church of Kenya 134
  Bible Institute 97
  education 47, 50, 97–8
  Friends College 111
  hospital 102, 110
  monthly meetings 56–7
  Native Prayer Conference 60–1
  natural centre 114–15, 117
  oppose Vihiga meeting 128–9
  support for Lung'aho 133
  Teacher Training College 112
  uncertainty over centrality 127–8, 137–9

Kakai, Joseph 107
Kakalelwa
monthly meetings 70
Kakamega 111, 128
Kalenjin people 79
Kalokol 111
Kampala 111
Kamusinga
school 98, 114–15
Kamwesa, George 135, 140
Kasiera, Ezekiel 29–30, 31
evangelism and social development 40
states evangelical message similiar to Pentecostals 64
Keller, Mr and Mrs 65
Kellum, Everett 41
Kenya
East Africa Protectorate 32, 36
education control 51
government steps in to settle conflict between East Africa and Elgon 131–2
government support for projects 101, 111
legally registers Elgon group 119
national independence 39, 74, 107–8
Quakers begin mission work 20–1
Kenya Missionary Council 113
Kenya Society of Friends
challenges of organization 155–7
context of spiritual community 161–2
formation 132–5
later disagreements and divisions 135–40
Kenyatta, Jomo 74
Kericho 111
Khaoya, Daniel 120
Kibabii
Catholics invaded by Dini ya Msambwa 72
Kidundu 127
yearly meetings 128–9
Kimball, Beatrice 104–7
Kimball, Herbert 104–7, 110
Kisia, Joseph 125, 130
Kiswahili language 45
Kitale region 111
Elgon split 125–6
Wanyonyi forms new group 135–6
Kitosh Education Society 69
Kobia, J.K. 131
Kwetu
teacher and translator 45

Lampman, Charles 100
Lirhanda region 127, 128
education 50
Litu, Joel 41, 95
Local Native Council 35
prohibits Christian villages 54
Logoli people 26, 30
Lonsdale, John 78
Lugari Rural Christian Training Centre 111
Lugulu 114
Bible Institute 69, 97
church burned 70
conflict between Elgon and other northerners 135–7
Elgon group moves to 136
health centre 110
monthly meetings 70
prayer meeting and revivalism 59
reorganization and Elgon split 120, 121–2, 125–6
yearly meeting changed to Kaimosi 117
Luisukha language 45
Lung'aho, Daudi 47
becomes evangelist 53
first to come to mission 45
Lung'aho, Thomas Ganira 55, 107, 108, 109, 113, 118
conflict with Dembede 138–9
on property and Elgon split 121
reconciliation with Elgon group 124–5, 126
subject of revolt 129
Wanyonyi tries to force retirement 133
Luragoli language
Bible translated into 41, 45, 158–9
foreign to northern region 115–16
Lusweti, B.M.W. 78
Lusweti, Jeremiah 126
Luyia people 158
arrival of missionaries and acceptance of Christianity 39–44
British colonial rule 32–9
contribute towards education 104
conversion to Quakerism 44–8
dislike Wanga ruler 34–5
greater prosperity and education 95–7
history, clans and religion 26–32

northern migration 111
on practising a new life 53–7
regional divide 115–16
rituals 28–9
and their religion 26–32

Malakisi
Dini ya Msambwa attack 72–3
Malava region 127, 128
monthly meetings 70
wants own yearly meeting 139–40
Maraga
first to come to mission 45
Maragoli people 35, 111
education 48–50, 115–16
monthly meetings 56–7
revolt against Lung'aho 129–30
vocational and business support 115
Masinde, Elijah 70–5, 77
Mau Mau 110–11
Mavuru, Kefa Ayub 60, 63
Mbakalo
disputed property 121
Mbale
monthly prayer meeting 62
Methodists 16
Mexico 19
Michener, Bryan 66–7
Michener, Edith 66
Miller, Clyde 64
Mombasa 111, 129
Moon, Lewis 66
Moon, Ruthanna 66
Morris, Rodney 102–3
Mount Elgon 71, 115
mourners' bench 15
Mugofu, Jeremiah 105, 140
Mumia, Wanga leader 33, 34–5
Murunga, Wanga leader 49
Mwaitsi, Maria 52
Mwangale, Philip 119
Lung'aho writes of reconciliation 124

Nabwana, Pascal 69
Nairobi 110–11
Nairobi Yearly Meeting 134–5
Nakuru 111, 129
Nandi people 39
Native Prayer Conferences 58–9, 60, 61
Ngaira, Benjamin 95, 107, 109
Ngaira, Joseph 52
Ngoya, Hezekiah 120, 126, 128, 129
North Kavirondo 36, 38
Dini ya Msambwa 41
North Kavirondo Central Association 37, 67, 69
North Kavirondo Taxpayers' Welfare Association 37
Nyang'ori 35
Nyanza Province 35
Nyasaye (god) 29

Oudo, Tadayo 129

pacifism 5–6
Parker, Margaret 66–7
Peace Committee 110
Penn, William 8
Pentecostal Assemblies 41, 45
education 50
and Holy Spirit movement 64–6
Pitman, Dorothy 105
Pkech, Lukas 73–4
Pokot people 73–4, 75
polygamy 70
Protestants 50
ecumenical relations 113
revivalism in America 14, 16
Punshon, John 17
Puritans 2, 4, 7–8

Quakers
Africans want own church 98
arrive in East Africa 39–44
begin foreign mission work 19–21
behaviour and prohibitions 54–5
British support for Kenyans 112
emergence 1–7
establishment of East Africa Yearly Meeting 94–101
evangelism 105–6
Gurneyites 10–13, 18
Hicksites 9–10, 12, 13, 18
historical summary 157–61
Holy Spirit movement 58–66
Inner Light 3–5, 8, 11, 16, 157
later missionaries in Africa 101–7
missionary zeal 6
movement for native church 53–7
pastoral work 17–18, 104
persecution 6–7, 8
principles and behaviour 5–6
professional versus evangelical 103–5
revivalism 14–17, 158
social reform and evangelism 40–1

spread in America 7–9, 13–14, 157
theory and conflict in organizations 155–7
Wilburites 11–13, 16

Rasmussen, Inga 103
Rasmussen, Sven 103
Rees, Deborah 46–7
Rees, Emory 41, 45, 46–7, 104
pastoral care and teachers 51
rejoices at converts' independence 52
translates Bible into Luragoli 115
Reeve, Fred 100–1, 104, 106, 108, 115
Retherford, John 99
Bible Institute 105
conflict over role in training 105, 106
on spiritual decline of teachers 104
Richmond Declaration of Faith 18
Roman Catholic Church 50, 53
discipline of converts 55
dominant force in the north 68
invasion by Dini ya Msambwa 72
relationship with Quakers 113
Roman Catholic Mill Hill Fathers 44–5
Rothe, Horst 102
Rural Service Programme 103

Salvation Army 45
Sangree, Walter 30
Sangura, Abraham 49
becomes evangelist 53–4
Second Coming of Jesus Christ 16, 44
experience of inner Light 3–5
Seventh-Day Adventists 45
Sirisia 126
slavery 7, 8
Smuck, Harold 107, 108, 126–7
social reform 7
alongside evangelism 40–1
inter-denominational co-operation 68–9
and mission work 20–1
Society of Friends *see* Quakers
South African Compounds and Interior Mission 44
speaking in tongues 60–1, 159–60
Standa, Jotham 108, 109
Staudt, Kathleen 39

Tachoni people 26, 56, 68
Teacher Training College, Kaimosi 112
Tiriki people 26, 27, 30, 35
fighting with Nandi 39
oppose Vihiga meeting 128–9
support for Lung'aho 133
vocational and business support 115
tithing 5
Turkana Friends Centre 111

Uganda 32, 95
Dini ya Msambwa 73
meeting houses 111
Ukambani people 20
United States
Protestant revivalism 14–17
spread of Quakerism 7–10, 13–14, 157

Vihiga 127–8
monthly meetings 56–7

Wagner, Günther 28–9, 30
Wakhisi, Charles 109, 120, 135
Wakube, Elisha 107, 118, 119, 120, 126–7
Lung'aho writes of reconciliation 124
Wanga people 27, 32–3
Wanyama, Petro 95
Wanyonyi, Ezekiel 132, 140
establishes northern group 135–6
tries to force Lung'aho out 133
Wegesa, Benjamin 49, 105
on Sangura 54
Wele (god) 29, 30–1
Were, Gideon S. 28–9, 30, 31, 74, 78
on Dini ya Msambwa 160
Wilbur, John 11–13
Wilson, James Q. 156
Wines, Leonard E. 97
Bible Institute 104–5
on growing pains of Africa 98–9
Wipper, Audrey 71, 74, 76, 77
witchcraft and sorcery 31
women
eating chicken and eggs 55, 159
educating 55–6
keen to join church 96–7
World Wars
Africans serve 36, 38, 94
bring changes 48–9, 159, 160
setback in mission activities 46
widen outlook 78, 94
Wyatt, Eric 107

Zal e Ambula, Japhet 61, 64